Lineages of Political Society

CULTURES OF HISTORY

CULTURES OF HISTORY

Nicholas Dirks, *Series Editor*

The death of history, reported at the end of the twentieth century, was clearly premature. It has become a hotly contested battleground in struggles over identity, citizenship, and claims of recognition and rights. Each new national history proclaims itself as ancient and universal, while the contingent character of its focus raises questions about the universality and objectivity of any historical tradition. Globalization and the American hegemony have created cultural, social, local, and national backlashes. Cultures of History is a new series of books that investigates the forms, understandings, genres, and histories of history, taking history as the primary text of modern life and the foundational basis for state, society, and nation.

Shail Mayaram, *Against History, Against State: Counterperspectives from the Margins*

Tapati Guha-Thakurta, *Monuments, Objects, Histories: Institutions of Art in Colonial and Postcolonial India*

Charles Hirschkind, *The Ethical Soundscape: Cassette Sermons and Islamic Counterpublics*

Ahmad H. Sa'di and Lila Abu-Lughod, editors, *Nakba: Palestine, 1948, and the Claims of Memory*

Prachi Deshpande, *Creative Pasts: Historical Memory and Identity in Western India, 1700–1960*

Todd Presner, *Mobile Modernity: Germans, Jews, Trains*

Laura Bear, *Lines of the Nation: Indian Railway Workers, Bureaucracy, and the Intimate Historical Self*

Vazira Fazila-Yacoobali Zamindar, *The Long Partition and the Making of Modern South Asia: Refugees, Boundaries, Histories*

Bernard Bate, *Tamil Oratory and the Dravidian Aesthetic: Democratic Practice in South India*

Lineages of Political Society

Studies in Postcolonial Democracy

Partha Chatterjee

Columbia University Press   New York

Columbia University Press
Publishers Since 1893
New York   Chichester, West Sussex
cup.columbia.edu

Copyright © 2011 Columbia University Press
All rights reserved

Library of Congress Cataloging-in-Publication Data

Chatterjee, Partha, 1947– Lineages of political society :
studies in post-colonial democracy / Partha Chatterjee.   p. cm. —
(Cultures of history) Includes bibliographical references and index.
ISBN 978-0-231-15812-1 (cloth : alk. paper) —
ISBN 978-0-231-15813-8 (pbk. : alk. paper) —
ISBN 978-0-231-52791-0 (ebook)
1. Democracy—India—History. 2. Democracy—Philosophy.
3. Postcolonialism—India. I. Title. II. Series.

JQ281.C47 2011
325'.3--dc23   2011032753

∞

Columbia University Press books are printed on permanent
and durable acid-free paper.
This book is printed on paper with recycled content.
Printed in the United States of America

References to Internet Web sites (URLs) were accurate at the time
of writing. Neither the author nor Columbia University Press is
responsible for URLs that may have expired or changed since the
manuscript was prepared.

To

ANJAN GHOSH

(1951–2010)

my comrade in many battles

Contents

List of Illustrations

Preface

Ever since *The Politics of the Governed* was published in 2004, my idea of "political society" has elicited much comment and discussion, some appreciative and a lot of it quite critical. The spread and intensity of the response has persuaded me that, regardless of my success or failure in explaining the phenomenon, I have been able to point to a problem that is exercising the minds of many, not only in India but in diverse countries of the world. Simply put, the problem is that democracy, perhaps in most of the present-day world, cannot be brought into being, or even fought for, in the image of Western democracy as it exists today. It is not just that existent democracies in Western Europe and North America (or in the white settler colonies of Australia and New Zealand) are all imperfect actualizations of the true normative ideal of democracy (it doesn't matter for my argument if one decides like a Platonist that the ideal is unachievable in the real world of human beings or if one prefers the Enlightenment view of the infinite perfectibility of Western man). Thus, it is not as though, irrespective of the imperfections of Western democracies, the normative model itself remains universally valid and should be regarded as a beacon for aspiring democrats around the world. Rather, the problem is that the experience of postcolonial democracy is showing every day that those norms themselves must be rethought.

This volume attempts to use the rapidly accumulating empirical evidence on the experience of postcolonial democracy to question the normative status of liberal democratic theory as it exists today. However, I must be clear about the very modest claims of this book. It does not offer an alternative normative model of the future political order. It is self-consciously realist and not utopian. Most of the time, it tries to understand the new practices of postcolonial democracy—those that were never experienced in the history of the modern state in the West—and conceptualize them in their difference from normative liberal theory. The paths to our normative future, I believe, will diverge from those taken in the past, but their direction remains uncertain and open. What this book shuns, however, is the preformed judgement—that is to say, the prejudice—that such difference is always the sign of philosophical immaturity and cultural backwardness.

I have discussed various parts of this book at numerous formal and informal meetings in many places, and I regret that it is not possible to individually acknowledge my debt to all my interlocutors. However, I should mention at least the following occasions when I presented drafts of specific chapters of this book: the workshop on "Postcolonial and Subaltern Studies" at the Instituto de Estudios Peruanos, Lima, Peru, and on "Postcolonial Transformations" at the Universidad Central de Venezuela at Caracas, Venezuela, in May 2006; the Crossroads Conference of the International Cultural Studies Association at Istanbul in July 2006; the two conferences on "Subaltern Citizens" at Emory University, Atlanta, in 2006 and 2007; the Asian International Cultural Studies Conference at Shanghai University in June 2007; the conference on "The Great Transformation: Indian Political Economy" at Columbia University in September 2007; the workshop on "Democracy in India and Beyond" at the University of Pennsylvania, Philadelphia, in October 2007; the two conferences in 2008 (in Berlin) and 2010 (in Calcutta) on "The Rule of Law and Democracy in Europe and India" organized by the Europe-India Advanced Research Network; the conference on "Postcolonial Democracy" at the New School for Social Research, New York, in April 2009; the discussions that followed my lectures at Bogaziçi University at Istanbul, the Delhi School of Economics, Yale University, the Madras Institute of Development Studies, the Graduate Centre of International Studies at Geneva, the Department of Politics at the University of Oxford, the Centre for the Study of Society and Culture at Bangalore, the Graduate Center of the City University of New York, and the University of Michigan; and, finally, the intensive and invigorating workshop on my writings held at the Centre for Political Studies, Jawaharlal Nehru University, New Delhi, in March 2010.

Sections of some of the chapters of this book were published earlier as articles in English and Bengali. An earlier version of Chapter Two was published in the *Economic and Political Weekly*, 33, 22 (May 30, 1998); Chapter Three and sections of Chapter Five were published in my Bengali book *Prajā o tantra* (2006); parts of Chapter Four were published in Timothy Mitchell, ed., *Questions of Modernity* (Minneapolis: University of Minnesota Press, 2000), and in Sudipta Kaviraj and Sunil Khilnani, eds, *Civil Society: History and Possibilities* (Cambridge: Cambridge University Press, 2001); a section of Chapter Six appeared in *Diacritics*, 29, 4 (Winter 2000); a version of Chapter Seven was published in Maria Antonella Pelizzari, ed., *Traces of India: Photography, Architecture, and the Politics of Representation, 1850–1900* (Montreal: Canadian Center of Architecture, 2003); Chapter Eight appeared earlier in *Public Culture*, 20, 2 (May 2008); versions of Chapters Nine and Ten were published in *Economic and Political Weekly*, 33, 6 (February 7, 1998) and 43, 16 (April 19–25, 2008); and a part of Chapter Eleven appeared in *Inter-Asia Cultural Studies*, 7 (2005). However, all the chapters have been so thoroughly rewritten and rearranged that they often bear little resemblance to their earlier incarnations. I should also mention the two symposia published in the *Economic and Political Weekly* in November 2008 and February 2009 that provided excellent occasions for empirically informed discussion on political society.

In the period when this book was written, the various departments, committees, institutes, and centres with which I am associated at Columbia University have given me some of the most exciting and challenging moments of my intellectual life. I thank all my colleagues and students of the last few years for enriching my ideas. I must, however, make special mention of Ruchi Chaturvedi, Ayça Çubukçu, Anush Kapadia, Rajan Krishnan, Lisa Mitchell, Poornima Paidipatty, Ravi Sriramachandran, and Antina von Schnitzler whose doctoral research taught me a great deal about the practices of political society on the ground. My colleagues at the Centre for Studies in Social Sciences, Calcutta (CSSSC), have been my intellectual companions for many years. I take this occasion to express once more my gratitude to them. It still comes as a shock to realize that Anjan Ghosh whom I had known for almost forty years is no longer with us: I will miss the remarks, both jocular and serious, that he might have made about this book.

The Hitesranjan Sanyal Memorial Archive at CSSSC has become an invaluable resource for my research in recent years. I particularly thank Abhijit Bhattacharya and Kamalika Mukherjee for their generous help with the visual material used for this book. I also remain indebted to the staff of the CSSSC Library and the Jadunath Sarkar Resource Centre.

Anne Routon of Columbia University Press and Rukun Advani of Permanent Black have been, as usual, immensely helpful and efficient. I thank Nicholas Dirks for including this book in his distinguished series with Columbia University Press. I must record here a special word of thanks for the anonymous readers of this manuscript: their comments and suggestions were extremely valuable.

Several chapters include translations into English from the Bengali. Unless otherwise specified, the translations are mine.

I am grateful to Christopher Pinney for giving me permission to reproduce images from his books *Camera Indica* and *Photos of the Gods*. I also thank the CSSSC Archive for letting me use images from its collection.

January 2011   P.C.

1

Lineages of Political Society

The Mythical Space of Normative Theory

It is sometimes said that modern political theory of the normative kind takes place in an ahistorical timeless space where perennial questions about the right and the good are debated. In fact, that is not quite the case. Rather, it would be more correct to say that these normative debates take place in a time-space of epic proportions which emerged fully formed only after the victorious conclusion of an epochal struggle against an old order of absolutist, despotic, or tyrannical power. There is, thus, a definite historical past that is posited by modern political theory as an era which has been overcome and left behind, even if it appears only as an abstract and negative description of all that is normatively unacceptable today. Sometimes, this abandoned past is given a location in real historical time, as, for instance, the absolutist order of the *ancien régime* overthrown by the French Revolution, or the restricted rules of suffrage extended by the Reform Acts in Britain in the nineteenth century, or the regime of racial discriminations undone by the Civil Rights legislation in the United States. But it is also clear that, in its abstract and negative character, this historical past is limitlessly elastic in its capacity to include virtually any geographical space and any historical period, and to designate these as the past that must be overcome for modern politics to become possible.

The curious fact is that this negatively designated historical past could even be found to coexist with the normatively constituted order of modern political life in a synchronous, if anomalous, time of the present. Thus, when the demand became vociferous in many Western countries in the early twentieth century in favour of unrestricted voting rights for women, the existing restrictions were described as unacceptable remnants of a past order. If there is, in some not too distant future, a serious campaign for the abolition of the House of Lords, the existing upper house of the British parliament will, I am sure, be similarly consigned to a pre-modern past. Thus, even in its apparent indifference to the historical mode of argument, modern political theory of the normative kind uses a definite strategy of historicization in order to demarcate and serially redefine its own discursive space.

If I am permitted to adopt, somewhat insincerely (but only partially so), a position of externality in relation to the space-time of Western political theory and take a panoramic view of its progress since the beginning of the modern age, I would end up with the impression that there is an elemental sameness in all of modern political theory over the last three hundred years. It is as if all the major political developments of the modern world were anticipated, indeed foretold, at the birth of modern political theory in late-seventeenth-century England. Thus, whether we speak of the abolition of feudal privileges, or independence from an imperial power that refused to grant representative government to its colonial subjects, or the abolition of slavery, or universal adult suffrage without discrimination on grounds of religion, race, class, or gender—the basic structure of arguments appears to be contained within modern political theory from the moment of its formation. Consequently, it doesn't really matter if John Locke could not even imagine women as fully rational members of the commonwealth, or if Immanuel Kant could do little more than hope that the Prussian monarch would be enlightened enough to rule according to the dictates of reason. Those views of individual political philosophers were remnants of a pre-modern political order that had managed, in a purely empirical sense, to coexist in the same contemporaneous time-space as modern political life. They could, by an appropriate historicizing strategy, be explained away from the normative space of modern political theory, which would then be left free to traverse the entire discursive field opened up by its epic victory over absolutism. Needless to say, this discursive field can only be abstractly constituted.

As someone from the postcolonial world introduced from a very young age to the normative verities of Western political theory, I must confess that I have found all this quite baffling. How was it possible, I have asked myself, that all the bitter and bloody struggles over colonial exploitation, racial discrimination, class conflict, the suppression of women, the marginalization of minority cultures, etc., that have dominated the real history of the modern world in the last hundred years or so, have managed not to displace in even the slightest way the stable location of modern political theory within the abstract discursive space of normative reasoning? How is it that normative political theory was never pushed into constructing a theory of the nation, or of gender, or of race, or indeed of class, except by marginal figures whose efforts were greeted at best with bare courtesy, and more often with open hostility? How could those contentious topics have been relegated to the empirical domains of sociology or history? How could it be that the entire conceptual history of modern politics was foretold at the birth of modern political theory? I have often heard it said, to the accompaniment of derisive sniggers, that Hegel's confident pronouncement in the early nineteenth century—"what the spirit is now, it has always been implicitly . . . the spirit of the present world is the concept which the spirit forms of its own nature"[1]—was only a piece of idealist mystification, or worse, German delusion. I am not sure that Hegel's detractors among contemporary political philosophers are necessarily free from that defect, even if they do not share the same national cultural traditions.

I should clarify that by normative Western political theory I mean the corpus of writings, principally in English, French, and German, that represents what is broadly called liberal thought and that has come to enjoy a position of dominance not only within the academy but in general public discourse in all contemporary democracies around the world. Needless to say, there have always existed contrary views to liberal political thought. The most important such tradition in Western intellectual life is Marxism, which we will have occasion to discuss several times in the subsequent chapters of this book. The reason why I think Marxist thought failed to offer an effective challenge to normative liberal political theory is, first, the tendency in a great deal of Marxist thinking of subordinating the political to the economic, and

---

[1] G.W. F. Hegel, *Lectures on the Philosophy of World History*, tr. H.B. Nisbet (Cambridge: Cambridge University Press, 1975), p. 150.

thus of regarding political principles as the instrumental means for securing economic ends; and second, the failure of Soviet socialism to offer a coherent normative account of its political institutions. The power of Marxist thought has been acknowledged in the Western academy mainly in its contribution to social history, political economy, political sociology, and cultural criticism, not to normative political theory. This is not to deny that there have been in the last three or four decades several innovative thinkers in the West who have challenged the claims of normative liberal theory by drawing upon the tradition of critical Marxism. One such figure is Michel Foucault, who will appear several times in the following chapters, but there are several others who will also be discussed and cited. Like postcolonial theorists, they too are engaged in the critique of globally dominant liberal political theory.

Having searched for several years both within and outside the domains of liberal normative political theory, I think I now have the outlines of a possible answer to the question—"How has normative political theory as practised in the West managed to fortify itself against the turmoil of the real world of politics and assert the continued validity of its norms as pronounced at its moment of creation?" The answer will take us well outside the philosophically well-tempered zones of the Western world.

Two Senses of the Norm

Although the epic time of modern political theory appears to begin in seventeenth-century England, the conceptual innovations that enabled that abstract time-space to be constructed and secured against the incursions of the real world of politics appeared, I think, only around the turn of the nineteenth century. By then, European countries had, of course, had the experience of conquering and ruling over vast territories in the Americas. But the European empires in the Western hemisphere never seriously posed the problem of having to incorporate within a European political order the forms of law, property, and government of the indigenous American peoples. The latter were not regarded as having a credible political society at all that needed to be integrated into the new imperial formation. Only the colonial settlements of Europeans and *mestizos* mattered—and these came to be organized on the most modern European normative principles of the time. In fact, the indigenous societies of the Amerindian peoples frequently served as examples of the pre-political natural condition of mankind that had to be superseded for the political and commercial societies of civilized people to emerge. But the European conquests in Asia that began in the second half of the eighteenth century posed entirely different problems. The existing political institutions of those defeated Oriental kingdoms could not be entirely set aside, for utterly "real" political reasons. They had to be given a place within the new imperial order of European rule over its Eastern colonies. Thus began a new journey of normative Western political theory.

A key moment in the British history of the emergence of its modern empire was the debate in Parliament from 1781 to 1792 over the conduct of Warren Hastings as governor-general of India. Charged with corruption and high crimes, Hastings, in his defence, argued that India could not be ruled by British principles. If he had, in his own conduct, deviated from British norms, it was because Indian conditions demanded it. "The whole history of Asia is nothing more than precedents to prove the invariable exercise of arbitrary power. . . . Sovereignty in India implies nothing else [than despotism]."[2] Edmund Burke, in his reply, was merciless. "[T]hese Gentlemen have formed a plan of Geographic morality, by which the duties of men in public and in private situations are not to be governed by their relations to the Great Governor of the Universe, or by their relations to men, but by climates, degrees of longitude and latitude . . ."[3] This was a license for corruption and abuse of power. "My Lords," Burke thundered in Parliament, "we contend that Mr. Hastings, as a British Governor, ought to govern upon British principles. . . . We call for that spirit of equity, that spirit of justice, . . . that spirit of safety, that spirit of protection, that spirit of lenity, which ought to characterise every British subject in power; and upon these and these principles only, he will be tried."[4] Burke's claim was that Indians had their own ancient

[2] Speech by Warren Hastings in his defence in the House of Commons on May 1, 1786, cited in P. J. Marshall, ed., *The Writings and Speeches of Edmund Burke*, vol. 6 (Oxford: Clarendon Press, 1991), pp. 348–9.

[3] "Opening of Impeachment," February 16, 1788, in Marshall, ed., *Writings and Speeches of Burke*, vol. 6, p. 346.

[4] Ibid., pp. 345–6.

constitution, their own laws, their own legitimate dynasties. A British governor, ruling by true British principles, ought to have respected those institutions and customs and not, like Hastings, arrogantly cast them aside in order to introduce British forms with the substance of despotism.

The impasse created by debates such as this in the domain of normative theory was resolved, in the tumultuous age of revolutions, by a set of conceptual innovations that had little to do with the great political conflicts of the time. Writing his *Principles of Morals and Legislation*, published in 1789, Jeremy Bentham declared that the methods and standards of legislation he was proposing were "alike applicable to the laws of all nations."[5] More interestingly for us, in an early essay, "The Influence of Time and Place in Matters of Legislation," Bentham proposed the following method:

> I take England, then, for a standard; and referring every thing to this standard, I inquire, What are the deviations which it would be requisite to make from this standard, in giving to another country such a tincture as any other country may receive without prejudice, from English laws? . . . The problem, as it stands at present, is: the best possible laws for England being established in England; required, the variations which it would be necessary to make in those of any other given country, in order to render them the best laws possible with reference to that country.[6]

In providing an instructive example of this method, Bentham chose a country that presented "as strong a contrast with England as possible."

> Such a contrast we seem to have in the province of Bengal: diversity of climate, mixture of inhabitants, natural productions, face of the country, present laws, manners, customs, religion of the inhabitants; every circumstance, on which a difference in the point in question can be

[5] Jeremy Bentham, *Principles of Morals and Legislation* (1789; Buffalo, N.Y.: Prometheus Books, 1988), ch. xvii, § 2.

[6] Bentham, "Essay on the Influence of Time and Place in Matters of Legislation," in John Bowring, ed., *The Works of Jeremy Bentham*, vol. 1 (Edinburgh: William Tait, 1843), p. 171. I have been unable to determine the exact date when this essay was written. It appears to have been written in the early 1780s.

grounded, as different as can be. . . . To a lawgiver, who having been bred up with English notions, shall have learnt how to accommodate his laws to the circumstances of Bengal, no other part of the globe can present any difficulty.[7]

But Bentham also insisted that "human nature was everywhere the same" and that different countries did not have "different catalogues of pleasures and pains." Then why should not the same laws hold good for all countries? Because the things that caused pleasure or pain were not the same everywhere. "The same event . . . which would produce pain or pleasure in one country, would not produce an effect of the same sort, or if of the same sort, not in equal degree, in another."[8] But these grounds of variation were not all of the same kind either. Some were physical, such as the climate or the nature of the soil, and these were invariant and insurmountable. Others, no matter how difficult or inexpedient, were subject to intervention and change, such as "the circumstances of government, religion, and manners."[9] Different sets of laws would be appropriate for different circumstances. Further, by the application of appropriate laws, the mutable circumstances could be subjected to the forces of change.

Bentham thought of these variations as amenable to more or less precise and detailed qualitative and quantitative comparison—that is to say, they were all subject to some common measure. He suggested that the legislator should be provided with two sets of tables relating to the country for which he was legislating. One set would consist of the civil code, the constitutional code, a table of offences and punishments, etc. and the other set would comprise tables of the moral and religious biases of the people, a set of maps, a table of the productions of the country, tables of the population, and the like.[10] Armed with these, he would be able to devise the best possible laws for any country.

Reading Bentham today, one can almost imagine an anticipation of the statistical handbooks of social indicators with which any undergraduate of the twenty-first century is now able to rank the countries of the world according to standards of living, mortality rates, quality

---

[7] "Influence of Time and Place," p. 172.
[8] Ibid.
[9] Ibid., p. 177.
[10] Ibid., p. 173.

of governance, human development, and dozens of other evaluative criteria. Unlike in the writings of eighteenth-century historians and travellers brought up on Montesquieu, cultural difference here is no longer incommensurable. Rather, it can now be seen in terms of its consequences, plotted as deviations from a standard and hence normalized. Governments everywhere have been brought within the same conceptual field. All deviations between states are now comparable according to the same measure. States could be divided into ranks and grades.

Moreover, once normalized, deviations could be tracked over time: the deviation of a state from the norm could close or widen. Thus, in time, a country could conceivably enter the grade of "advanced societies" or drop out of it. The important innovation here was the handle that was afforded for the intervention of "policy" to affect the distance of an empirical state from the desired norm. Indeed, as the philosopher Ian Hacking has shown, the statistical elaboration of the idea of normality in the nineteenth century would establish two senses of the norm: one, the normal as the right and the good—the normative, as political philosophy, for instance, would have it—and the other, the normal as the empirically existent average or mean, capable of improvement.[11]

Norms and Exceptions

The significance of this conceptual innovation for the emergence of the new practices of government in the nineteenth century has not been adequately stressed. We see the concepts elaborated for the first time in Jeremy Bentham and his "utilitarian" theories of legislation. But these formal properties of the comparative method would become part of the background assumptions of virtually all schools of thought on the subject of modern government, including many that had no truck with utilitarianism as a political philosophy. Notwithstanding Bentham's exaggerated confidence in the ability of his method to provide exact and unimpeachable solutions to every policy problem, what it did mark out was a conceptual field that could in principle integrate into a single theoretical domain all questions of governance in every society that exists in the world. Its comparative method of

[11] Ian Hacking, *The Taming of Chance* (Cambridge: Cambridge University Press, 1990), pp. 160–9.

normalization would establish an enduring modality of relating the domain of the normative to that of the empirical, something that would long outlast the limited appeal of utilitarian political philosophy. The norm-deviation structure has provided, from the nineteenth century to the present day, an enduring framework for addressing policy questions of improvement, progress, modernization, and development.

However, Bentham's comparative method would also establish a second global paradigm. If constitutionally established representative government was to be recognized as the universally valid normative standard, then the universally valid and legitimate exception to that norm could only be some form of enlightened despotism. Despotism is unlimited and arbitrary power, unconstrained by constitutional rules. In this sense, it was often distinguished in the classical literature of the seventeenth and eighteenth centuries from absolutism—which was unlimited power but legitimately constituted within certain fundamental laws. The form of government recommended by the new normative theory for European colonies in the East was absolutist in the sense that while it did not recognize any limits to its sovereign powers within the occupied territory, it did claim to be constituted by, and to function within, certain fundamental laws. But it was despotic in its foundational assumptions since the authority that was to lay down those fundamental laws was arbitrarily constituted and was not in any way responsible to those whom it governed. But when despotism claims to be enlightened, it places a limit on itself and promises to itself to be responsible: it becomes limited by and responsible to enlightened reason. When that happens, there is effectively no difference between despotism and absolutism. Despotism has to justify its actions to itself by their results.[12] Since the empirically prevailing average social conditions in the "backward" colonies were different from those in the advanced countries, the normative standard of the latter would have to be altered to suit the former. The universally valid norm would have to be withheld in favour of a colonial exception.

The ground for declaring the exception is the empirical deviation of prevailing institutions and practices in a particular country from the

---

[12] Leonard Krieger, *An Essay on the Theory of Enlightened Despotism* (Chicago: University of Chicago Press, 1975), p. 39.

universally desirable norm. Bentham spoke of the moral and religious biases of the people; today we might label the deviations as the products of culture. Electoral democracy, or freedom of speech, or the secular state, or equal rights for women might be universally desirable norms but they could be suspended in countries where prevailing cultural practices deviate significantly from the norm. As we will see, the application of the norm-deviation and norm-exception structures is not restricted only to international comparisons; they could be, and indeed are, applied to heterogeneous population groups within the nation-state.

This structure of norm and exception can be seen in virtually every justification of colonial empires in the nineteenth and twentieth centuries. The puzzle posed by postcolonial political theory—by Uday Singh Mehta, for example—of liberal democratic governments in Europe holding overseas territories under their despotic rule, thus apparently contradicting their cherished normative principles, dissolves when one realizes the power of the norm-exception construct.[13] Thus, John Stuart Mill, one of the greatest liberal political theorists of all time, while making an extended case for the universal superiority of representative government, specifically argued that it could not apply, at least not yet, to dependencies such as India and Ireland.[14] The latter were exceptions; hence there was really no contradiction in Mill's normative liberal theory. He recommended a paternal British despotism for those countries until such time as their peoples became mature enough to govern themselves. Of course, neither Mill nor any other liberal could suggest an impartial way of deciding when and if such a stage had been reached. Apparently, there was no alternative but to rely on the good sense of the paternal guardians to grant self-government to their wards. Or rather, the only alternative was to acknowledge the right of a subject people to announce its attainment of maturity by rebelling against its masters—a right somewhat incompatible with liberal doctrines of good colonial governance.

From the nineteenth century, therefore, the two senses of the norm

---

[13] Uday Singh Mehta, *Liberalism and Empire: A Study in Nineteenth-century British Liberal Thought* (Chicago: University of Chicago Press, 1999).

[14] John Stuart Mill, *Considerations of Representative Government* (1861; Buffalo, N.Y.: Prometheus Books, 1991), ch. xviii.

encoded the basic political strategy of relating the normative to the empirical. The norm-deviation structure would establish the empirical location of any particular social formation at any given time in relation to the empirically prevailing average or normal. The corresponding normative framework could then provide, by means of a norm-exception structure of justification, the ground for the application of "policy" to intervene and bring the empirical average closer to the desired norm. Normalization was the theoretical key to this political strategy.

The norm-deviation method as a crucial aspect of modern disciplinary practices is, as Michel Foucault has shown, ubiquitous in the operations of the modern regime of power.[15] The norm-exception formula too is used widely to deal with the exigencies of heterogeneity and uncertainty in a policy field that has been presumably normalized. What I am also suggesting through my thumbnail sketch of the conceptual history of political institutions in the modern West is that, contrary to the long-enshrined received narrative, those institutions and their normative principles were not the products of an exclusively endogenous development but the result of Europe's encounters with its colonial territories, first in the Americas and then in Asia and Africa. Let me now move to our times and look at formerly colonized parts of the world to see how the universal verities of Western political theory have fared in those places.

The Civil and the Political in Alien Spaces

I will have to be somewhat schematic in laying out the background conditions that made postcolonial political theory possible. The period of decolonization following the end of the Second World War made the nation-state the universally normal form of the modern state. Popular sovereignty became the universal norm of legitimacy: even military dictators and one-party regimes began to claim to rule on behalf of the people. But decolonization was achieved not necessarily because the paternal guardians decided that their immature wards had at last achieved adulthood. On the contrary, in most colonial countries

---

[15] Especially Michel Foucault, *Discipline and Punish: The Birth of the Prison*, tr. Alan Sheridan (Harmondsworth: Penguin, 1977).

the people declared their determination to rule themselves by rebelling against their masters. This meant that the pedagogical role of those who were the guardians of the norm and the declarers of the exception came to be questioned. As we shall soon see, this would have important implications for the relation between the norm and the exception.

The normative principles of modern politics as established in the West held enormous sway over the new ruling elites in postcolonial countries, not least because of the influence of colonial education. But decades of colonial rule did not necessarily close the deviation of the empirical social indicators from the universally desirable norm. The sociologically grounded theories that now came into vogue rephrased the old arguments of colonial difference in a new language of modernization, calling the deviation a historical lag that had to be made up. Underlying these theories was, as Sudipta Kaviraj has pointed out, an assumption of symmetrical development, that is to say, an expectation that all of the functionally interrelated processes within modernity should emerge simultaneously.[16] If they did not, then it was a case of imperfect or failed modernity. A little reflection will show that this expectation of symmetrical development is not unrelated to the abstract homogeneous discursive space cleared out and occupied by normative political theory.

But soon there began to emerge arguments about alternative or multiple modernities. These, Kaviraj has shown, are better understood as implying a sequential theory of development. This theory suggests that the particular sequence in which the different processes of modernity occurred in Western history need not be repeated elsewhere. In that case, the resultant forms of the modern in those places might look quite different. Thus, to take an example, if the particular sequence "commercial society—civic associations— rational bureaucracy—industrialization—universal suffrage—welfare state," which may be taken as a schematic representation of the trajectory of the modern democratic state in the West, is replaced by a sequence in which rational bureaucracy and universal suffrage precede the others, then it is likely that the form of the state that would result would not

---

[16] Sudipta Kaviraj, "An Outline of a Revisionist Theory of Modernity," *Archives européennes de sociologie*, 46, 3 (2005), pp. 497–526.

be a replica of the state in the West. It is from a consideration of these alternative sequences of modernity rather than from that of multiple or post-modernity that postcolonial political theory was born. It created the possibility, not necessarily of resolving the debate launched, for instance by Fredric Jameson, of whether modernity is necessarily singular, but of leaving its normative structure underspecified and open to future determination.[17]

But this raised entirely new theoretical problems regarding the relation between the two senses of the norm, namely, the empirical average and the normatively desirable. Let me illustrate this with reference to two sets of issues—the first of legality, and the second of violence.

Leaving out the white settler colonies, the domain of civil social institutions and modern representative politics was, in most parts of the colonial world, restricted to only a small section of the colonized population. Mahmood Mamdani has described how in Africa there emerged a modern civic space that was racially divided but regulated by a modern code of civil law, while a huge domain of traditional society was organized under customary law.[18] Karuna Mantena has explored the foundations of indirect rule in the anthropological theories of Henry Maine drawn from his comparative studies of ancient societies and colonial social formations in India.[19] Following the decolonization of Africa, the conservative nationalist regimes de-racialized civil society while leaving the traditional sphere of customary law largely intact, while the radical regimes tried to impose uniform citizenship on all by authoritarian methods, leading to resistance and conflict. In India, the new republic was founded on a liberal democratic constitution, universal suffrage, and competitive electoral representation. But the space of politics became effectively split between a narrow domain of civil society where citizens related to the state through the mutual recognition of legally enforceable rights and a wider domain of political society where governmental

[17] Fredric Jameson, *Singular Modernity: Essay on the Ontology of the Present* (London: Verso, 2002).

[18] Mahmood Mamdani, *Citizen and Subject: Contemporary Africa and the Legacy of Late Colonialism* (Princeton: Princeton University Press, 1996).

[19] Karuna Mantena, *Alibis of Empire: Henry Maine and the Ends of Liberal Imperialism* (Princeton: Princeton University Press, 2010).

agencies dealt not with citizens but with populations to deliver specific benefits or services through a process of political negotiation. I have elsewhere described the anomalies that result in the application of the norm of equality of all citizens before the law and how those anomalies are sought to be resolved through the intervention of politics.[20]

Take the familiar example of squatter settlements of the poor in numerous cities of the postcolonial world. These urban populations occupy land that does not belong to them and often use water, electricity, public transport, and other services without paying for them. But governmental authorities do not necessarily try to punish or put a stop to such illegalities because of the political recognition that these populations serve certain necessary functions in the urban economy, and that to forcibly remove them would involve huge political costs. On the other hand, they cannot be treated as legitimate members of civil society who abide by the law. As a result, municipal authorities or the police deal with these people not as rights-bearing citizens but as urban populations who have specific characteristics and needs and who must be appropriately governed. On their side, these groups of the urban poor negotiate with the authorities through political mobilization and alliances with other groups.

On the plane of governmentality, populations do not carry the ethical significance of citizenship. They are heterogeneous groups, each of which is defined and classified by its empirically observed characteristics and constituted as a rationally manipulable target population for governmental policies. Consequently, if, despite their illegal occupation of land, they are given electricity connections or allowed to use municipal services, it is not because they have a right to them but because the authorities make a political calculation of costs and benefits and agree, for the time being, to give them those benefits. However, this can only be done in a way that does not jeopardize the legal order of property and the rights of proper citizens. The usual method is to construct a case such that the particular illegality associated with a specific population group may be treated as an exception that does not disturb the fundamental rule of law. Governmental decisions aimed at regulating the vast populations of the urban poor

---

[20] Partha Chatterjee, *The Politics of the Governed: Reflections on Popular Politics in Most of the World* (New York: Columbia University Press, 2004).

usually add up to a huge pile of exceptions to the normal application of the law.

Populations respond to the regime of governmentality by seeking to constitute themselves as groups that deserve the attention of government. If as squatters they have violated the law, they do not necessarily deny that fact, nor do they claim that their illegal occupation of land is right. But they insist that they have a right to housing and livelihood in the city, and, if they are required to move elsewhere, they must be rehabilitated. They form associations to negotiate with governmental authorities and seek public support for their cause. Their political mobilization involves an effort to turn an empirically formed population group into a moral community. The force of this moral appeal usually hinges on the generally recognized obligation of government to provide for the poor and the underprivileged. This obligation may be seen as part of the general democratic temper of our age. But I believe it is also specifically a consequence of the anti-colonial movement that overturned the paternal despotism of imperial rule and established the formal sovereignty of the people.

If we consider the example of elections in India, for instance, we will find that the overwhelming bulk of the political rhetoric expended in election campaigns concerns what governments have or have not done for which population groups. The function of rhetoric here is to turn the heterogeneous demands of populations into the morally coherent and emotionally persuasive form of popular demands. In this sense, as Ernesto Laclau has argued, populism is the only morally legitimate form of democratic politics under these conditions.[21] It is important to emphasize that, unlike the symmetrical theory of modernity which would regard such populism as a perversion of modern democratic politics, the sequential theory would consider it with utter seriousness as a new and potentially richer development of democracy.

However, the negotiations that take place in political society frequently involve an invitation to the authorities to declare an exception. Thus, when squatters claim that they be allowed to occupy their settlements, or hawkers that they be allowed to set up stalls on the streets, they do not demand that the laws of property be abolished or that all trade licenses and regulations be set aside. Rather, they demand

---

[21] Ernesto Laclau, *On Populist Reason* (London: Verso, 2005).

that the authorities make a political judgement to use the sovereign power of the state to declare their case an exception to the norm laid down by the law.

It is true, of course, that the law is also frequently broken by the propertied and the wealthy, that is, by those who claim to be proper citizens inhabiting civil society. Thus, municipal building regulations, trade regulations, and tax laws are widely believed to be broken by the urban rich, many of whom, being influential and well connected, even flaunt their impunity. But these violations are unable to mobilize the moral justification that the illegalities of the poor manage to do in the arena of democratic politics. Indeed, the urban poor point to the violations practised by the rich as evidence not of the irrelevance of a moral order but of the unfair exceptions made by the authorities in favour of the rich; and, to restore the balance of fairness, they demand that similar exceptions be made for the poor. The rich usually defend their violations by corruption, evasion, or the blatant use of force; rarely can they make them objects of negotiation in political society.

We should also remember that vast sections of the poor in postcolonial economies find a living in the so-called informal sector of employment, which is largely unregulated and in which production or service units frequently violate labour, tax, and environmental laws. Quite often such enterprises include owners who are themselves workers, and it is not unusual for them to value the survival of their units above the making of profits for accumulation. They frequently use collective political mobilization and seek the help of political parties and leaders to ensure conditions for their survival, often by demanding that the usual tax, labour, and environmental regulations not be applied in their case. Here again politics intervenes to suspend the norm and create an exception, supposedly in a justified cause.

This raises another interesting problem for contemporary political theory. Is justice better served by non-arbitrary procedures which entail an equal application of the law, or by contextual and possibly arbitrary judgements that address the peculiarities of a particular case? It is useful to recall here de Tocqueville's observation in the early days of the modern democratic state. Distinguishing between tyranny and arbitrary power, he says, "Tyranny may be exercised by means of the law itself, and in that case it is not arbitrary; arbitrary power may be exercised for the public good, in which case it is not tyrannical."[22] We could say that political society, operating under conditions of electoral democracy in India, affords the possibility of inviting the arbitrary power of government to mitigate the potentially tyrannical power of the law. As a matter of fact, it could even be said that the activities of political society in postcolonial countries represent a continuing critique of the paradoxical reality in all capitalist democracies of equal citizenship and majority rule, on the one hand, and the dominance of property and privilege, on the other.

It is relevant to point out that this critique has a genealogy going all the way back to the origins in the eighteenth century of British colonial attempts to impose a regime of the non-arbitrary rule of law in the newly conquered territories of India. Ghulam Husain Tabatabai, the most perceptive Indian historian of the eighteenth century, and Mirza Abu Taleb who travelled to Britain at the turn of the nineteenth, both wrote extensively and critically on what they thought was an expensive, slow, distant, and unconscionably inflexible judicial system introduced by the British in Bengal. Both thought that direct access to an impartial judge who was knowledgeable about and sensitive to the specific circumstances of a case was far more likely to serve the cause of justice.[23] The critique has continued to inform popular beliefs and practices about the judicial system of modern India. Thus, for example, one of the most sought after services of elected local bodies in rural West Bengal is arbitration in property, family, and community disputes. Even though this is not one of their statutory functions, elected local representatives are preferred by rural people for resolving

[22] Alexis de Tocqueville, *Democracy in America,* vol. 1, tr. Henry Reeve, revised by Francis Bowen, ed. Phillips Bradley (New York: Vintage, 1990), p. 262.

[23] Abu Taleb Khan, *Travels of Mirza Abu Taleb Khan in Asia, Africa, and Europe during the Years 1799 to 1803,* tr. Charles Stewart (1814; New Delhi: Sona Publications, 1972), ch. xxii, p. 196. There is a four-volume edition of the 1788 translation of Ghulam Husain's work *Sair ul-mutakkherin* published in 1902: *A Translation of the Sëir Mutaqherin; or View of Modern Times, being an History of India, from the Year 1118 to the Year 1194, (this Year answers to the Christian Year 1781–82) of the Hedjrah; etc. by Seid-Gholam-Hossein-Khan,* vols 1–4 (Calcutta: R. Cambray, 1902). An edition published in 1926 is now available as a facsimile edition from New Delhi: Inter-India Publications, 1986.

conflicts to the slow, opaque, and frequently corrupt institutions of the police and courts.[24] The latter are seen as instruments that only the wealthy can manipulate to their advantage; the poor avoid them to the best of their ability.

It is also worth mentioning here, in a comparative spirit, the analysis offered by Achille Mbembe of the postcolonial state in Africa. He argues that the specific form of sovereignty claimed over the territory and resources of Africa by the colonial powers frequently led to the authoritarian postcolonial state form characterized by the *étatisation* of society, the socialization of state power, and the privatization of public prerogatives. These three features of the postcolonial state were all marked, Mbembe says, by the socialization of arbitrariness.[25] Although the Indian state is nowhere near as authoritarian as many of the African states, the continuing social legitimacy of arbitrary power is an important and under-researched aspect of the practices of Indian democracy.

If one then thinks of this widely shared popular critique of the modern normative idea of the non-arbitrary and equal application of the law within a sequential rather than symmetrical framework, one could be led in some unexpected directions. Thinking symmetrically, one might conclude, like many conservative colonial officials of British India, that the impersonal procedures of rational law and bureaucracy were unsuited to backward societies habituated to customary rather than contractual obligations, and that the exercise of personal but impartial authority was more appropriate. This would be the familiar declaration of a colonial exception. But if we take the sequential logic more seriously, we might be moved to suggest not the irrelevance of the norm of the impersonal and non-arbitrary application of the law but its critical revaluation in the light of emergent practices in many postcolonial countries that seek to punctuate or supplement it by appealing to personal and contextual circumstances. There is enough ground here to speculate, for instance, that the enormous powers of judicial review of legislation and active surveillance of executive acts

[24] Dwaipayan Bhattacharya, Partha Chatterjee, Pranab Kumar Das, Dhrubajyoti Ghosh, Manabi Majumdar, and Surajit Mukhopadhyay, *Strengthening Rural Decentralization* (Calcutta: Centre for Studies in Social Sciences, 2006).

[25] Achille Mbembe, *On the Postcolony* (Berkeley: University of California Press, 2001), pp. 24–65.

assumed by the Indian law courts—powers unknown in any other liberal constitutional system in the world—is a response to this popular critique of procedural non-arbitrariness.

It is important to stress that the normative principles of Western political theory continue to enjoy enormous influence all round the world as models worthy of emulation. The actual practices of modern political life have resulted, however, not in the abandonment of those norms but in the piling up of exceptions in course of the administration of the law as mediated by the processes of political society. The relation between norms and practices has resulted in a series of improvisations. It is the theorization of these improvisations that has become the task of postcolonial political theory.

One other area in which such improvisations have led to a distinct reformulation of the received norm is the secular state. The French republican ideal of *laïcité*, having travelled to Turkey as *laïque*, has in recent years provoked much controversy and conflict over state recognition of religious practices, without as yet producing any redefined norm.[26] In India, while the secular state is a central feature of the constitutional structure, its practice has come to mean neither the mutual separation of state and religion nor the strict neutrality of the state. Rather, an altogether new norm of the modern secular state seems to have emerged. This Rajeev Bhargava has theorized as that of principled distance, which implies the disavowal of a state religion but not the strict non-intervention of the state in religion.[27] In this context, one must also mention the massive but as yet untheorized process of the establishment of modern secular states all over East Asia, apparently without any serious debate over the question of secularism. What is it about the sequence of modernity in that part of the world that made this possible?

The Political Management of Violence

A study of squatter settlements in the city of Calcutta carried out by Ananya Roy brings out an interesting gender dimension of political

---

[26] Nilufer Gole and Ludwig Ammann, eds, *Islam in Public: Turkey, Iran and Europe* (Istanbul: Istanbul Bilgi University, 2006).

[27] Rajeev Bhargava, ed., *Secularism and Its Critics* (Delhi: Oxford University Press, 1998).

society.[28] The livelihood of families living in these illegal settlements greatly depends on the employment of women as domestic help in neighbouring middle-class houses. This is, of course, an informal sector of employment lacking any form of self-organization of labour. The men of the settlements often do not have regular jobs. But they form associations to seek the support of political parties in order to protect their settlements. The associations are entirely male. The reason is not merely that political work is traditionally seen as a male pursuit, but also that politics in the slum neighbourhoods is thought to be dangerous, involving frequent incidents of violence. Political society, consequently, tends to be a masculine space.

The point is illustrated graphically in Thomas Blom Hansen's study of the Shiv Sena in the towns and cities of Maharashtra, especially Mumbai.[29] The political effectiveness of the Shiv Sena as a right-wing populist party claiming to defend Marathi interests and Hindu dominance has crucially depended on its control over the urban slum population and the informal sector of labour. Hansen shows that a key figure here is the local *dada*, the strongman who builds a personal network of loyalty and protection and projects the image of masculine, assertive and often violent power. The modality of this power is performative; it is effective precisely to the extent that it works as a demonstrated threat that brings about the desired result. The issues on which the Shiv Sena intervenes are everyday matters of political society among the urban poor—jobs, housing, living conditions in the slums, prices of essential items of consumption, dealing with the police and the authorities. The methods are direct and often theatrical: the image of local strongmen projecting raw power to secure instant justice is what is expected to attract their followers. For the most part, the actual violence is kept within carefully controlled limits. Only rarely is there widespread organized violence, and that happens only after a decision of the central leadership of the party, as in the 1992 killings of Muslims in Mumbai.

The subject of violence brings into view the dark underside of political society. It is clear that the real world of politics is quite far

[28] Ananya Roy, *City Requiem, Calcutta: Gender and the Politics of Poverty* (Minneapolis: University of Minnesota Press, 2003).

[29] Thomas Blom Hansen, *Wages of Violence: Naming and Identity in Postcolonial Bombay* (Princeton: Princeton University Press, 2001).

removed from the Weberian ideal of the state possessing a monopoly of the means of legitimate violence. Since many of the practices of political society involve transgressions of the law, it follows that agents other than the state authorities must also acquire the means of using force to defend those practices when necessary. Once again, political parties and leaders try to mobilize such means, with or without the acquiescence of the authorities. This is undoubtedly the principal reason why there has emerged the phenomenon of what is often called the "criminalization" of politics, that is, the increasing presence of persons with criminal records among elected representatives at local, state, and even national levels. That violators of the law can become legitimate representatives of the people is not necessarily a symptom of popular foolhardiness or of the perversion of electoral democracy. Rather, it is a sign of the inability of the normative regime of law to fully bring under its order the real heterogeneity of power relations in society. It is also significant that, in most local formations of political society, a certain "normal" level of violence tends to be established which represents some sort of empirical equilibrium among prevailing power relations, and that there are recognized thresholds beyond which violence would be regarded as having crossed the limits of normality. On the other hand, when a situation has to be demonstrated as intolerable or outrageous, there is frequently a spectacular show of violence, usually involving the destruction of public property or attacks on government institutions and personnel. Violence here is not mindless or blind, but rather, even in its most passionate expressions, calculated to elicit the desired response from the government and the public.

Redefining the Norms

A consideration of postcolonial politics against the background of Western normative theory might suggest that moral norms should be abandoned in favour of realist politics. However, this would mean a trivialization of the challenge posed for postcolonial political theory. Even though the demand for realism has much merit, it cannot mean, as Raymond Geuss has pointed out, the claim that morality has no place in politics.[30] Rather, as we cannot fail to see in numerous

---

[30] Raymond Geuss, *Philosophy and Real Politics* (Princeton: Princeton University Press, 2008).

accounts, postcolonial politics frequently presents a moral critique of the normative standards upheld by Western political theory and improvises practices that run parallel or counter to the approved forms. The theoretical challenge that is thereby posed is twofold. The first is the challenge to break the abstract homogeneity of the mythical time-space of Western normative theory by emphasizing the real history of its formation through violent conflict and the imposition of hegemonic power. The second is the even greater challenge to redefine the normative standards of modern politics in the light of the considerable accumulation of new practices that may at present be described only in the language of exceptions but which in fact contain the core of a richer, more diverse, and inclusive set of norms.

As far as the first challenge is concerned, the work of many historians and literary scholars has brought together in recent decades a mass of evidence to show that several key political and economic institutions of the modern West were produced not endogenously but through interaction with the colonial worlds across the Atlantic and in the East. Thus, Michel-Rolph Trouillot argued that the idea of universal citizenship was indeed *first* posed in the age of revolutions by the Haitian uprising of black slaves.[31] Susan Buck-Morss has pushed the argument further by showing that the consciousness of emancipation that inspired the idea of equal citizenship in the modern state, as elaborated by philosophers such as Hegel, was directly the product of an engagement with the challenge posed by the Haitian revolution.[32] Buck-Morss has also drawn our attention to the fact, long known to scholars of colonial trade but never remarked upon, that the factory, that central institution of the industrial revolution, was invented as the European merchant company's foreign trading station.[33] We also know that the joint stock company, another pillar of modern capitalism, was first developed as an institution of colonial trade, the English East India Company being the most successful pioneer.[34] Such

[31] Michel-Rolph Trouillot, *Silencing the Past: Power and the Production of History* (Boston: Beacon Press, 1995).

[32] Susan Buck-Morss, *Hegel, Haiti, and Universal History* (Pittsburgh: University of Pittsburgh Press, 2009).

[33] Ibid., pp. 101–3.

[34] K.N. Chaudhuri, *The Trading World of Asia and the English East India Company, 1660–1760* (Cambridge: Cambridge University Press, 1978).

instances can be multiplied and extended to institutions of bureaucracy, diplomacy, international law, penal administration, surveillance, crowd control, emergency relief, and a host of other aspects of modern government.

The point is not merely to insist upon an acknowledgement that the institutions of economic and political life in the modern West have a historical genealogy that extends into the formerly colonial world. It is to explore the further implication of that history for the authoritative status of the normative claims of Western political theory for our contemporary world. If we know that the principal hegemonic strategy for establishing the universal claims of the normative standards of Western political institutions is to combine a norm-deviation paradigm in the empirical domain with a norm-exception paradigm in the policy domain, what has been the consequence of decolonization and the emergence of postcolonial thinking for the continued relevance of this strategy?

One has heard several voices in recent times that reject, on ideological grounds, the claims of normative Western political theory. Thus, representative electoral democracy has been rejected as Western or bourgeois and therefore unsuited to conditions in non-Western countries. The idea of human rights has been similarly rejected as Western or Christian and therefore inapplicable to other societies. There have been claims on behalf of "Asian values" or "Islamic principles" as having greater universal validity than the Western norms of modern democratic government. While the conflicts rage over these questions in the field of ideology, what should be of greater interest to political theory are the ways in which actual practices in the field of government and politics cope with the realities of power in a world in which no society has the option of entirely escaping the tentacles of modern economic, political, and cultural institutions. Once we recognize this, we have no alternative but to return to the problem of symmetrical versus sequential accounts of modernity. If by tracing the historical genealogy of Western political institutions we have established the sheer historical contingency of Western modernity, there can be no reason left to demand the symmetrical repetition of that configuration of institutions in other parts of the world. Hence, political theory is left with the task of describing the varied products of different sequences of development in different countries as novel but ineluctably modern practices of government and politics. Such descriptions cannot avoid the question of normative evaluation. However, since many of these practices imply a critique of the normative standards of Western political practice, political theory cannot any more proceed with its normal business of endlessly elaborating and refining its normative principles supposedly established from the moment of its birth. That is the challenge posed by postcolonial politics.

The second task of redefining the universal normative standards set by Western political theory in the light of the experience of postcolonial politics involves serious moral evaluation. We have noticed that the divergent practices that have emerged in postcolonial countries are frequently justified as exceptions to the normative rule. Could the accumulation of exceptions justify a redefinition of the norm? Take the example of citizenship. The normative rule under the Indian constitution is equal citizenship for all. But from the very beginning, exceptions were made to provide for special representation and reserved places in government service and education for Scheduled Castes and Tribes and for the personal laws and special educational institutions of minority religious communities. Initially, these exceptions were justified as transitional measures to be removed when a reasonable equality of opportunity was established between all groups and communities. As these practices have unfolded in the last half a century, even though the constitutional language of exceptions continues, the democratic politics of caste and religious minorities proceeds by taking these exceptional provisions of differentiated citizenship as enduring background conditions that lay the ground for new strategies of negotiation with government. The question is: can the contemporary practices be framed as a redefined norm that endorses differentiated rather than equal citizenship as the normative standard for the modern state?

The question becomes more worthy of our attention when we realize that differentiated citizenship has, in some form or other, become normal practice in the empirical sense in most Western countries, even though it is still described as exceptional in relation to the legal norm. Thus, the practices that have evolved to deal with new immigrants, including undocumented ones, in the countries of Western Europe and North America are no different from what we have described as characteristic of political society in postcolonial India. Has there been a redefinition of citizenship in actual practice that is awaiting a political theorist to put into normative language?

Interestingly, the growing phenomenon in contemporary Western democracies of deep and pervasive mistrust of elected representatives and apparent voter apathy has led theorists to look closely at practices such as popular vigilance, denunciation, negative coalitions, mock trials, etc. Pierre Rosanvallon has called such non-electoral forms "counter-democracy."[35] If one turns to postcolonial democracies, one will find many of these counter-democratic forms in the domain of civil society of the urban middle classes, as seen most recently in the campaigns that led twice to the ouster of popularly elected governments in Thailand in 2006 and 2009. In India, while mistrust of representatives and the forms of counter-democracy can be widely observed, the urban middle classes show a marked lack of faith in the efficacy of elections, while those who most use the instruments of political society to deal with government—the poorer sections of people in both cities and villages—are the ones who persistently vote in large numbers. Once again, the postcolonial is marked by difference.

The emergence of postcolonial states in the latter half of the twentieth century appeared to affirm the determination of formerly colonial peoples not to allow the imperial powers to point to an empirical deviation from the norm and declare an exception in relation to the universal normative standard. But, as we have seen, postcolonial regimes have adopted the same norm-deviation and norm-exception paradigms in governing their own populations. Not only that, the politics of the governed operates within the same paradigms, inviting governmental authorities to declare an exception and suspend the norm in their case. The question that pervades postcolonial politics today is: who should get to declare the exception? That is the question debated every day in this part of the world—not always, I might add, by entirely peaceful means. The question that appears to have receded from view is one that used to be asked in the twentieth century: is

---

[35] Pierre Rosanvallon, *Counter-democracy: Politics in an Age of Distrust*, tr. Arthur Goldhammer (Cambridge: Cambridge University Press, 2008).

it possible to think of modern politics outside the norm-deviation and norm-exception paradigms? That question does not seem to be thinkable today except in a non-realist theoretical mode. Since I am able to deal with politics only when it is real, whether in the past, present, or future, I must warn the reader that the following chapters will not attempt to answer that utopian question.

I
Genealogies

2

Five Hundred Years of Fear and Love

Misrecognitions

When Vasco da Gama arrived on the coast of Malabar in 1498 with four relatively small vessels, he was, it is traditionally said, "looking for Christians and spices." The latter motive seems obvious to us now, from all that we know of the importance of trade in the European search for sea routes and new continents in the so-called age of discovery. Indeed, soon after the Cape route to Asia was opened up, the composition of the return cargo to Lisbon in the early years of the sixteenth century shows the overwhelming dominance of items such as pepper, ginger, cinnamon, and cloves, although this composition was to change fairly soon.[1] Regarding the other objective of the visit, however, we may well wonder why anyone should accept the hazards of sailing across uncharted and dangerous seas to seek out Christians in India. Here, we have to remind ourselves of the ideological world inhabited by men like da Gama. Our current ideas that associate European expansion with rational economic activity and modern statecraft gloss over the fact that the connection only emerged gradually during the course of the five hundred years we are talking about, and that it does not hold for the early part of this period in the same way that it might for the later. As a matter of fact, an important motive for the Portuguese expeditions to India was shaped by the legends and rumours concerning a certain Prester John, a Christian ruler supposedly living somewhere in the Orient, who was said to be

[1] Sanjay Subrahmanyam, *The Portuguese Empire in Asia, 1500–1700: A Political and Economic History* (London: Longman, 1993), p. 63.

keen to join forces with the kings of Europe in their crusade against Islam. In an atmosphere charged with memories of the recent "reconquest" of the Iberian peninsula from the hands of the so-called Moors, and a strategic situation in which Muslim rulers and traders along the African, Arabian, and Persian coasts were seen as the principal hurdles to European expansion into the Indian Ocean region, it should be understandable why the prospect of finding a Christian ally in the East seemed so compelling to the ruling groups in Lisbon. Of course, recent historians have warned us that the motives of trade and religion did not operate in the same manner or with the same force in all influential sections of the Portuguese court, and that there is a much more complex political story of how da Gama was finally chosen to lead the expedition to India.[2] Nevertheless, the two motives do explain many curious aspects of what happened in the course of the argonaut's journey.

Vasco da Gama's ships anchored off the coast of Calicut on Sunday, May 20, 1498. The first Portuguese went ashore the next day and reported thus:

> This city of Calecut is of Christians, who are dark men, and some of them go about with large beards, and long hair on the head, and others have shaven heads, and still others cropped. And they have certain topknots on their crowns, as a sign that they are Christians, and moustaches with their beards. And they have their ears pierced, and in the holes they wear much gold, and they walk about naked from the waist up, and below they wear certain very delicate cotton-cloths.

Over the next few days, the Portuguese obviously became a great curiosity in town since they were followed by large crowds of people, including women and children. They saw a large building which they thought was a church. It had a large tank beside it and a pillar at its entrance with the figure of a bird on it. Small bells hung from the doorway which led into an inner chamber inside which, the visitors reported, "was a small image which they [the locals] said was Our Lady." The Portuguese were not allowed entry into the inner chamber and had to say their prayers from the outside, after which some men

---

[2] See especially Sanjay Subrahmanyam, *The Career and Legend of Vasco da Gama* (Cambridge: Cambridge University Press, 1997), pp. 24–75.

wearing cords of thread from their shoulders sprinkled them with holy water and a white ash which, the visitors noticed, "the Christians of this land have the habit of putting on their foreheads, and bodies, and around the neck and along their upper arms." The report mentions that Vasco da Gama took the ash offered to him but managed to avoid putting it on.[3]

I relate this story in order to bring up a question that is inextricably connected with relations between Europe and India in the last five centuries—that of cultural misrecognition. In this case, the error is blatant, indeed ridiculously so. The explanation, too, is not far to seek. As Sanjay Subrahmanyam, da Gama's most recent biographer, tells us, the Portuguese were expecting to meet oriental Christians whose practices were different from their own. "Since they were convinced that they were in the land of some sort of deviant Christians, anything that was not explicitly Islamic appeared, residually, to be Christian."[4] As contacts became more regular and intimate over the succeeding centuries, there would of course be a huge accumulation of European knowledge about India. Indeed, from the age of enlightenment onwards, European scholars and administrators would claim a distinctly privileged position as the authoritative scientific interpreters of information on the natural resources and social life of India. Needless to say, the new experts would not make the same sorts of errors as the first Portuguese visitors.

And yet, the question is still asked: how have the preconceived and unexamined cultural assumptions of Europeans shaped and perhaps distorted even the supposedly scientific understanding of India in the modern disciplines of social knowledge? To pursue the example provided by the report on the first Portuguese visit to Calicut, although no informed person today will make the mistake of identifying as Christian priests men wearing white ash on their foreheads and sacred threads around their torsos, yet what is the validity of supposing that what those men represented was a religion? Could it be merely a cultural prejudice of enlightened Europe to suppose that religion is a cultural universal? Why do we assume that all human societies, or at

---

[3] My knowledge of the details of da Gama's visit is derived entirely from his latest biography: Subrahmanyam, *Vasco da Gama*, pp. 76–163.

[4] Ibid., p. 133.

any rate societies with a certain degree of civilizational complexity, must have something that answers to the concept "religion"? The matter is more serious than a mere error in identification. It is possible for us to laugh at the mistake made by Vasco da Gama's men. What would we say if it turns out that after being educated for a few generations in the modern scientific disciplines, the descendants of the men with sacred threads now go about their business imbued by the sincere conviction that what they have, or indeed must have, is a religion? The problem is central to the complexities of the relations between Europe and India, and we will have occasion to return to it later.

How did Indians react to their encounter with the first European visitors across the seas? I am not a historian of this period and it is possible that there exist sources that answer that question. The secondary literature I have seen, however, appears to be based entirely on the Portuguese accounts. What can be inferred from them is that the visitors were greeted at first with warmth mixed with curiosity, followed by growing caution as the Portuguese, racked by the fear of walking into some heinous oriental trap, began to act with great suspicion and obstinacy, and culminating in a sense of outrage when they began to take captives and bombard the shores and other vessels. It must have taken some time for the truth to sink in that a new era had dawned over the Indian seas—one that a reputed historian has rather delicately named the era of "hostile trade."[5] K. N. Chaudhuri sums up the change as follows: "[T]he arrival of the Portuguese in the Indian Ocean abruptly ended the system of peaceful oceanic navigation that was such a marked feature of the region. . . . The importation by the Portuguese of the Mediterranean style of trade and warfare, by land and sea, was a violation of the agreed conventions and certainly a new experience."[6]

Within a decade of Vasco da Gama's first visit, the Portuguese were seeking to exercise by force some sort of monopoly over the Indian Ocean trade and compelling others to navigate only with their

[5] Sanjay Subrahmanyam, *The Political Economy of Commerce: Southern India, 1500–1650* (Cambridge: Cambridge University Press, 1990).

[6] K. N. Chaudhuri, *Trade and Civilisation in the Indian Ocean: An Economic History from the Rise of Islam to 1750* (Cambridge: Cambridge University Press, 1985), pp. 63–4.

permission.[7] By the 1580s, Zain al-Din Ma'bari was writing at length about the "infamous deeds" of the Portuguese which had brought ruin upon Malabari society—the burning of cities and mosques, the interruption of the *hajj*, and the killing of nobles and learned men. His response was to inspire the Muslims of Malabar to launch a jihad against these "vile and disgusting infidels."[8] Moving to the eastern end of India's coastline along the Bay of Bengal, where the Portuguese presence was more prominent in the form of private traders and adventurers, two words entered the Bengali language as popular synonyms for sea pirate—*harmad* (from *armada*) and *bombete* (from *bombardier*). Summing up the reactions in that part of India to the Portuguese arrival, a nationalist historian from Bengal writes: "With a strange and perverse consistency, the Portuguese continued to offend the susceptibilities of a civilized society and a cultured court by their failure to conform to the higher standard of international conduct prevailing in India."[9]

The question might be asked: how did Europeans justify the continued violent disruption, well into the seventeenth century, of a region of relatively peaceful maritime trade when in Europe itself the effort was already on to secure some sort of agreed "law of the seas"? The answer is supplied by João de Barros, a Portuguese scholar. Writing in 1552, he states quite clearly:

> For even though there does exist a common law which allows all navigators to sail the seas freely . . . this law applies only to the whole of Europe and its Christian inhabitants, who have been placed within the fold of the Church of Rome by baptism and by faith, and who are also governed by Roman law in their polity. . . . But as regards Muslims and

[7] Indian vessels could sail only with the *cartaz* or pass issued by the Portuguese and this was enforced, often quite brutally, by the power of Portuguese boats fitted with guns. It seems Indian merchants and rulers in the end found it cheaper to accept Portuguese dominance rather than embark on a project to build their own fleet to take on the Portuguese. M. N. Pearson, *The Portuguese in India* (Cambridge: Cambridge University Press, 1987), pp. 57–9.

[8] *Tuhfat al-Mujahidin*, cited in Stephen Frederic Dale, *The Mappilas of Malabar 1498–1922: Islamic Society on the South Asian Frontier* (Oxford: Clarendon Press, 1980), pp. 50–3.

[9] Surendra Nath Sen, "The Portuguese in Bengal," in Jadunath Sarkar, ed., *The History of Bengal*, vol. 2 (Dhaka: University of Dacca, 1948), p. 354.

Heathens, who are outside the law of Jesus Christ, . . . if these are condemned in their souls, being the principal part of them, their bodies which are animated by those souls cannot plead the privileges of our laws, since the adherents of those creeds are not members of the evangelical congregation, even though they may be our neighbours as rational beings and though they may live to be converted to the true Faith.[10]

Today, it might seem that these words were penned by some fanatical medieval warmonger, but the historian Charles Boxer assures us that Barros was a humanist and a distinguished member of the somewhat aborted Portuguese renaissance of the sixteenth century.[11] I do not find this either strange or contradictory. Rather, I see in this justification of aggressive overseas expansion an early example of a structure of argument produced by what I have elsewhere called "the rule of colonial difference."[12] This occurs when a normative proposition of supposedly universal validity (and many such propositions would be asserted in the centuries separating us from the early Portuguese expeditions) is held not to apply to the colony on account of some inherent moral deficiency in the latter. Thus, even as the rights of man would be declared in the revolutionary assemblies of Paris in 1789, the revolt in Saint Domingue (now Haiti) would be put down on the ground that those rights could not apply to black slaves. John Stuart Mill would set forth with great eloquence and precision his arguments establishing representative government as the best possible government, but would immediately add that this did not hold for India. The exception would not detract from the universality of the proposition; on the contrary, by specifying the norm by which universal humanness was to be recognized, it would strengthen its moral force. In the case of the Portuguese expedition, the norm was given by religion. Later, it would be supplied by biological theories of racial character or historical theories of civilizational achievement or socio-economic theories of institutional development. In each case, the colony would be made

[10] Cited in C. R. Boxer, *João de Barros: Portuguese Humanist and Historian of Asia* (New Delhi: Concept, 1981), p. 100.

[11] Ibid., pp. 100–1.

[12] Partha Chatterjee, *The Nation and Its Fragments: Colonial and Postcolonial Histories* (Princeton: Princeton University Press, 1993), pp. 16–18.

the frontier of the moral universe of normal humanity; beyond it, universal norms could be held in abeyance.

I have referred earlier to the ideological world of the men of the early Portuguese expeditions. There is a common understanding which treats this world as marked more by Europe's medieval tradition of religious bigotry than its modern ethic of rational innovation and profit making. Accordingly, a distinction is made between the early phase of European overseas expansion, characterized by the banditry, intolerance, and cruelty of the Portuguese who were unable, because of their backwardness, to establish a large and durable empire in the East, and a later phase of Dutch, English, and French colonialism whose lasting effects, distributed over two hundred years, were supposedly the spread of capitalism, technological progress, and modern governance. Sanjay Subrahmanyam has recently argued against this proposition.[13] If cultural backwardness was responsible for the Portuguese failure to establish extensive colonies in Asia, then how were the same Portuguese in the same period able to do so in the Americas? If they came up against superior resistance from the local powers in India, then surely what they lacked was not some mysterious ethic of rational organization and technical innovation but rather the ability to mobilize a sufficient force of arms.

The point needs stressing because it constitutes one more element of continuity in the history of the European presence in South Asia in the last five centuries. Whether in its early phase or later, armed force has always been a constitutive element of that presence. It was not the only element, but it was a foundational and necessary part of European colonialism in India. There had been many earlier states in India founded on conquest, but none had been held as a colony. When those empires collapsed, there was no "decolonization," as happened in the middle of the twentieth century. There is thus some historical significance to the fact that when the last European colony on Indian soil was brought down in Goa in 1961, it needed a mobilization of armed force, albeit a rather small one by the standards of our war-besotted century. I do not see the terror and violence of the early Portuguese expeditions as a medieval hangover soon to be obliterated by civilized trade and modern education. I see it as spelling out in somewhat

[13] Subrahmanyam, *Portuguese Empire in Asia*, pp. 270–7.

coarse and brutal terms a condition of Europe's dominance in the modern world.

Territorial Conquest

Despite attempts from time to time to press for larger territorial acquisitions, allegedly on the model of the Spanish in America, the Portuguese presence in India remained confined mainly to its power over the sea routes, exercised from a few fortified centres on the coasts of the Arabian Sea and the Bay of Bengal. Already by the 1540s, historians tell us, there was a "crisis" in the Portuguese enterprise in India. The second half of the sixteenth century saw the rise and consolidation of a great territorial empire—that of the Mughals— which, though based primarily on an agrarian economy, was by no means uninterested in maritime trade. Following the incorporation of Gujarat and Bengal into the empire, the Mughals became an impassable barrier to Portuguese ambitions, which were now reduced to the fanciful hope that the Jesuit priests invited to the Agra court might succeed in converting the emperor Akbar to Christianity. Soon, even the Portuguese dominance over the seas was threatened by the entry of the Dutch and the English chartered companies. In the 1660s, the Dutch managed to oust the Portuguese from their bases in Sri Lanka, and from Cochin and Cannanore, to establish themselves as the dominant power on the Indian seas. From this time onwards, the story of Europe in India is one of maritime rivalry between the European powers, their involvement in local politics and the founding in the mid-eighteenth century of the British Indian empire.

We all know this story, because it has been told many times, although recent historians have raised some new questions about it. The imperialist version of the familiar story is one in which the English, initially interested in nothing more than a fair chance to profit from trade, almost accidentally get embroiled in the intrigues of Indian rulers and their decadent courts, and end up having to take responsibility for establishing justice and the rule of law. What they build is a new order characterized by a modern economy and the institutions of modern governance. In the nationalist version of the same story, the English capture power from the Indian rulers by force and trickery, destroy the old institutions of economic production and social order, and, by deepening the processes of colonial exploitation, perpetuate poverty and close off the possibilities of industrial development. Recent historians such as Burton Stein, Muzaffar Alam, Sanjay Subrahmanyam, and C.A. Bayly among others have, first of all, questioned the assumption of a general decline in the Indian economy and polity in the eighteenth century. They have argued that, on the contrary, this was a period of considerable economic dynamism with new rights, new sources of capital, new methods of revenue extraction, an increased use of money, and the intensification of control over labour. Second, there arose at this time several regional regimes that were militarist, pursuing mercantilist policies that depended greatly on foreign trade and advanced banking methods. Third, already by the seventeenth century, the European trading companies were important players in the politics surrounding these regional economies because of their control over the flow of bullion from abroad. Fourth, the English East India Company was able to overpower these regional kingdoms in the eighteenth century because of its dominance over the sea routes and its superior ability to finance warfare. Fifth, following its assumption of power, the English company also inherited the institutions and practices on which the earlier regimes were based and thus in effect became one more indigenous regime: in Bayly's words, "the Company became an Asian merchant, an Asian ruler and an Asian revenue-farmer."[14] In short, or so these historians have argued, the radical break that is supposed to characterize the advent of British rule is overstated; there was more continuity than discontinuity in the eighteenth-century transition.[15]

It is not possible here to get into the empirical details of this debate. But I do want to argue that there is reason to disagree with this revisionist suggestion in one very important sense. However, before I make that argument, I need to bring into my story one more figure from sixteenth-century Europe, a person who was exactly the same age

[14] Christopher Bayly, *Imperial Meridian: The British Empire and the World 1780–1830* (London: Longman, 1989), p. 74.

[15] For a short statement of these arguments, see Burton Stein, "Eighteenth Century India: Another View," *Studies in History*, 5, 1 (January–June 1989), pp. 1–26. Other statements are: C. A. Bayly, *Indian Society and the Making of the British Empire* (Cambridge: Cambridge University Press, 1988); Bayly, *Imperial Meridian*; D. A. Washbrook, "Progress and Problems: South Asian Economic and Social History, c. 1720–1860," *Modern Asian Studies*, 22 (1988), 1, pp. 57–96.

as Vasco da Gama but who, as far as we know, had nothing at all to do with India.[16]

The Goodwill of the Colonized

Niccolò Machiavelli, like Vasco da Gama, was born in 1469. In 1513, when Afonso de Albuquerque was consolidating the empire in India and da Gama was whiling away his so-called "wilderness years" somewhere near the Spanish–Portuguese border, the Florentine was writing a manual of statecraft for his prince. In it, among many other topics that would bring him both acclaim and notoriety for several centuries, Machiavelli considered this question: is it better for the prince to be loved more than feared or feared more than loved? His answer was:

> . . . one ought to be both feared and loved, but as it is difficult for the two to go together, it is much safer to be feared than loved, if one of the two has to be wanting. For it may be said of men in general that . . . as long as you benefit them, they are entirely yours. . . . [But] men have less scruple in offending one who makes himself loved than one who makes himself feared; for love is held by a chain of obligation which, men being selfish, is broken whenever it serves their purpose; but fear is maintained by a dread of punishment which never fails.
>
> Still, a prince should make himself feared in such a way that if he does not gain love, he at any rate avoids hatred; for fear and the absence of hatred may well go together. . . .
>
> I conclude, therefore, with regard to being feared and loved, that men love at their own free will, but fear at the will of the prince, and that a wise prince must rely on what is in his power and not on what is in the power of others. . . .[17]

The above advice is, of course, part of an analysis by Machiavelli of the strategy and techniques of power whose relevance to the development of the state in post-renaissance Europe has been the subject of

[16] I acknowledge my debt to the epigram in Ranajit Guha's collection of essays entitled *Dominance without Hegemony: History and Power in Colonial India* (Cambridge, Mass.: Harvard University Press, 1997) which provided me with a way of introducing my argument in Machiavellian language.

[17] Niccolò Machiavelli, *The Prince*, tr. Luigi Ricci (New York: Mentor, 1952), pp. 98–100.

much controversy. One of the most perceptive readings of these manuals of statecraft, some Machiavellian and others avowedly anti-Machiavellian, appearing in Europe between the sixteenth and the eighteenth centuries has been proposed by Foucault.[18] He argues that whereas the ostensible purpose of these texts was to give advice to the sovereign on how to retain possession over his territory, there is a completely different concern that also animates these discussions—which is to develop an art of government. The latter is not about sovereignty over territory, but rather about the proper disposition of people and things to produce a range of desired effects. Foucault shows how the notion of "economy," originating in the idea of the proper management of the household, begins to permeate the discussions on government, and how it remains hamstrung by the limited model of the family until there occurs, in the political economy of the early nineteenth century, the rise of the concept of population. Population emerges as a descriptive and empirical category, as distinct from the moral idea of rights-bearing citizens who share in the popular sovereignty that is supposed to be the basis of the new notion of the legitimate state. The growing knowledge about populations revealed their characteristic features and regularities—the aggregate patterns of births and deaths, of cycles of growth and scarcity, of the movements of labour and wealth, and above all of the ways in which, by intervening at one or more of these points, "policy" or the art of government could produce a specific constellation of economic effects. Population gradually became "the ultimate end of government"—its welfare, its improvement—and these ends were to be brought about by acting upon that population, by inducing it through suitable policies to behave according to its own needs and proclivities and yet to produce in the aggregate the desired effects.

Foucault has traced the genealogy of the modern art of government to the practices of the Christian pastor in Europe, looking after the spiritual and material well being of his flock by attending to the minute details of its everyday and even intimate lives. This "pastoral power," if one judges it by Machiavelli's terms, is more about love than about

---

[18] See especially Michel Foucault, "Governmentality," and "Politics and Reason," in Foucault, *Power*, ed. James D. Faubion (New York: New Press, 2000), pp. 201–22 and 298–325.

fear. It is possible, I am sure, to find similar ideas about a ruler being loved by his subjects in many of the traditions, whether Hindu or Buddhist or Islamic, of paternalist kingship circulating in South Asia over the centuries. But these genealogical antecedents must be distinguished from the forms that would be elaborated in Europe from the early nineteenth century into the modern governmental regimes that Foucault describes. And it is in this context that I wish to advance the hypothesis that in the elaboration of the modern art of government—of the management of populations by policy rather than of the representation of the sovereignty of citizens—Europe's colonial theatres in Asia and later Africa were at least as important as the metropolitan territories themselves as sites of experimentation and theorizing. The reconstituted idea of pastoral power was, I strongly believe, a persistent theme in modern Europe's colonial project, and most exemplarily so in the case of British rule in India. Which is why I will make the argument that what is new about the English rulers of India, as distinct from earlier indigenous regimes, is their need, already apparent from the late eighteenth century, to be loved by their alien Indian subjects.

This, then, is the second part of my story about Europe and South Asia in the last five hundred years. The first part was about fear—domination by the exercise of superior force. I have insisted that this is an element that does not disappear from the relationship between Europe and South Asia during the entire period, even after the supposedly more rational and modern forms of power are introduced by the British. The new element—love—comes in with British rule. It is not born in India, which is why it will not be found if one looks for it in the archives of eighteenth-century Indian history. Its genealogy lies in certain radically new ways of thinking about society and power in late-eighteenth- and nineteenth-century Europe. It affects India because the new imperial project is henceforth to be thought out in European terms, and very often in Europe itself. Of course, what is projected is not always what comes about, which is why it seems to the historian of colonial rule that the grand designs of European statesmen and philosophers were ultimately irrelevant, because what actually happened in India carried the unmistakable stamp of native artifice—the final products were makeshift, ramshackle, and imperfect. I read this to mean that whereas the desire to be loved by the colonized always remained the coveted moral goal of the colonial project, other less exalted norms were accepted in the interim—"if [the prince]," to recall Machiavelli, "does not gain love, he at any rate avoids hatred." Using Gramscian language, we can say with Ranajit Guha that what was built by the colonial power was a "spurious hegemony."[19] Both the desire for hegemony and its spurious substitute are important for understanding colonial history. Without them, we would not know why British rule in India, unlike any of its indigenous precursors, was a "dominance without hegemony": no earlier regime had had the need to think of the moral foundation of its rule as hegemonic in this sense. Without them, once again, we would not discover another secret—why we, the once-colonized, continue to this day to harbour an apparently insatiable need to love Europe.

The Knowledge of the Colonized

The story of love can be told from the late eighteeenth century—from William Jones and the Asiatic Society and the European discovery of the greatness of Indian civilization. To love India and to be loved by Indians, one had first to know India. But I would say the story actually begins at a much more mundane level with the surveys of land revenue and economic products, and of the characteristics of the population. "Statistics," we know, literally means "the science of the state," and already by the turn of the century the word is being used in colonial India to describe the systematic collection of data on diverse subjects that might be of interest to the state. Strange as it may sound, we could say that statistics was a new language of love between ruler and ruled, and I know of few more remarkable tomes of love than the gigantic series of ethnographic-statistical surveys of the districts of eastern India carried out in the early nineteenth century by Francis Buchanan-Hamilton, child of the Scottish enlightenment, physician, botanist, and intrepid traveller. He was one of the first of a series of British scholar-administrators who built up the massive edifice of official knowledge about India which still remains one of the most valuable archives for historical scholarship.

If to love was to know, then to be loved one had to do good to one's subjects: "if you benefit them," said Machiavelli, "they are entirely

[19] Ranajit Guha, *Dominance without Hegemony*, p. 72.

yours." William Jones, who was in love with the imaginative world of the Orient, thought of his professional work in the Indian law courts as "doing very great and extensive good to many millions of native Indians who look up to me not as their judge only, but as their legislator."[20] The most common term used in British India to describe this work of benefiting the population was "improvement." It occurs, as Ranajit Guha described in his first book, from as early as the debates over the "permanent settlement" of the land in Bengal:[21] indeed, by Guha's count, the word "improve" occurs as many as nineteen times in the two brief minutes written by Cornwallis on this subject in 1789 and 1790.[22] Again, William Jones had no doubts about the significance of his work of compiling the laws of India; he declared: "The natives are charmed with the work, and the idea of making their slavery lighter, by giving them their own laws, is more flattering to me than the thanks of the King [of England], which have been transmitted to me."[23] From the time of Jones and Cornwallis, for the next hundred and fifty years, cutting across many policy changes from zamindari to ryotwari to utilitarianism to liberal reform to welfarism, it would become a commonplace of colonial rhetoric to assert that the British were in India to improve it, to civilize it, to make it fit for the modern world, to give it the rule of law and the railways, Shakespeare and modern science, hospitals and parliaments, until in the end, with an almost ridiculous twist of historical irony, it would be declared that the British had been in India to make Indians fit for self-government, which is to say that the latter had first to be robbed of their autonomy in order to qualify to receive it back from the robbers.

What about Indians? Did they return the love their new masters so generously showered on them? For the sake of simplicity, I will divide Indians into two sections, although, as I will also indicate, the matter was more complicated than that. One section consisted of those who collaborated. It is obvious, even though some historians still find it necessary to stress this obvious fact with monotonous regularity, that

[20] Cited in S. N. Mukherjee, *Sir William Jones: A Study in Eighteenth-Century British Attitudes to India* (Cambridge: Cambridge University Press, 1968), p. 122.

[21] Ranajit Guha, *A Rule of Property for Bengal: An Essay on the Idea of Permanent Settlement* (Paris: Mouton, 1963).

[22] Guha, *Dominance without Hegemony*, p. 32.

[23] Cited in Mukherjee, *Sir William Jones*, pp. 122–3.

a handful of British officials and soldiers could not have ruled India for almost two hundred years if Indians, indeed many Indians, had not collaborated. Who were they? In the early period of the East India Company's rise to power, we know of Indian princes and nobles and merchants who sided with the English against other Indian princes and nobles and merchants. We must regard these alliances as situated within a military-diplomatic context—they were strategic relations whose logic Machiavelli would have recognized instantly, for they were imbued with no other sentiment than calculations of self-interest. By the 1830s, when British power was virtually paramount in the subcontinent, these classes were left with little choice except to collaborate or perish. This was demonstrated with savage ruthlessness in the putting down of the revolt of 1857. The landed and merchant collaborators of the late colonial empire, despite their often exaggerated fondness for the European accoutrements of status, were abject in their political subservience, and would make themselves even more ludicrous by becoming increasingly irrelevant to the new forms of political power emerging within the anti-colonial movement. For this group of collaborators, certainly, it would be absurd to say that they loved the British "out of their own free will."

There was another group, however, of those who collaborated. This is a group about which a great deal has been written, not the least by its members themselves. I am referring, of course, to the new Indian middle classes, the new literati or intelligentsia, or whatever else one wishes to call them. A long line of historical scholarship has identified the introduction of English education in India as the crucial process that created this class, instilled in it the values of European modernity, secured the translation of those values into the vernaculars, and thus produced the movements of modern nationalism that would in the end claim self-government for Indians. Needless to say, this argument ties up neatly with the colonial view that it was British rule itself that prepared the ground for Indian independence. But strangely enough (or if we think carefully, perhaps not so strangely), this is also the running theme of a long tradition of liberal nationalist historiography in India. It is only in the last two decades that a serious attempt has been made in the academic historiography of South Asia to question the assumed connection between English education, the rise of the middle classes, and the anti-colonial movements. But this is a debate that is still on, and I myself have been a participant in it. To avoid repeating myself, therefore, I will approach this subject of the Indian middle classes and their collaborative role by looking at a relatively less noticed body of literature—the writings of Indian visitors to Europe. This may also set up a useful contrast with the account of the first Portuguese visitors to India with which I began this discussion.

Starting with the celebrated visit of Rammohan Roy to England in 1831, many members of the new Indian intelligentsia, some illustrious and others relatively inconspicuous, visited Europe in the nineteenth century. Many of them wrote travelogues meant to inform and educate their compatriots about Europe as they had seen it. I will make a few observations here about travellers from Bengal, with whose writings I have some familiarity.[24] But before that, let me refer to a couple of travelogues by Indian visitors to England in the eighteenth century— members of an older literati entirely unschooled in the ways of the European intellectual world.

Mirza Shaikh Ihtisamuddin went to England with a group of emissaries sent by the Mughal emperor Shah Alam to the English king in 1765, by which time the East India Company had firmly established its political hold over Bengal. Ihtisamuddin stayed in England for three years and, several years after his return to Bengal, wrote an account of his travels.[25] At the turn of the century, Mirza Abu Talib of Lucknow visited Europe between 1799 and 1803 and also wrote about

[24] I was led to this subject by Simonti Sen, "Views of Europe of Turn of the Century Bengali Travellers 1870–1910," PhD dissertation, University of Calcutta, 1995. This has been now published as Simonti Sen, *Travels to Europe: Self and Other in Bengali Travel Narratives 1870–1910* (Hyderabad: Orient Longman, 2005).

[25] Although the original Persian manuscript of Ihteshamuddin's (the name is also spelt thus and in other ways) travelogue was never printed, several translations have been published over the years. The earliest is *Shigurf Namah i Velaët, or Excellent Intelligence concerning Europe; being the Travels of Mirza Itesa Modeen, in Great Britain and France*, translated from the Original Persian Manuscript into Hindoostanee, with an English Version and Notes, by James Edward Alexander (London: Parbury, Allen and Co., 1827). Alexander's book contains the English and Urdu translations in a single volume. A Bengali translation was published by A.B.M. Habibullah in 1981 under the title *Bilayetnama* (Dhaka: Muktadhara, 1981). A new English translation has been recently published by Kaiser Haq:

his visit.[26] Neither knew English or any European language when he left for England; neither had a prior mental map imprinted in his mind telling him how England ought to be seen. I say this because the travellers of the nineteenth century would have a completely different orientation both to their visits and to the way they described them.

What is striking about the descriptions by Ihtisamudddin and Abu Talib of the "wonders and curiosities" they encountered during their travels is their passion to find out how things were made and how they worked. Ihtisamuddin starts with a series of detailed descriptions of how the direction and speed of a ship is regulated, how the compass is made and functions, how a logbook is maintained, how the sails are put up and down, how different kinds of winds are negotiated, all the time making comparisons with how things are done on Indian boats. "The people of England are extremely skilled in the art of sailing and work very hard to improve their skills even further."[27] In London, he was greatly interested in how the wooden ceilings of houses were constructed, how piped water was supplied, what sorts of plants he saw in the botanical gardens, the stuffed animals and fish displayed in the museum, and the collection of Arabic, Persian, and Turkish books in an Oxford college where, incidentally, he met a certain Mr Jones who was aiming to go to India as a judge and who sought his help in reading some difficult Persian manuscripts. (Indeed, Ihtisamuddin even suggests that his translations were later used by the Oxford scholar, who was, needless to say, our familiar William Jones, to write a book from which he made a lot of money.) Both Ihtisamuddin and Abu Talib were appreciative of many wonderful things that the English were capable of making or doing, but nowhere do they give the impression that these wonderful things might be examples of an entire culture or civilization that had attained a superior level of perfection. Indeed, neither of our travellers was much persuaded by theoretical explanations. When Abu Talib's ship approached the Car Nicobar islands in the Bay of Bengal,

---

Mirza Sheikh I'tesamuddin, *The Wonders of Vilayet: Being the Memoir, Originally in Persian of a Visit to France and Britain,* tr. Kaiser Haq (London: Peepal Tree Press, 2001).

[26] *Travels of Mirza Abu Taleb Khan,* tr. Charles Stewart (1814; rpnt New Delhi: Sona Publications, 1972).

[27] Ihteshamuddin, *Bilayetnama,* p. 37.

he was mystified by the fact that he could see vegetation in the horizon but no land. The captain of the ship tried to explain to him the spherical surface of the sea and the properties of refraction of light through water and even demonstrated this by dropping a ring in a bowl of water, all of which Abu Talib faithfully recorded. But he was convinced that the ship's telescope was faulty or that the men on the ship had played a trick on him.[28]

Compare this with a typical travelogue from the second half of the nineteenth century. The gentleman from Bengal stepping on to the ship now has a concept of Europe firmly planted in his mind. Indeed, the ship is for him the first place he encounters the real Europe and the exercise of comparing it to his conceptual Europe begins in earnest. The voyage acquires for him the moral significance of a rite of passage: "On 12th March 1886, the steamer 'Nepaul' left Bombay for England. No mailboat ever felt the throbbing of so many Hindu hearts. . . . Prouder was she now at the result of the moral influence of England in her vast empire in India, which enabled so many of her sons to break through the trammels of caste, to rise above old prejudices and superstitions and to seek education and enlightenment at the fountainhead of modern civilisation."[29] Setting foot on English soil, the gentleman would declare: "I am now in that Great England of which I had been reading from my childhood and among the English people with whom Providence has so closely united us."[30] Not everything he would see in England would necessarily meet with his approval; indeed, often he would be disappointed because the real England would sometimes fail to measure up to the conceptual image. But overall, he would have no doubt that what he was experiencing, and what he would need to convey to his countrymen back home, was a moral and civilizational essence, expressed in such virtues of the modern English people as the spirit of independence, self-respect and discipline, their love of art, literature and sport, and above all, their cultivation of knowledge. Observing the success of the Colonial Exhibition of 1886, our traveller from Bengal would remark: "The myriads of visitors that

[28] Cited in Simonti Sen, "Views of Europe," p. 21.

[29] Trailokya Nath Mukherjee, *A Visit to Europe* (Calcutta: Arunodaya Roy, 1902), cited in Simonti Sen, "Views of Europe," p. 66.

[30] Simonti Sen, "Views of Europe," p. 98.

daily flocked to the exhibition revealed to us the great mysterious cause of European progress. It is the constant search after knowledge and a constant readiness to accept a better state of things, whenever that is discovered and understood." It was this that lay at the heart of modern European civilization and what set it apart from and above colonized countries such as India. Indeed, it was the knowledge that the Europeans had acquired of the natural and social resources of India that had given them the power to rule over the "natives."

> The real inequality between Europeans and "natives" rests not on the fact of the former filling a few high posts in the country. . . . The European knows more of our mountains and rivers than we do; he knows more of the plants that grow around us, their names, their properties, even the size and shapes of their leaves; he knows more of what is interred in the bosom of our earth; he knows more about the capabilities of our land; in everything he knows more than we do of our own country. Then he knows better how to use that knowledge for the benefit of men. We do not know these things; hence we are "natives."[31]

I present this text here as one of the most sincere declarations of love by a modern Indian for modern Europe. Its author—the Bengali gentleman we have followed from the time he embarked on his voyage to England—was Trailokyanath Mukherjee, curator of a museum in Calcutta, a recognized expert on the agricultural products and craft manufactures of the different parts of India and an outstanding humorist in the world of Bengali fiction. If he did not, like Ihtisamuddin a hundred years before him, write about the compass and the sails and the wonderful machines that the Europeans had invented, it was not because he did not know how they were made or how they worked. Rather, he knew too much. He was already an insider in the world of European knowledge, converted, disciplined, and full of admiration. For men and women like Trailokyanath, we could say without fear of contradiction that they loved Europe "of their own free will," because indeed their wills had been adequately produced to make that choice. We would be right, of course, to add that although Trailokyanath was an insider, he was nevertheless standing only at the margins, acutely conscious of the fact that he and his countrymen would now have to

[31] Ibid., p. 168.

learn this new knowledge from the European, indeed learn even about their own country.

To avoid any confusion, let me add that politically Trailokyanath was a loyalist. He did not question the fact that the British had acquired the right to rule India because they knew how to use their knowledge for the benefit of Indians. Not everyone from the middle classes would remain a loyalist though, at least not from the turn of the century. What is it that would change? Let us refer back to Foucault's discussion on the anti-Machiavellian tracts and his distinction between the sovereign power of the ruler over his territory and the art of governing populations. Unlike Trailokyanath, many educated Indians would now question, on the strength of modern Western political theory itself, the legitimacy of an alien power that was unrepresentative of the people and unwilling to recognize them as citizens with rights. Not only that, some would also argue that the people were not in fact being benefited as much as they ought to be, and that that was so because the government was unrepresentative: if sovereignty were to pass to the Indian people, the art of modern governance could be utilized to yield them far greater benefits.[32]

As it happened, political opposition to British rule grew stronger within the Indian middle classes in the first half of the twentieth century. In that period, the middle classes built connections with the anti-colonial demands of other sections of the people, especially peasants and workers, and spearheaded the process that finally led to the transfer of power, and also the partition of the country, in 1947. Their opposition to British rule did not in any way diminish their love for the concept of Europe that was planted in their minds—the Europe of Shakespeare and the steam engine, of the French Revolution and quantum mechanics. They rejected the sovereignty that the British claimed over India, but did not question the superiority of Europe in cultivating the arts of modernity. The subtlety of this attitude was beyond the comprehension of many late colonial officials, who took

---

[32] The economic critique of colonial rule in India was launched by Dadabhai Naoroji and R.C. Dutt at the turn of the nineteenth century, whereas the foundations of a nationalist strategy of industrialization for ending poverty and creating general prosperity were laid at around the same time by G.V. Joshi, M.G. Ranade, and G.K. Gokhale. These set up an intellectual framework of nationalist economic thinking in India that would stay relevant for almost a hundred years.

the climate of political opposition in the last days of British rule as a signal of impending danger to their lives. Thus, Field Marshall Auchinleck was still insisting in June 1947 that the British army must stay on in India until the following year to protect British lives,[33] little realizing that, once the question of sovereignty was settled, there would be no reason left for Indians to hate Europeans.

I have not yet talked about the other section of Indians—those who did not collaborate. On them, I will be brief. I believe that the mass of the Indian people, those who were subjects under British rule, whether in British India or in the princely states, never collaborated. This is not to say that they did not respect the authority of the British, or obey them, or look up to them for justice and protection. Despite many large and small revolts by tribals and peasants in British India, it is correct to say that for the most part rebellion was more the exception than the rule. But the mass of the people did not give the British the love that they so much wanted—love that would flow from their own free wills—because within the structure of colonial rule the British could never recognize these lowly subjects as possessing wills with that quality of free rationality that could invest their apparent docility with the aura of love. They were, in short, incapable of loving the concept of Europe.

Of the many Indians who collaborated with British rule or acknowledged its dominance, therefore, only some became familiar with the full range of knowledges and practices that constituted its intellectual wherewithal and accepted its rationality. But they too ultimately rejected the colonial claim to political dominance while making their own the project of building a modern state and society. Mohandas Karamchand Gandhi, with his characteristic acuteness, saw through the strategy at its moment of birth. As early as in 1909, in *Hind Swaraj*, he described this as wanting to have "English rule without the Englishman."[34] Those who follow Gandhi believe that that is exactly what the rulers of independent India have tried to do in the last sixty years.

I have now come to my final consideration, which is about Europe

[33] Leonard Mosley, *The Last Days of the British Raj* (1961; rpnt Bombay: Jaico, 1971), pp. 155–66.

[34] M.K. Gandhi, *Hind Swaraj*, in *The Collected Works of Mahatma Gandhi*, vol.10 (New Delhi: Publications Division, 1958).

and South Asia today. One major transformation that took place in the middle of the twentieth century, alongside the collapse of Europe's colonial empires, was the decisive shift in world dominance from Europe to the United States. For the most part and for most people in South Asia, the concept of Europe today seems to be encompassed within the concept of the West, of which the United States is the dominant focus. There is little doubt that force remains a foundation of that dominance, and although a contemporary Machiavelli will argue that the threat of the use of devastating force is a more efficient guarantee of dominance than its actual use, we have only to remember the televised spectacles of the first Gulf War, the bombing of Sarajevo, and the invasion of Iraq to perceive the concentrated terror that can be unleashed by those who regard themselves as policemen of the world.

In the meantime, the rulers of the newly independent countries of South Asia have continued with their project of building modern nation-states. Winning sovereignty from the colonial powers has unplugged among the expanding middle classes the springs of love for the concept of the West. I am not referring here to the alleged infatuation of young Indians with designer clothes and pop music which many feel is threatening our national tradition. My understanding of the history of the colonial encounter in the last two centuries leads me to believe that if there is the importation of a Coca-Cola culture into this country, it will soon acquire a distinctly Indian character and blend imperceptibly into that ever-changing entity called Indian tradition. I am more concerned with the invocation of Western modernity that tells us that in practising the latest arts of managing populations, Indians are losing the race because they are bogged down in politics. There is growing impatience among the middle classes who feel India is not catching up with the West fast enough because it has too much democracy. Alongside, there is a renewed attempt to impose a particular brand of the modernized upper-caste brahminical culture as the true national culture on the ground that all great nations of the West were built through a process of cultural homogenization. The same logic leads the political establishment of each South Asian country to regard its neighbours as rivals and potential enemies. And, needless to say, it is the same logic that is now driving those establishments into a nuclear arms race, bolstered by the belief that that is the only way to gain the respect of the great powers of the West. I have to say that this does not reflect the wisdom of Machiavelli's prince. Rather, it reflects the mentality of the small-time street corner thug who believes that the world is ruled by big thugs and lives on the fantasy that by imitating the swagger and brashness of the big guys he will one day be invited to join their club. This is a parody—a pathetic parody—of the chauvinism of the great powers designed to make postcolonial elites feel good about themselves, but one whose price, as always, will be borne by the poor and the powerless.

I have said before that the postcolonial love for the West flows out of a concept of the West. This concept has congealed in postcolonial minds over the last five hundred years. It has survived the brutalities of the Portuguese armada, the intrigues of Robert Clive, the viciousness of the counterinsurgency in 1857–8, and the callousness that caused the Bengal famine of 1943. The fact that the most devastating wars in human history and the atrocities of Nazism, fascism, and apartheid took place in the twentieth century and were integral to the historical dynamics of modern Europe has not, for postcolonial Indians, pushed that concept to a crisis. Large sections of India's elites still repose enough faith in that concept to insist that one should strive harder than one has so far to copy those old models of modernity in their own country.

I am convinced that the concept of the West that has been so lovingly nourished is in deep crisis in the West itself. The idea of participatory democracy and active popular sovereignty which was the moral foundation of modern politics since the time of the French Revolution has been largely eroded by the instrumentalist doctrine that political choice is only about how much benefit can be reached to how many people at what cost. The social consensus around which the idea of national identity had been built in the countries of Europe and North America has been put under severe stress with the entry from other cultures of new immigrants who were not part of that earlier consensus. And now that the neo-liberal storm has blown over, it has left behind a capitalist social order with few ideological resources to cope with the moral embarrassment of managerial irresponsibility and greed, unemployment, sickness, and destitution. I do not believe that the collapse of the socialist regimes in Eastern Europe and the Soviet Union has meant the vindication of the liberal capitalist order as we have known it so far. On the contrary, I see that collapse as one more sign of the crisis of the old project of modernity inaugurated in Europe in the late eighteenth century.

It is incumbent upon those who are still marginals in the world of modernity to use the opportunities they have to invent new forms of the modern social, economic, and political order. There are many experiments that have been carried out in the last hundred years or so. Many of the forms that have been fashioned are regarded as imperfect adaptations of the original—unfinished, distorted, perhaps even fake. It is worth considering whether many of these supposedly distorted forms—of economic institutions, laws, political organizations, cultural practices—might not in fact contain the possibility of entirely new forms of economic organization or democratic governance never thought of by the old forms of Western modernity. For this, however, one must have the courage to turn one's back on the history of the last five hundred years and face the future with a new maturity and self-assurance born of the conviction that Vasco da Gama must never appear on our shores again.

The chapters that follow in this book will examine some of these apparently deviant and distorted forms of modern politics in India and consider whether they might carry in them the potential for new democratic practices.

3

The Rule of Subjects

Righteous Action

There has been much discussion on satyagraha in modern Indian politics. Inaccurately translated into English as "passive resistance," the idea found its most famous and elaborate expression in the political movements led by Gandhi from the 1920s. But political struggles with similar features can be found in several other types of movements that were not explicitly Gandhian. The historian Sumit Sarkar has shown that, several years before the entry of Gandhi into Indian politics, the political tactics adopted in the Swadeshi movement in Bengal in 1905–9 prefigured many of the techniques of Gandhian satyagraha.[1] Such techniques have also been widely used in India's leftist and socialist movements.

Put simply, satyagraha is resistance to oppressive rule by disobeying unjust laws or orders, to accept the punishment that might result without retaliating with violence, but to resist again. Properly organized, satyagraha can assume the form of mass popular resistance to state authority. But it explicitly avoids the path of violence. In a violent conflict, the scales are generally tilted in favour of the organized power of the agencies of the state. But if an unarmed mass can demonstrate its resolve to face repeated and violent punishment and still not give up its resistance, then the modern state is often put in a difficult situation. Confronting the laws of the state, there then emerges the *satya* or "truth" of the satyagrahi whose value to the resisters far outweighs that of the laws of the state.

---

[1] Sumit Sarkar, *The Swadeshi Movement in Bengal 1903–1908* (1973; rpntd Ranikhet: Permanent Black, 2010).

Where does the satyagrahi get his or her truth? On what ground does he or she conclude that the laws of the state are unjust because they violate some higher truth? The concept that is most often cited in this connection in Indian political thinking is dharma. In this sense, dharma does not mean religion. Rather, it means right or appropriate conduct, righteous action. It means rules that are for the good of the community. The rules of dharma are not promulgated by any ruler: they are, as it were, eternal rules that are eternally valid. There have been many recent discussions on the role of dharma in political movements, both violent and non-violent, from eighteenth-century peasant revolts to twentieth-century anti-colonial struggles. Since modern historians have been fascinated by the evidence of popular resistance to state authority, it is not surprising that they should have been particularly interested in tracing the presence of dharma in the consciousness of rebellious chiefs and peasants.

More pertinent to our discussion are the leaders of such political struggles inspired by the sense of dharma. The ideal leader is a renouncer, uninterested in furthering his or her individual interest. Shouldering the principal part of the sacrifices and punishments, he or she sets exemplary standards that others joining the movement might follow. Gandhi often reminded his followers that even if ordinary participants in the movement were unable to live up to the exacting standards of the truth, the satyagrahi must at all times strive to do so. The personal sacrifices of the satyagrahi must set an example for others and give them courage. The highest sacrifice for a satyagrahi was meeting death in the fight against unjust domination. This ideal of exemplary sacrifice, including death if necessary, was not confined to the Gandhian movement. It remains present to this day in many strands of political struggle in India. Thus, just as modern political movements have often been inspired by the righteous ideals of dharma, so have notions of leadership and sacrifice been shaped by those ideals.

Policy

In this chapter, I will talk about a very different tradition of political thinking in India that has little to do with dharma. V. Narayana Rao and Sanjay Subrahmanyam have recently drawn our attention to a genre of writing, mostly in Telugu, that was called *nīti* literature and which, apparently quite self-consciously, distinguished itself from the canonical *dharmaśāstra* literature explicating the principles and rules of right conduct.[2] *Nīti*, as explicated in the *Mahābhārata*, consists of the principles of *rājadharma* by which the king was meant to preserve his rule and protect his subjects. In the classical tradition, it was always asserted that *nīti* must be contained within the broader rubric of dharma. Nevertheless, there are many political tactics spoken of in the *Mahābhārata* that would have embarrassed even a Machiavelli. Yet the accepted interpretation of the concept of *nīti* in the *Mahābhārata* is that it is subordinate to dharma. Nrisingha Bhaduri says that the intended meaning is not merely the king's interest (*artha*) in preserving or expanding his kingdom but a notion of kingship that is encompassed within the concept of dharma.[3] The *Arthaśāstra* of Kautilya, of course, states quite explicitly that the objective of *rājadharma* is to further the material interests (*artha*) of the king. Although it does say that the ruler must give equal attention to the pursuit of dharma, *artha*, and *kāma* (pleasure), the three goals of human life, there is reason to suspect that this is no more than a conventional gesture towards scriptural orthodoxy because the *Arthaśāstra* clearly occupies a field of knowledge autonomous from the study of dharma, and that autonomy is based on the clear distinction between *artha* and dharma. Indeed, Kautilya states quite clearly his view that of dharma, *artha*, and *kāma*, *artha* is the most important because it provides the foundation for the pursuit of the other two goals.[4]

The *arthaśāstra* literature of Kautilya and others was known to the scholar-bureaucrats of pre-colonial India, especially southern India. The particular text of Kautilya that we now use was, of course, discovered in Mysore at the beginning of the twentieth century. But even though such a comprehensive text may not have been in circulation,

---

[2] Velcheru Narayana Rao and Sanjay Subrahmanyam, "History and Politics in the Vernacular: Reflections on Medieval and Early Modern South India," in Raziuddin Aquil and Partha Chatterjee, eds, *History in the Vernacular* (Ranikhet: Permanent Black, 2008), pp. 25–65.

[3] Nrisingha Prasad Bhaduri, *Daṇḍanīti: prācīn bhāratīya rājśāstra* (Calcutta: Sahitya Samsad, 1998).

[4] Kautilya, *The Arthasastra of Kautilya*, vol. 1, tr. R.P. Kangle (Delhi: Motilal Banarasidass, 1986), adhikaraṇa 1, adhyāya 7.

Kautilya's views were well known through citations and criticism in many other texts. And other compendia in Sanskrit such as the *Śukra-nītisāra* were widely used and cited by scholars.

The *nīti* literature that Rao and Subrahmanyam cite from the Kakatiya and Vijayanagara periods, i.e. roughly from the twelfth to the fifteenth centuries, pays no obeisance at all to dharma and appears to claim an autonomous field of application for its principles. Thus, a fifteenth-century Telugu compilation called *Sakala-niti-sammatamu* proclaims the following principles: "If serving a ruler causes incessant pain to the servant, the servant should leave such a master right away;" "He may be rich, born in a good caste, a strong warrior beyond comparison, but if a king is an ignoramus, his servants will no doubt leave him;" "A bad king surrounded by good people turns out to be good, but even a good king is difficult to serve if his advisers are bad."[5] It would be hard to find statements of this kind in any *dharma-śāstra* text.

The distinctive feature of a *nīti* text is that it was aimed at providing instruction to a ruler in order to further his interests in consolidating and expanding his rule. It was concerned with *artha*, i.e. worldly material goals, not with the moral or spiritual goals of dharma or *mokṣa* (liberation from the cycle of life). It also spoke of reaching those worldly goals exclusively through the use of instruments of power, and never appealed to the intervention of any superhuman or divine force. These *nīti* texts also did not refer to the *dharmaśāstra* as authoritative texts that needed to be cited. The *Sakala-niti-sammatamu*, for instance, is an anthology of nearly a thousand extracts drawn from seventeen *nīti* texts, but not a single quotation is from a dharma text. Rao and Subrahmanyam also stress that this specific genre of *nīti* texts was composed and read by the group of scholar-bureaucrats whom they refer to broadly as the *karanam*. These were usually Niyogi Brahmins or Kayasthas who worked as ministers or advisers to minor princes or feudatories in Andhra, Karnataka, and Orissa. They were usually literate in Sanskrit but not necessarily well read in the legal literature of the *smṛti* or the *dharmaśāstra*. They did not assume that their readers would be conversant with that canonical literature either. Indeed, their intended readers were princes, noblemen, and other *karanam* functionaries. In other words, these texts comprised a

---

[5] Cited in Rao and Subrahmanyam, "History and Politics," p. 46.

literature on statecraft produced by and for the practitioners of statecraft. Further, they were composed not in Sanskrit but in regional vernaculars such as Telugu and Kannada, another sign of their distance from the canonical body of *dharmaśāstra* texts.

In northern or western India, the group corresponding to the *karanam* was the *munshi*. As functionaries in the administration of Mughal governors or local rulers, *munshis* were the practitioners of statecraft and wrote about its principles in the Indo-Persian genre of *t'arikh* or history, as well as in instruction manuals for princes called *akhlaq*. A *munshi* could be Muslim or Hindu and his concern in such writings was not the discourse of *shari'a* but the political realm of *siyasat*. Muzaffar Alam has pointed out the characteristic features of the *akhlaq* literature produced in India in the Sultanate and Mughal periods.[6] The prime consideration here was to formulate principles of rule that would be normative for an Islamic monarch ruling over an overwhelmingly non-Muslim body of subjects. The problem had been posed earlier in Iran in the context of rule by the infidel Mongols. The political literature of Nasr-al-din Tusi and others was known in India in the Mughal period. As Alam shows, the crucial quality that was demanded of such a monarch was not Islamic piety but *aqal*, i.e. good sense and judgement. If the sultan had *aqal*, then the subject, irrespective of sect or religion, would get *adil* or justice and there would be cooperation, adjustment, and peace among the communities in the realm.

Narayana Rao and Subrahmanyam have suggested that the *nīti* literature continued in southern India into the early nineteenth century. Elsewhere, the eighteenth century seems to have been a time of considerable rethinking of the foundations of the Mughal political order. An excellent example is the *Sair ul-mutakkhirin* of Ghulam Husain Tabatabai.[7] Ghulam Husain was an administrator and diplomat attached to several rulers and governors in Bengal and Bihar in the middle of the eighteenth century. He witnessed from close quarters the "revolution in Bengal" when the British took over the reins of power in 1757. The *Sair* covers the history of Hindustan from the death of

[6] Muzaffar Alam, *The Languages of Political Islam in India, c.1200–1800* (Delhi: Permanent Black, 2004).

[7] As mentioned in ch. 1 above, I have used the four-volume 1788 translation published in 1902.

Aurangzeb in 1707 to 1780. Steeped in the political doctrines and cultural ethos of the Mughal order, Ghulam Husain confronts the question of political principles in the age of decline of empire. The death of Aurangzeb is followed by a succession of incompetent monarchs on the throne of Delhi. How is the integrity of the political order to be maintained under such circumstances? Ghulam Husain argues that those with knowledge and experience of statecraft, especially scholar-nobles with vision and resolve, must take it upon themselves to provide the necessary advice to those who sit on the throne. If needed, they should even capture power themselves. Ghulam Husain's heroes of the eighteenth century are Husain Ali Khan, Alivardi Khan, Shuja-ud-daulah, and Shitab Rai. None of them occupied positions of power by dynastic succession. Rather, by virtue of their political skill, determination, and wisdom, they had seized power to save the state and protect its subjects. If uncertainty and anarchy descend on the kingdom because of the misrule of the monarch, then it is a legitimate act, according to Ghulam Husain, for a competent statesman to overthrow the ruler and seize power. However reprehensible this might be from the standpoint of religion, it was the right thing to do from the standpoint of political reason. Alivardi Khan, for instance, took up arms against his own master Sarfraz Khan, an act of grievous sin in the eyes of religious law. But the study of history shows that Sarfraz had no talent for administration, and that had he continued to rule Bengal would have been plunged into misery. Under Alivardi's rule, the people of Bengal enjoyed security and prosperity unmatched either before or after.

It must be pointed out that although different from religious law, the domain of politics is not devoid of ethical principles. Ghulam Husain discusses this topic at length. Thus, he argues that the ruler must have personal honesty and integrity, not because of the fear of punishment on Judgment Day but in order to strengthen the legitimacy of his rule. A ruler who is known to be honest and faithful is not vulnerable to criticism even from his enemies and many would come to his aid in times of danger and uncertainty. An important reason why the political regime collapsed in Bengal so soon after Alivardi Khan's death was, according to Ghulam Husain, the terrible moral reputation of his daughters and grandchildren, because of which once the fires of disloyalty were lit, no one came forward to put them out.

Ghulam Husain clearly saw that the edifice of political obligation within the Mughal order, built around notions of promise, trust, and loyalty, was breaking down. One could no longer rely on rules and practices established over two hundred years. The first rule of political ethics under these new and uncertain conditions was, he explained, self-preservation, that is to say, ensuring one's own security and that of one's family, property and dependants. But one's actions today could have consequences tomorrow. Therefore, even for securing one's immediate self-interest, it was necessary to exercise judicious foresight. One should remember that disloyalty or treachery today could bring about retribution tomorrow. Yet for the same reason it was important for rulers not to rely on ties of kinship or fealty but instead to appoint officials of competence and integrity.

There is a striking section in the *Sair* in which Ghulam Husain is trying to explain the new political ethics of the time to his aged father Hidayat Ali, a Mughal nobleman then serving Prince Ali Gauhar, the future Emperor Shah Alam II. Ali Gauhar was then in Allahabad, moving with his troops towards Bengal where the British had established their supremacy in 1757. Ghulam Husain was then an adviser to Ram Narayan, governor of Patna and an ally of the British. Sent as an emissary to Ali Gauhar to try and persuade him to conclude a peace treaty with the British, Ghulam Husain meets his father in Allahabad. He tells the aged nobleman that the Mughal army was in terrible shape and that its generals were incompetent. If there was a battle, the British were certain to win. The prince ought to be advised to come to an agreement with the British. If the prince refused, Hidayat Ali at least should leave his service in order to save his own life and property. The old man refused to accept his son's argument. Echoing a traditional sense of political morality, he replied that the descendants of Timur had never been faithless with those who had served them and that he would never betray his master. This encounter between two generations of practitioners of statecraft at a transitional moment in Indian history seems to reflect the conflict between dharma and *nīti*.

The Return of Dharma

If elements of the practice of what may be broadly called *nīti* or policy were visible in India in the eighteenth century, what happened to them in the nineteenth? I believe that the tide of English education that swept British India in the nineteenth century also prepared the soil for the rebirth of dharma in politics. *Nītiśāstra* was largely ignored and soon forgotten. There are many reasons for the political revival of dharma. One was the persistent criticism by European observers throughout the eighteenth and nineteenth centuries of the principles of Oriental government. They alleged that Eastern rulers were constitutionally corrupt, arbitrary, and tyrannical. One could never trust their word, nor did their decisions ever have any basis in morality. Not only that, the immorality of their rulers had percolated deep into all sections of Oriental society. No one spoke the truth, and the slightest opportunity of self-seeking was enough for them to resort to lies and cunning. Regardless of the moral principles expounded in their religious texts, in practical life they took to immoral ways from childhood. Confronted by this storm of criticism raised by colonial administrators and Christian missionaries, Indian nationalist reformers began to insist that these allegations were motivated and false. The Indian social system was guided not by cunning and the pursuit of self-interest but by the ideals of dharma and truth. If corruption and immorality had entered into social life, they were deviations that would have to be removed by modern religious reform.

The second reason for the decline of *nīti* was that as the field of modern government and politics expanded in India, the ideas of entitlement and rights of subjects began to take hold. Soon the question began to be raised: if the consent of the subjects was the legitimate foundation of the modern state, then how could foreign rule be legitimate? Was the fundamental issue of politics merely good governance or was it a question of sovereignty? To illustrate how the relation between *nīti* and dharma came to be posed in the early phase of nationalism in India, let me consider a text on politics from 1876.

The book is called *Byabahār darśan*, written by Anandachandra Mitra. The Bengali book carries a subtitle in English: "An Introduction to the Science of Politics."[8] I have discussed this remarkable book at length on another occasion.[9] Anandachandra, a schoolteacher in

---

[8] Anandachandra Mitra, *Byabahār darśan* (Calcutta: Ray Press, 1876).

[9] "A Modern Science of Politics for the Colonized," in Partha Chatterjee, ed., *Texts of Power: The Disciplines in Colonial Bengal* (Minneapolis: University of Minnesota Press, 1995), pp. 93–117.

Mymensingh in eastern Bengal, belonged to the reformist Brahmo Samaj and was influenced by the reformer Sibnath Sastri. He was quite familiar with the classical *nīti* literature in Sanskrit, but, imbued with the new political ideas coming from Europe, he began a search for a new "science of politics" to which he gave the name *byabahār darśan* (*vyavahāra* being the Sanskrit term for the discipline of adjudication of disputes in law). Looking for such a science, he discovered that "there is no science called *byabahār darśan* in India." Not only that, the study of scientific philosophy generally was very poorly developed in this country. "Everyone will acknowledge that Indians, more than any other people, are god-fearing and pious, and that their literature contains the highest qualities of emotion. This proves that those attributes of the heart such as faith, devotion, affection, bravery and love of beauty are most powerfully developed among Indians. This emotional bent is the main reason why scientific philosophy is virtually absent in this country."[10]

Thus, it is futile, Mitra thinks, to look for a "science of politics" in India. However, that did not mean that there was no practice of politics. "Despite the absence of a scientific discourse of *byabahār*, the art of *rājnīti* flourished in India."[11] But notice now how, in Anandachandra's rendering, the distinction between dharma and *nīti* is virtually erased:

> Because there was no proper discussion of the science of politics in this country, all subjects were brought under the rubric of the *dharmaśāstra*. In India, the king is regarded as the very embodiment of dharma. . . . In fact, the corpus of *nīti* narratives that emerged describing the duties of the ruler and his subjects is what I will call politics in India. Even though all of these dicta of *nīti* are not entirely sound according to the science of politics, they do contain ideas that are both profound and elevated, that are a joy to read and show signs of sophisticated thinking.[12]

But here too the influence of dharma spoils everything: "When the subject of government is discussed, these books, by ignoring the opinions of the subjects and instead recommending that the ruler

[10] Mitra, *Byabahār*, p. 28.
[11] Ibid., p. 32.
[12] Ibid., p. 34.

be worshipped like a god and announcing the supremacy of Brahmins and other high castes, strike at the root of any true concept of politics."[13]

The science of politics that Anandachandra was looking for, it becomes clear from his text, is founded on the rights of the *prajā*, i.e. the subjects. He had already obtained from his study of European philosophy the idea that the sovereignty of the state must be grounded in the rights of subjects: "If a state founded on *prajāśakti* (the power of subjects), that is to say, on the general will, and on *prajāsvattva* (the entitlement of subjects), that is to say, on the general well being, is the best possible state, then one has to accept that a state constituted according to the principles of the science of politics is the only proper state. There can be no doubt that such a system of administration is the best one possible."[14] As a matter of fact, Anandachandra had no doubt at all about what sort of state was the most preferable according to the science of politics. Even as a colonized Indian in 1876, he proposed the following unambiguous definition:

> That which brings into mutual combination the aggregate power of the *prajā* [subjects], in which the power of subjects is contained, by which it is regulated and that which it cannot exceed, is called the *rājā* [ruler]. One or several individuals who represent the combined power of the *prajā* or subjects is the *rājā* or ruler.[15]

The next definition follows with equal certainty:

> That society in which *rājśakti* [the power of the ruler] and *prajāśakti* [the power of subjects] act in unison is called a *rājya* [state]. The combined power of subjects comes together to create the power of the ruler and of its own will accepts the obligation to obey the ruler. The latter too remains so much under the influence of the power of subjects that the ruler cannot act by ignoring the subjects. The society which conducts its affairs in this way is a proper state.[16]

How is the ruler to act by coming under the influence of the power of subjects? "The will of the majority is the general will and acts that are

13 Ibid., p. 35.
14 Ibid., p. 23.
15 Ibid., p. 70.
16 Ibid., p. 72.

in accordance with the general will are for the general well being."[17] In fact, Mitra makes it quite clear that the ruler conceived of by the science of politics is not the traditional king of the past; it is in fact a modern republic. "With the rapid advance of the general will in recent times, one trusts that all established monarchies will soon be abolished."[18]

It is important to note that despite proclaiming what was essentially a Rousseau-inspired theory of popular republican sovereignty, Mitra continues to work with the concepts of ruler and subjects. The power of the ruler (*rājśakti*) and the power of subjects (*prajāśakti*) are, as it were, distinct forces. In imperfect states, they come into conflict and cause disunity and disorder. In the perfect state, where the will of the ruler is identical with the general will of the subjects, the two forces become united: the power of subjects is willingly contained within the power of the ruler. However, even in this perfectly constituted republic, ruler and subjects seem to continue to maintain their distinct forms; they do not merge and mingle into a single formation. Even in the perfect republic, subjects do not become the ruler.

One is tempted to remark that there is a hint here of the distinction that would be made in German political debates of the 1920s between the constituent and the constituted powers. The latter is the power enshrined in an actual constitutional state. But it is founded on the prior consent of a constituent power, i.e. the people, which, at least in the argument of Walter Benjamin, always reserves its right to withdraw its consent.[19] Without stretching the point too far, it is arguable that Anandachandra at least took his Rousseau seriously.

It is also interesting to point out, as a genealogical curiosity, that the current term for the modern republic in several South Asian languages is *prajātantra*, which literally means the rule of subjects. One could speculate why, despite embracing the modern republican ideal of the sovereignty of the people, the republican nation-states of South Asia continue to carry in their political language an implicit distinction

[17] Ibid., p. 22.

[18] Ibid., p. 23.

[19] Walter Benjamin, "Critique of Violence," in Walter Benjamin, *Selected Writings*, eds Marcus Bullock and Michael W. Jennings (Cambridge, Mass.: Harvard University Press, 1996), pp. 244–300.

between *rājśakti* (the power of the ruler) and *prajāśakti* (the power of subjects).

To return to Anandachandra Mitra, he is sceptical of the role of religion in modern politics. "Just as bile helps digest our food, keeps our blood healthy and sustains our lives, so is it impossible to have a national life without dharma [in this case, religion]. However, the task of the science of politics is to ensure that excess of religious zeal and bigotry does not harm society or disturb its sanity."[20] Anandachandra was well aware of the fact that religious fervour could create a collective enthusiasm whose force could drive nations to win wars or achieve major national success. But such success was short-lived. "We do not call that the true life of a nation, but rather its perversion. Just as an excess of blood causes hysteria and drives an individual to display as much strength as that of five people, so have these nations acted hysterically. Their achievements have not lasted and the consequences have generally been unfortunate. The conquests of the Muslims are a good example."[21]

However, despite his doubts about religious zeal, Anandachandra is not happy with the mere defence of self-interest. "Indians are today only concerned with their self-interest. They have resolved to fill their own bellies even by destroying their neighbours. There are two reasons for this: one, the lack of religious knowledge, and two, the absence of a science of politics."[22] There is no point blaming Anandachandra for this rather confusing conclusion. In the 1870s, at the moment of the emergence of nationalism, it was not possible for him to set aside the powerful spiritual appeal of Indian dharma which was pitted against the Western proclivity for the mere pursuit of self-interest. Notwithstanding his intellectual preference for a true science of politics, Anandachandra was unable to suggest a mode of national life that did not give pride of place to dharma, even though this was not to be allowed to reach the extreme stage of religious fanaticism. As a matter of fact, the *prajāśakti* or the power of subjects whose efflorescence he so eagerly looked for could never have united with the *rājśakti*, or the power of the ruler, under the given conditions of colonial rule. The

[20] Ibid., p. 55.
[21] Ibid., p. 56.
[22] Ibid., p. 58.

subjects would first have to enter into a contest over sovereignty and oust the foreign rulers before a true state based on the science of politics could emerge. That struggle for national sovereignty, in turn, would be greatly influenced by the emotive force of self-sacrifice, faith, and dedicated service to the nation, all articulated in the spiritual language of dharma. The mundane details of administrative policy and proce-dures of governance that comprise the subject matter of *nīti* were not the major concern of the politics of anti-colonial resistance. It is for this reason that, during the movement against the partition of Bengal in 1906, the radical nationalist newspaper *Bande Mataram* could announce: "The new movement is not primarily a protest against bad Government—it is a protest against the continuance of British con-trol; whether that control is used well or ill, justly or unjustly, is a minor and inessential consideration."[23] The contest for sovereignty had begun. There was little opportunity then to distinguish between the separate and autonomous spheres of dharma and *nīti*.

I believe this situation continued through most of the twentieth century until the period of the 'Emergency' in 1975–7. In fact, until the 1980s there was a predominant style of politics in India, nurtured since the days of the nationalist struggles, which valued ideological integrity and demanded consistency between ends and means. The acceptability of political leaders depended greatly on the sacrifices they had made for the cause of the nation and the people. In the last three decades or so, however, a different style of politics has rapidly made a place for itself in India's democratic arena. I would say that the more the will of the subjects has shifted from an engagement with sovere-ignty to a concern for the daily nitty-gritty of governmentality, the more the principles of dharma have yielded to those of *nīti*. A mode of political reasoning that had been suppressed since the early nine-teenth century is now proudly flaunting its virtues in the democratic spaces of provincial politics. There is no canonical literature yet on this new style of politics. But while it may lack the high spiritual appeal of dharma, it is not necessarily devoid of its own ethical rules. In the rest of this chapter, I will try to illustrate these new principles of democratic *nīti* with some examples.

[23] "Nationalism not Extremism," *Bande Mataram*, April 26, 1907, in Sri Auro-bindo, *Bande Mataram: Early Political Writings* (Pondicherry: Sri Aurobindo Ashram, 1973), pp. 296–9.

New Practices of *Nīti*

To begin with the state of 'Emergency' of 1975–7, the event marked an important watershed in the evolution of the democratic system in India. The period is widely remembered for Indira Gandhi's authoritarianism, the suspension of constitutional and civil liberties, the imprisonment of thousands of opposition leaders and activists, and the programmes of forcible sterilization and slum clearance. Also remembered are the astonishing results of the 1977 elections in which the voters of mainly northern India used the power of the vote to remove from office the apparently invincible regime of Indira Gandhi's Congress Party. The usual narrative about the Emergency is that of an authoritarian state defeated by popular resistance. Many remember the frequent use by opposition activists of terms like *dharmayuddha* (righteous war) and the battle between right and wrong to describe their resistance to the Emergency.

For most of us, the Emergency was an extraordinary and exceptional event. But we must not forget that even during that exceptional year and a half numerous ordinary people carried on with their daily lives. Indeed, even those whom we regard as the victims of the Emergency—those hapless residents of the squatter settlements and slums of the old city of Delhi—had to cope with the compulsions of daily living. After all, they were not heroic political actors, not even political activists. What did they make of their experiences during the Emergency? The anthropologist Emma Tarlo gives us an insight into this domain of subaltern consciousness.[24] Conducting her fieldwork more than twenty years after the event, she asked former slum residents displaced during the Emergency to recall that period. The answers were unexpected, to say the least.

Welcome Colony, across the River Jamuna, is a government housing project where many of the displaced slum dwellers of Old Delhi were given plots of land. Official records show that most were allotted land on the basis of certificates of sterilization under the population control programme carried out during the Emergency. According to the rules, only those displaced by the slum clearance drive were meant

---

[24] Emma Tarlo, *Unsettling Memories: Narratives of India's 'Emergency'* (Delhi: Permanent Black, 2003).

to be given land in this estate, but the records show that many who were not slum residents had managed to obtain land on behalf of the genuinely displaced, by using the latter's documents. In other words, the piece of paper certifying the fact of displacement had become a commodity. If the original displaced person entitled to a resettlement plot lacked the resources to build a house there, he or she would have sold his or her papers to someone else and probably moved into another slum. The one who bought the certificate was also a poor slum dweller who now had to grease the palms of a few officials to get the land allotted in his or her name. And then there was the notorious sterilization certificate, which too entitled the holder to a plot of land and which, unsurprisingly, was also bought and sold, as Tarlo was able to observe even from the official records.

The surprising thing is that for these displaced persons now living in resettlement colonies across the river from Delhi, the memory of the Emergency is not one of oppression. Rather, it is a collection of stories of how they sought out opportunities for coping with the vagaries of administrative measures and the pressures of the market. One woman, for instance, recounted, "At that time, I had the [tubectomy] operation done. Because of that, I was able to get a permanent job as cleaning staff in a government office. These days they only give you a watch or an electric fan which is why no one gets the operation done." In the course of her fieldwork, Tarlo came across a remarkable woman who, after being ousted from her slum residence, had, along with her husband, taken shelter with another family in Welcome Colony. After some time, she produced an affidavit stating that she was married to the owner of the house where she was staying and managed to get the property transferred to her name. A few days later, the original owners of the house found themselves on the street while the displaced woman became the legal owner of the house. She apparently became quite adept at finding opportunities for extracting benefits from the system of regulations and policies that governed the settlement and even advised others on the subject, needless to say for a fee.

It may be asked: what has this to do with politics? Such stories could be told of any place in any historical period. How does this help us understand the politics of the Emergency? My answer is: the intimate connection between the daily lives of the urban poor and the practices of governmentality exemplified by the above story is a new experience in the history of the Indian state. It may be recalled that one of the key findings of the early phase of *Subaltern Studies* was that the state was always a distant entity in peasant consciousness. Peasants generally wanted to have nothing to do with magistrates or courts, police stations or hospitals. In the same way, the relation of the urban poor, many of whom were migrants from the villages, to the agencies of the state was also distant. The historian Dipesh Chakrabarty, for instance, analysed the politics of the early industrial working class of Calcutta mainly as an instance of peasant resistance.[25] The activities of the developmental state did begin after Independence, but specific administrative practices for reaching targeted benefits to specific population groups did not quite take off until the 1970s. This process properly began with the poverty removal programmes of Indira Gandhi's government in the early 1970s. The so-called 20-point programme undertaken during the Emergency was a further episode in the evolution of the practices of governmentality in India. That is why the everyday stories of the Emergency unearthed by Tarlo seem so important to me.

I have elsewhere discussed the new "politics of the governed" spawned by the spread of governmental activities and the deepening of democratic demands in the last three decades in India.[26] We will again look at various aspects of that politics in the last section of this book. There are just two features of what I have called "political society" that I need to mention here. First, the administrative policies used to deal with demands in political society often tend to hover around a grey zone between legality and illegality. To take the case of the evicted slum dwellers of Old Delhi, their original residences in the squatter settlements were illegal. But when they were thrown out and given official certificates of displacement, they became legal claimants to the category of "displaced persons." This certificate could now be traded in the market. That might seem illegal. But there could be good administrative reasons for recognizing, in certain circumstances, the illegal holders of legal entitlements. Thus, if it is the case that many

[25] Dipesh Chakrabarty, *Rethinking Working Class History* (Delhi: Oxford University Press, 1989).

[26] Partha Chatterjee, *The Politics of the Governed* (New York: Columbia University Press, 2004).

genuine claimants to land meant for the resettlement of displaced persons did not have the resources to build houses on their plots, the likely result would be that the allotted plots would be covertly sold to others, leading to a black market in resettlement plots. It could be a wiser policy to allow the de facto transfer of the displacement certificate, even as a market transaction, and register the plots of land only with those who would actually build houses on them. Here, it is hard to decide what is strictly legal and what is not. There are many such conundrums that can be found in the administrative practices of governmentality.

The second point that needs to be made is that in this negotiation between claims and benefits, it is hard to distinguish between voluntary and coercive acts. We know as a general principle that the basic strategy of modern governmentality is to secure the intended result through a system of rewards and penalties, and to avoid the use of force as far as possible. By this logic, if a forcibly evicted person accepts a plot of land meant for such displaced people, it becomes, in the language of governmentality, a case of "voluntary resettlement." It could be pointed out that the eviction was an act of coercion. True enough. But when an illegal squatter, after eviction and resettlement, becomes the legally recognized owner of a plot of land, how strong can the charge be of the oppressive use of force? Many residents of Welcome Colony still describe graphically the traumatic scenes of bulldozers crashing through their huts and shanties. And yet, those of them who now have houses in the new colony are fulsome in their praise for the government which made them legitimate owners of their own property. The same goes for the sterilization campaign. There too a system of rewards and penalties was in place. Take the case of the daily wage labourer, unsure of finding work the next day, who agreed to be sterilized because it would fetch him a permanent job in a government office. Did he use his own judgement to weigh his available options and choose voluntarily, or was he coerced? It is difficult to tell, especially for those among the urban poor whose range of available opportunities is so severely constrained.

There has been a fair amount of discussion on the significance of the period of Emergency in the evolution of Indian democracy. In these accounts, the Emergency is seen as an exceptional and aberrant event that did not represent the normal conditions of democratic politics in India. The resistance against the Emergency and the subsequent electoral defeat of Indira Gandhi's Congress cannot but display the signs of a righteous battle of justice against tyranny. Most characters in that story are either heroes or villains. And that nameless, formless mass of voters whom we call the Indian people will always remain the superhero in the drama of the end of the Emergency. But if we move away from this dharma-inspired heroic history to the mundane details of daily life under the Emergency regime, we find a very different process in operation. This is the process of the expansion and deepening of governmentality in India. In this other history, the Emergency was no exception. Or rather, to put it more carefully, it was exceptional only in the sense that it marked out the limits that needed to be observed in order to carry out governmental functions most effectively within the constitutional framework, by employing flexible mechanisms of rewards and penalties and without using force. The outrage caused by forcible evictions or the sterilization programme had lessons for government which, I believe, were learnt in devising subsequent policies of urban planning and population control. New and more sophisticated governmental techniques were developed to achieve administratively more effective and politically less expensive results. Most politicians in India today will agree that the Emergency should never happen again. But that does not mean that slum evictions have stopped or that the population control programme has been abandoned: only the techniques have changed.

There is one more thing to be said about Welcome Colony and its residents. Researching their case, Tarlo found that they were over-whelmingly reverential towards Indira Gandhi, who enjoyed an almost divine status in their memories. Even though they still remem-bered their forcible eviction during the Emergency, they did not hold her responsible for it. This seems to be counterintuitive: how could the direct victims of the excesses of the Emergency have such a positive view of the political leader who headed the Emergency regime? The Welcome Colony residents, however, believe that the oppressions of the Emergency were carried out by corrupt officials and overzealous party activists; Indira Gandhi, they insisted, could not be blamed for those misdeeds. Indeed, they believed that Indira Gandhi was the saviour of India's poor and had paid the ultimate price for her commitment by falling to an assassin's bullet. In their eyes, she held a position well beyond the mundane bickering of politics; she was a goddess inhabiting the world of myth, a symbol of righteous virtue.

Nrisingha Prasad Bhaduri in his book *Daṇḍanīti* has drawn our attention to the fact that the word *netā* which is widely used today to refer to political leaders shares the same etymological root √*nī* with the word *nīti*.[27] Both words carry the sense of pulling forward, driving, or steering. The person who pulls something towards a goal is a *netā*, while the knowledge that allows someone to pull is *nīti*. The business of governmentality involves moving forward towards a certain intended direction or goal. The leader who must carry out this task need not have a deep sense of dharma but must necessarily have a keen understanding of *nīti*. I will argue that the new crop of political leaders that have emerged in Indian democracy in the last three decades or so are skilled in the art of *nīti*. It is futile to expect them to match up to the high ideals of dharma. Indeed, compared to the moral stature of leaders of the nationalist or Left movements, the present generation of leaders will appear to be self-interested, opportunist, venal, and acquisitive. We often refer to such leaders in the lower rungs of provincial politics as fixers, touts, etc., and look upon them with much derision. And yet, these are the people to whom ordinary men and women having to cope with the daily intricacies of governmental procedures must turn. One should not be surprised by this. Then again, when one such "fixer" fails to get the job done, it is not surprising that people should abandon him and turn to someone else. This is, in some ways, the basic storyline of everyday democratic politics.

There is one more topic that deserves more extended treatment than is possible in the space of this chapter. This concerns the question of violence. Politics inspired by dharma has always had a place for the righteous use of force. All wars in modern history have carried with them some justification in the name of the good, the right, or the just. The recourse to armed resistance against an oppressive regime is still widely regarded as a legitimate political method. The national movement in India saw much spirited debate on this question and the *Bhagavad Gītā* was widely cited as a canonical text justifying the righteous use of force against injustice. Even the Gandhian movement which expressly abjured the use of violence had a place for the exercise

[27] Bhaduri, *Daṇḍanīti*, p. 7.

of force. The intention behind the non-violent satyagrahi breaking the unjust laws of the state was to bring the violence of the state on his or her own body; indeed the intention was to invite the agents of the state to use force against the satyagrahi. When the state refused to employ force, the last weapon of the satyagrahi was the fast unto death, which was a way of doing violence to one's own body and holding the state responsible for it. The relation between violence and the politics of dharma is, I think, deep and inseparable.

If we move from the domain of dharma to that of *nīti*, we will still find a role for the use of force. But unlike in dharma-inspired politics, the key consideration in the calculations of *nīti* is the effectiveness of force, i.e. its cost as compared to the expected consequences. Hence, only that much force is admissible as is required to achieve the desired objective. It is in keeping with the dictates of *nīti* that we see in contemporary warfare the technologies of precision bombing whose intention is to hit the exact target while keeping the "collateral damage" to a minimum. If we look at the new expressions of the power of subjects in India's democratic politics, we will find that there is a place in it for the calculated use of force. Indeed, there is frequent resort to violence, on behalf of state power as well as in opposition to it. In opposing the policies of government, groups of subjects often take recourse to violent demonstrations, even taking on the armed agents of the state in confrontations. The calculation is that a round of violent agitation will force the rulers to turn their attention to the demands of the agitating subjects and force the government to start negotiations. This pattern has been repeated several times in the north-eastern states of India over the last three decades. Needless to say, there is no fixed rule that lays down how much violence will prove effective, and how much excessive. It has often been said that violence between religious groups is the result of planned operations designed to elicit a particular political result; so, apparently, are decisions to delay the intervention of the armed force of the state to put down such communal violence. Sometimes there are instant results of planned acts of violence; at other times it becomes clear that the violence was excessive and counterproductive. In the case of the everyday demonstrations of violence, there is in many local situations a certain acknowledged equilibrium of violence between state and non-state actors. Certain recognized limits to the use of violence are accepted. Often, as I mentioned in an earlier chapter in relation to the Shiv Sena in Mumbai, the theatrical demonstration of the threat of violence may turn out to be more effective than the actual use of force. Following that logic, it could be said that the pose of violence is the proper application of *nīti*; its actual use becomes a violation of *nīti*. But the complex use of violence in the new political process of dealings between the power of subjects and the power of the rulers in India's democracy needs to be studied in much greater detail.

In this chapter I have used, following Anandachandra Mitra, the twin ideas of *rājśakti* (the power of the ruler) and *prajāśakti* (the power of subjects). By his definition, the power of subjects emerges from their sense of claims or rights on government, and it is made effective by the desire of the rulers to promote the security and well being of their subjects. On the other hand, the power of the rulers derives from their position as representatives of the subjects. There is no doubt that there has been in the last three decades an efflorescence of the power of subjects in India. But this *prajāśakti* has failed to become united with *rājśakti* or the power of the ruler. The most obvious evidence of this is the widespread mistrust and lack of credibility of politicians among virtually all sections of the people. Whether urban or rural, people in India are vocal about the incompetence, corruption, and lack of integrity of politicians at all levels of government. One might say that the disillusionment with *rājśakti* is today almost universal. But the curious fact is that the expectations from government for the provision of various services has not diminished at all; rather, it has increased at all levels. The more *prajāśakti* asserts itself, the more the demands mount for governmental services, just as ever-newer methods of politics are devised to secure them. This domain of the rise of the power of subjects is, I have argued, the domain of *nīti*; it is in terms of *nīti* that it needs to be analysed.

The trouble is that those who inhabit the world of *rājśakti* are thoroughly sceptical of the recent rise of *prajāśakti*. And the more this suspicion deepens, the greater the tendency to resort to arguments inspired by dharma. After all, why else would a judge of the high court claim that to offer rehabilitation to an illegal squatter was the same as rewarding a thief? This is straight out of a text of dharma, not of *nīti*.

There was a time when the distinction between dharma and *nīti* was both understood and appreciated. Now, as those who used to be mere subjects increasingly learn to handle the levers of democratic politics, there is a renewed attempt on the part of the rulers to trump the considerations of *nīti* by resort to principles of dharma. It is through this tussle between the power of subjects and that of rulers that the future practices of Indian democracy will be defined.

4

Two Poets and Death

The Condolence Meeting

Bankimchandra Chattopadhyay, the most renowned literary figure in nineteenth-century Bengal, died on April 8, 1894. Three weeks after his death, a memorial meeting, organized by the Chaitanya Library and the Beadon Square Literary Club, was held at Star Theatre. It was decided that the speakers would be Rajani-kanta Gupta, the historian; Haraprasad Sastri, the famous scholar of Buddhism and early Bengali literature; and Rabindranath Tagore, then a young but already much acclaimed poet. Nabinchandra Sen, one of the most respected senior figures on Bengal's literary scene and a younger contemporary of Bankim in the provincial civil service, was asked to preside. To the surprise of the organizers, Nabinchandra refused. In his place, Gurudas Banerjee, judge of the Calcutta High Court, presided over the meeting. The address on Bankim delivered by Rabindranath that day later went on to become something of a landmark essay in Bengali literary criticism. Memorized by generations of schoolchildren, it has been for more than a century a staple of the formation and transmission of aesthetic canons in Bengal's new high culture.

What will concern us here is not the assessment of Bankim's literary output or of his historical role, on which much has been written.[1] Instead, our concern will be the reasons for Nabinchandra Sen's refusal

---

[1] Most recently, and brilliantly, by Sudipta Kaviraj, *The Unhappy Consciousness: Bankimchandra Chattopadhyay and the Formation of Nationalist Discourse in India* (Delhi: Oxford University Press, 1995).

to come to Bankim's memorial meeting. The poet Nabinchandra was known to have been close to Bankim and, although he did not often share what he thought were the latter's excessively Westernized literary tastes, he clearly deferred to his superior erudition, intellect, and public standing. The reasons for Nabinchandra's refusal had nothing to do with Bankim. Nabinchandra objected to the very idea of a public condolence meeting.

"Imitating the English, we have now begun organizing 'condolence meetings','" Nabinchandra wrote. "As a Hindu, I do not understand how one can call a public meeting to express one's grief. A meeting to express grief, think of it!" "How many buckets have you arranged for the public's tears?" he is said to have remarked to one of the organizers. "Our" grief, he claimed, was "sacred;" it drove one into seclusion. "We do not mourn by wearing black bands round our sleeves." A meeting in a public auditorium could only create, he thought, the atmosphere of a public entertainment; this was not "our way of mourning the dead."[2]

Soon after the memorial meeting, Rabindranath Tagore wrote an essay in the journal *Sādhanā*.[3] Entitled "The Condolence Meeting," the essay began by mentioning the objection that had been raised to the public condolence of Bankim's death. It was true, he said, that the practice was hitherto unknown in the country and that it was an imitation of European customs. But, like it or not, because of European contacts, both external conditions and subjective feelings were undergoing a change. New social needs were arising, and new ways would have to be found to fulfil them. Because of their unfamiliarity, these might seem artificial and unpleasant at first. But merely because they were European in origin was not a good reason for rejecting them outright.

The main point of objection to the idea of a public condolence meeting seems to have been its *kṛtrimatā*, artificiality. That which is *kṛtrim* is a product of human action: it is an artifice—fabricated, unnatural. Sometimes it indicated a "mere" form, empty within;

[2] Nabinchandra Sen, *Āmār jiban*, vol. 5 (1913), in *Nabīncandra racanābalī*, vol. 2, eds Santikumar Dasgupta and Haribandhu Mukhati (Calcutta: Dattachaudhuri, 1976), p. 253.

[3] Rabindranath Thakur, "Śoksabhā" (May–June 1894), in *Rabīndra-racanābalī*, vol. 10 (Calcutta: Government of West Bengal, 1989), pp. 291–9.

sometimes it could even describe behaviour that is insincere, false. This is what Nabinchandra would have meant when he referred to the showing of grief by wearing a black armband. The *kṛtrim* form of a public meeting was inappropriate, he must have said, for expressing an emotion as intense and intimate as grief at the death of a loved one.

In his essay, Rabindranath straightaway took up the question of artificial social forms. A certain *kṛtrimatā* was unavoidable if social norms were to be followed, he said. Surely, not everything could be left to individual taste and feeling. Artificiality could be said to be a defect in matters that were strictly internal to the self, where individual feelings reigned supreme. But society being a complex entity, it was not always easy to determine the boundary between the domain of the individual and that of society. In matters pertaining to society, certain universally recognized rules had to be followed if social relations were not to degenerate into anarchy. For example, Rabindranath pointed out, grief at the death of one's father, or—another example— the feelings of a devotee towards god, could be said to involve some of the most intimate and intense emotions in human life. And yet society claims to lay down the procedures of funerary and other associated rites to be followed on the occasion of a father's death, or, in the other case, the procedures of worship to be followed by all devotees, irrespective of individual preference or taste. This is so because society deems it necessary to regulate and order these aspects of life in a way that is beneficial for all of society.

Having made this general point about the necessary "artificiality" (borrowing our contemporary language, we might even say "constructedness") of all social regulations, Rabindranath then goes on to argue that Indian society was for long largely a "domestic society" or a "society of households" (*gārhasthyapradhān samāj*), a society in which the strongest social bonds rested on the authority of parents and other elders within the family. The specific forms of social regulation in India reflect this domestic character of traditional society. But this was now changing.

Recently there had been some changes in this society of households. A new flood had swept into its domain. Its name was the public.

It is a new thing with a new name. It is impossible to translate it into Bengali. The word "public" and its opposite "private" have now come into use in Bengali. . . .

Now that our society consists not only of households but also of an emergent public, the rise of new public responsibilities has become inevitable.[4]

One such new public responsibility was the public mourning of the death of those who had devoted their lives not just to the good of their own households but to the good of the public. The form of mourning was "artificial," as before, but it was now a form in which not just the members of the household but members of the public were required to participate.

What is interesting about this part of Rabindranath's argument is the explicit identification of a new domain of social activity involving "the public" and of new social regulations ordering these public practices. But he then goes on to make some observations about this emergent public domain that are still more interesting.

I do not deny the fact that the public in our country is not appropriately grief-stricken by the death of great men. Our public is still young; its behaviour bears the mark of adolescence. It does not recognize its benefactors, does not realize the true value of the benefits it receives, easily forgets its friends and thinks it will only receive what is given to it but will not incur any obligations in return.

I say such a public needs to be educated, and discussions in public meetings are a principal means of such education. (p. 293)

What we have here is a public that is not *yet* a proper public and a group of social leaders who think of their role as one of guiding this public to maturity. Rabindranath, as we can now recognize easily, is only restating here the fundamental problematic of the nationalist project of modernity under colonial conditions. The driving force of colonial modernity is a pedagogical mission.

What a "proper" public must look like is also, needless to say, given by world history. Rabindranath has no doubt about this. The examples that come to his mind in the context of Bankim's death are from the literary world of Europe and the relationship there between eminent literary figures and the public.

---

[4] Ibid., p. 293.

We do not have a literary society in our country and in society itself there is no cultivation of literature. Social practices in Europe make it possible for eminent persons to appear on numerous occasions at numerous public meetings. Their circle of acquaintances is not restricted to their family and friends; they are at all times present before the public. To their compatriots, they are close at hand and visible. Which is why at their death, a shadow of grief falls over the whole country. (p. 294)

By contrast, great men in India, despite their greatness, are not similarly visible in public. "Especially since women have no place in our outer society, our social life itself is seriously incomplete." The kind of intimate knowledge of a great person's life, habits, and thoughts that can evoke love and gratitude among ordinary people is completely lacking in our society. Instead of loving and respecting our great men, we turn them into gods to be worshipped from afar. The condolence meeting, argued Rabindranath, was precisely the occasion at which those who were close to a great person could tell the public what he was like as a human being, with faults and idiosyncrasies. They could make the great man as a private person visible to the public.

It is easy to recognize the sort of public sphere Rabindranath was wishing for. It was a public sphere consisting of not only books and journals and newspapers but also active literary societies, literary gatherings, an involvement of the public with things literary and cultural, an interest among ordinary people in greatness not as a superhuman gift but as a human achievement. Following Habermas, we can even sense here a hint of that new conception of personhood where the private and the intimate are, as it were, always oriented towards a public. Rabindranath, we can see, was imagining for his own country a world of literary activity embedded in a public sphere constituted by a variety of civil social institutions, the sort of world he himself had seen at first hand when, some fifteen years before, he had lived in England for more than a year as a student.

Did Nabinchandra not value a public sphere of this kind? What was the older poet objecting to? Many years after this incident, when writing his autobiography, Nabinchandra Sen returned to the subject. He was, as can be expected, strongly derisive of literary societies and literary gatherings, dismissing them as places where people met for idle talk, or rather idle listening. His idea of commemorating great literary figures was a very different one.

> If instead of these utterly wasteful meetings and speeches, the organizers were to preserve the birthplaces of the ancient and [modern] poets of Bengal and hold a sort of religious festival [*debpūjar mata utsab*] every year at those places, then we can pay our respects to our great writers, hold a community gathering and at the same time bring credit to the cause of Bengali literature. Mendicant *bairagis* and itinerant singers have in this way turned the birthplaces of the Vaisnava poets Jayadeva, Chandidas, and Vidyapati into places of pilgrimage where they hold annual festivals. But we, instead of following this sacred and "indigenous" [*svadeśī*] path, thanks to English civilization and education, spend our time organizing these laughable condolence and memorial meetings devoid of all true compassion. (p. 208)

Indeed he suggested that the birthplaces of modern writers like Madhusudan, Dinabandhu, and Bankim, like those of the Vaisnava poets of old, be turned into places of pilgrimage where devotees might gather once every year.

Nabinchandra also gave in his autobiography a particularly caustic description of Bankim's condolence meeting.

> The condolence meeting was held. When Rabi Babu finished his long, meandering lament, wiped the tears from his eyes and sat down, the audience—so I was told—started shouting from all sides, "Rabi Thakur! Give us a song!" The eminent Gurudas Babu, who was chairing the meeting, was much annoyed by this and said that Rabi Babu had a bad throat and would not be able to sing today. . . . They say in English that people go to church not to worship but to listen to the music. Perhaps it is truer to say that they go there to display their clothes. Similarly, in our condolence meetings, people walk in chewing *pān*, humming a tune from Amrita Babu's latest farce, asking for a song in Rabi Thakur's effeminate voice and generally expecting a good evening's entertainment. (p. 253)[5]

---

[5] Nabinchandra's description of this incident, though coloured by his prejudices, is not entirely far from the truth. Tagore's most recent biographer quotes another source which gives a similar account. Prasantakumar Pal, *Rabijībanī*, vol. 4 (Calcutta: Ananda, 1988), p. 3.

Nabinchandra seems clearly unwilling to accept that a public condolence meeting, like many formal occasions in modern European social life (including churchgoing), is any more than mere show. Indeed, he is unprepared even to accept that humanization of greatness which is part of the celebration of ordinary life that lies, as Charles Taylor has pointed out, at the heart of the transformation in social consciousness brought about by Western modernity.[6] Nabinchandra would rather have the great deified after their death, their birthplaces turned into places of pilgrimage, their statues "worshipped with flowers and sandalpaste." This, he would say, was "our" way of collectively expressing our gratitude to the great.

We have here the seeds of a serious disagreement. Does modernity require the universal adoption of Western forms of civil society? If those specific forms have been in fact built around a secularized version of Western Christianity, then must they be imitated in a modernized non-Christian world? Are the normative principles, on which civil social institutions in the modern West are based, so culturally particular that they can be abandoned in a non-Western version of modernity? These questions have been raised often enough in recent discussions. I wish to discuss here only a particular aspect of the matter.

Condolence Today

I have not brought up this incident at the beginning of this chapter merely to present one more curiosity from the history of colonial modernity in nineteenth-century Bengal. I think this largely forgotten disagreement can be shown to have an interesting significance for us today, one that was not clear to any of the antagonists a hundred years ago. In order to bring this out, let me first state that the question of condolence meetings is not, as far as I can see, a matter of debate today. Their form is largely the same as in the West, with the laying of wreaths, observing a minute's silence, and memorial speeches. These practices of a secularized Western Christianity are rarely recognized as such in India today: they have been quite thoroughly domesticated in the secular public life of the country's civil institutions. Of course, it is not

---

[6] Charles Taylor, *Sources of the Self: Making of the Modern Identity* (Cambridge: Cambridge University Press, 1992).

unusual to find a few indigenous touches added on, such as the garlanding of portraits or the burning of incense sticks. Music can be part of such a secular function: in West Bengal as well as in Bangladesh, by far the most likely music on such an occasion would be something composed by Rabindranath Tagore himself. However, the atmosphere would not be one of a public entertainment: Nabinchandra's fears on this count have proved to be unfounded. Rabindranath's hopes of grooming a public into maturity seem to have been borne out.

This, of course, only concerns public institutions of civic life whose formal practices are recognized as being secular. In other collective institutional contexts, which it would be grossly misleading to call "private," there is, needless to say, on an occasion such as the death of a prominent person or of someone closely connected with the institution, the continued observance of practices that are clearly recognized as religious. In the domain of the state itself, however, the political pressure to be scrupulously "secular" requires state authorities to assemble, paradoxically enough, a representative collection of practices from a variety of religions. Each of these—recitations, prayers, discourses, music—is presented in a state mourning as representing a religion; what makes it a part of a "secular" state function is the simultaneous presence within a single event of all of these representative religious performances. We will return to this difference between secular public practices in civil institutions and state institutions when we talk about the relation today between civil society and political society.

Civil and Political Society

Let me bring these up here: family, civil society, political society, and the state. These are classical concepts of political theory, but used, we know, in a wide variety of senses and often with much inconsistency. I must clarify here the sense in which I find it useful to employ these concepts in talking about contemporary India.

Hegel's synthesis in the *Philosophy of Right* of these elements of what he called "ethical life" spoke of family, civil society, and the state, but had no place for a distinct sphere of political society. However, in understanding the structure and dynamics of mass political formations in twentieth-century nation-states, it seems to me useful to think of a domain of institutions mediating between people and the state but standing parallel to civil society. The sharpness of the nineteenth-century distinction between state and civil society, developed along the tradition of European anti-absolutist thinking, has the analytical disadvantage today of either regarding the domain of the civil as a depoliticized domain in contrast with the political domain of the state, or of blurring the distinction altogether by claiming that all civil institutions are political. Neither emphasis is of help in understanding the complexities of political phenomena in large parts of the contemporary postcolonial world.

I find it useful to retain the term civil society for those characteristic institutions of modern associational life originating in Western societies that are based on equality, autonomy, freedom of entry and exit, contract, deliberative procedures of decision-making, recognized rights and duties of members, and such other principles. Obviously, this is not to deny that the history of modernity in non-Western countries contains numerous examples of the emergence of what could well be called civil social institutions which nevertheless do not always conform to these principles. Rather, it is precisely to identify these marks of difference, to understand their significance, to appreciate how by the continued invocation of a "pure" model of origin—the institutions of modernity as they were meant to be—a normative discourse can still continue to energize and shape the evolving forms of social institutions in the non-Western world, that I prefer to retain the more classical sense of the term civil society rather than adopt any of its recent revised versions.[7] Indeed, for theoretical purposes, I find it useful to hold on to the sense of civil society used in Hegel and Marx as bourgeois society (*bürgerliche gesellschaft*).

An important consideration in thinking about the relation between civil society and the state in the modern history of countries such as India is the fact that whereas the legal-bureaucratic apparatus of the state has been able—by the late colonial and certainly in the postcolonial period—to reach as the target of many of its activities virtually all of the population that inhabits its territory, the domain of civil social institutions as conceived above is still restricted to a fairly small section

[7] An account of some of these versions is given in Jean L. Cohen and Andrew Arato, *Civil Society and Political Theory* (Cambridge, Mass.: MIT Press, 1994).

of "citizens." This hiatus is extremely significant because it is the mark of non-Western modernity as an always incomplete project of "modernization" and of the role of an enlightened elite engaged in a pedagogical mission in relation to the rest of society.

But then, how are we to conceptualize the rest of society that lies outside the domain of modern civil society? The most common approach has been to use a traditional/modern dichotomy. One difficulty with this is the trap, not at all easy to avoid, of dehistoricizing and essentializing "tradition." The related difficulty is one of denying the possibility that this other domain, relegated to the zone of the traditional, could find ways of coping with the modern that might not conform to the (Western bourgeois, secularized Christian) principles of modern civil society. I think a concept of political society, distinct from and lying alongside civil society, could help us see some of these historical possibilities.

By political society, I mean a domain of institutions and activities where several mediations are carried out. In the classical theory, the family is the elementary unit of social organization: by the nineteenth century, this is widely assumed to mean the nuclear family of modern bourgeois patriarchy. Hegel, we know, strongly resisted the idea that the family was based on contract, but by the late nineteenth century, the contractually formed family became the normative model of most social theorizing in the West as well as of reformed laws of marriage, property, inheritance, and personal taxation. Indeed, the family became a product of contractual arrangements between individuals who were seen to be the primary units of society. In countries such as India, it would be completely unrealistic to assume this definition of the family as obtaining universally. In fact, what is significant is that when formulating policies and laws that must reach the greater part of the population, even the state does not make this assumption.

The conceptual move that seems to have been made very widely, even if somewhat imperceptibly, is from the idea of society as constituted by the elementary units of homogeneous families to that of a *population*, differentiated but classifiable, describable and enumerable. Foucault has been more perceptive than other social philosophers of recent times in noticing the crucial importance of the new concept of population for the emergence of modern governmental technologies. Perhaps we should also note the contribution here of colonial anthropology and colonial administrative theories.

Population, then, constitutes the heterogeneous material of society. Unlike the family in classical theory, the concept of population is descriptive and empirical, not normative. Indeed, population is assumed to contain large elements of "naturalness" and "primordiality;" the internal principles of the constitution of particular population groups is not expected to be rationally explicable since they are not the products of rational contractual association but are, as it were, pre-rational. What the concept of population does, however, is make available for governmental functions (economic policy, bureaucratic administration, law, and political mobilization) a set of rationally manipulable instruments for reaching large sections of the inhabitants of a country as the targets of "policy."

Civil social institutions, on the other hand, if they are to conform to the normative model presented by Western modernity, must necessarily exclude from its scope the vast mass of the population. Unlike many radical theorists, I do not think that this "defect" of the classical concept needs to be rectified by revising the definition of civil society in order to include within it social institutions based on other principles. Rather, I think retaining the older idea of civil society actually helps us capture some of the conflicting desires of modernity that animate contemporary political and cultural debates in postcolonial countries such as India.

Civil society in such countries is best used to describe those institutions of modern associational life set up by nationalist elites in the era of colonial modernity, though often as part of their anti-colonial struggle. These institutions embody the desire of this elite to replicate in its own society the forms as well as the substance of Western modernity. We can see this desire working quite clearly in the arguments of Rabindranath Tagore quoted at the beginning of this chapter. It is indeed a desire for new ethical life in society, one that is in conformity with the virtues of the enlightenment and of bourgeois freedom and whose known cultural forms are those of secularized Western Christianity. All these are apparent in Rabindranath's argument for new secularized public rituals. It is well recognized in that argument that the new domain of civil society will long remain an exclusive domain of the elite, that the actual "public" will not match up to the standards required by civil society and that the function of civil social institutions in relation to the public at large will be one of pedagogy rather than free association.

Countries with relatively long histories of colonial modernization and nationalist movements often have a quite extensive and impressive network of civil social institutions of this kind. In India, most of them survive to this day, not as quaint remnants of colonial modernity but often as serious protagonists of a project of cultural modernization still to be completed. However, in more recent times, they seem besieged.

To understand this, we will need to historicize more carefully the concepts of civil society, political society, and the state in colonial and postcolonial conditions.

Modernity and Democracy

The explicit form of the postcolonial state in India is that of a modern liberal democracy. It is often said, not unjustifiably, that the reason why liberal democratic institutions have performed more creditably in India than in many other parts of the formerly colonial world is the strength of its civil social institutions that are relatively independent of the political domain of the state. But one needs to be more careful about the precise relationships involved here.

Before the rise of mass nationalist movements in the early twentieth century, nationalist politics in India was largely confined to the same circle of elites that was then busy setting up the new institutions of "national" civil society. These elites were thoroughly wedded to the normative principles of modern associational public life and criticized the colonial state precisely for not living up to the standards of a liberal constitutional state. In talking about this part of the history of nationalist modernity, we do not need to bring in the notion of a political society standing alongside civil society.

However, entwined with this process of the formation of modern civil social institutions, something else was also happening. I have explained elsewhere how the various cultural forms of Western modernity were put through a nationalist sieve and only selectively adopted, and then combined with the reconstituted elements of what was claimed to be indigenous tradition.[8] Dichotomies such as spiritual/material, inner/outer, alien/indigenous, etc. were applied to justify and legitimize these choices from the standpoint of a nationalist

[8] Partha Chatterjee, *The Nation and Its Fragments: Colonial and Postcolonial Histories* (Princeton: Princeton University Press, 1994).

cultural politics. We would have noticed in the debate between the two poets cited above a clear example of this politics. What I wish to point out here in particular is that even as the associational principles of secular bourgeois civil institutions were adopted in the new civil society of the nationalist elite, the possibility of a different mediation between the population and the state was already being imagined, one that would not ground itself on a modernized civil society.

The impetus here was directly political. It had to do with the fact that the governmental technologies of the colonial state were already seeking to bring within its reach large sections of the population as the targets of its policies. Nationalist politics had to find an adequate strategic response if it was not to remain immobilized within the confines of the "properly constituted" civil society of urban elites. The cultural politics of nationalism supplied this answer by which it could mediate politically between the population and the nation-state of the future. In the debate between the two poets, Nabinchandra's arguments anticipated this strategic answer. It would, of course, be explicated most dramatically and effectively in what I have elsewhere described as the Gandhian moment of manoeuvre.[9]

This mediation between the population and the state takes place on the site of a new political society. It is built around the framework of modern political associations such as political parties. But, as researches on nationalist political mobilizations in the Gandhian era have shown repeatedly, elite and popular anti-colonial politics, even as they came together within a formally organized arena such as that of the Indian National Congress, diverged at specific moments and spilled over the limits laid down by the organization.[10] This arena of nationalist politics, in other words, became a site of strategic manoeuvres, resistance, and appropriation by various groups and classes, many of them unresolved even in the present phase of the postcolonial state. The point is that the practices that activate the forms and methods of mobilization and participation in political society are not always consistent with the principles of association in civil society.

[9] Partha Chatterjee, *Nationalist Thought and the Colonial World* (London: Zed Books, 1993).

[10] One set of studies of Indian nationalist politics that explicitly addresses this "split in the domain of politics" is contained in the volumes of *Subaltern Studies* and in several monographs written by historians contributing to that series.

What then are the principles that govern political society? The question has been addressed in many ways in the literature on mass mobilizations, electoral politics, ethnic politics, etc. In the light of the conceptual distinctions I have made above between population, civil society, political society, and the state, we will need to focus more clearly on the mediations between population on the one hand, and political society and the state on the other. The major instrumental form here in the postcolonial period is that of the developmental state which seeks to relate to different sections of the population through the governmental function of welfare, although we should remember that these welfare entitlements do not flow from the universal rights of citizenship—as in the post-War welfare state in Western Europe or North America. Correspondingly, if we have to give a name to the major form of mobilization by which political society (parties, movements, non-party political formations) tries to channelize and order popular demands on the developmental state, we should call it democracy. The institutional forms of this emergent political society are still unclear. Just as there is a continuing attempt to order these institutions in the prescribed forms of liberal civil society, there is probably an even stronger tendency to strive for what are perceived to be democratic rights and entitlements by violating those institutional norms. I will argue later in this book that the uncertain institutionalization of this domain of political society can be traced to the absence of a sufficiently differentiated and flexible notion of community in the theoretical conception of the modern state. In any case, there is much churning in political society in the countries of the postcolonial world—not all of which are worthy of approval—which can nevertheless be seen as an attempt to find new democratic forms of the modern state that were not thought out by the post-enlightenment social consensus of the secularized Christian world.

It is also worth pointing out that the two apparently conflicting trajectories of liberal civic modernity on the one hand and communitarian or populist democracy on the other can be easily connected to Sudipta Kaviraj's argument about symmetrical and sequential trajectories of modernity discussed in Chapter One. The genealogical history of postcolonial democracy in India highlights the fact that democratic mass mobilization, universal adult franchise, and the developmental state have preceded the generalization of civil social institutions or universal school education. The resulting practices of modernity and democracy are, not surprisingly, quite different from the familiar practices of modern Western democracy.

But improvisations seldom have a smooth passage to recognition as legitimate innovations. In concluding this chapter, I wish to suggest three theses that I will pursue in the following chapters of this book. These are three theses that arise from the historical study of modernity in non-Western societies.

1. The most significant site of transformations in the colonial period is that of civil society; the most significant transformations occurring in the postcolonial period are in political society.

2. The question that frames the debate over social transformation in the colonial period is that of modernity. In political society of the postcolonial period, the framing question is that of democracy.

3. In the context of the latest phase of the globalization of capital, we may well be witnessing an emerging opposition between modernity and democracy, i.e. between civil society and political society.

Before ending this section, I should make a final remark on my story about the two poets and death. Rabindranath Tagore won the Nobel Prize for literature in 1913 and went on to become by far the most eminent literary figure in Bengal. In his long and active career, he held steadfastly to his early commitment favouring an ethical life of public virtue, guided by reason, rationality, and dedication to a modern spirit of humanism. Since his death in 1941, however, he of all modern literary figures has been the one to be deified. On the day he died, when his body was taken through the streets of Calcutta, there was a huge stampede: people fought one another to collect relics from the body. Since then his birthplace has been turned into a place of pilgrimage where annual congregations are held every year—not religious festivals in their specific ceremonial practices, and yet not dissimilar in spirit. We could easily imagine the older poet Nabinchandra Sen chuckling with delight at the predicament of his more illustrious junior. The disagreement over "our" way of mourning for the dead, it would appear, has not yet been resolved.

Civil and Political Society Contrasted

Commenting on my distinction between civil and political society, Nivedita Menon has urged that it should be kept at the level of a conceptual distinction and not interpreted to suggest a distinction that divides up empirical spaces into middle-class civil society and lower-class political society.[11] Surely she is right, but not if the admonition is taken to mean that the conceptual distinction must never be applied to any empirical situation, for then of what use would such concepts be? The question is: how can the conceptual distinction be made to work in a particular empirical case? I would argue that there may indeed be cases (such as the one I will refer to in the following chapters of middle-class groups approaching courts of law to protect the civic rights of tax-paying law-abiding citizens against squatters, hawkers, vagrants, ticketless travellers, polluting auto-rickshaws, etc.) where the middle-class identification with civil society as against political society may be exactly relevant. On the other hand there may be many instances when that may not be the appropriate empirical marker. Menon's suggestion that civil and political society indicate "two styles of political engagement," with the former more available to an urbanized elite and the latter to the rest, is a useful methodological dictum. Stuart Corbridge and others, after a detailed empirical study of civil and political society in Bihar and West Bengal, suggest that "they may be thought of as a set of interlocking political practices that are arranged along a continuum."[12] These are analytical refinements obtained through productive engagement with actual empirical situations on the ground. They keep the concepts theoretically relevant only to the extent that they can be used to elucidate actual politics and prevent them from becoming ossified by the weight of ideology.

However, some scholars have questioned the analytical distinction itself in order to uphold a political project of strengthening and

[11] Nivedita Menon, "Introduction," in Partha Chatterjee, *Empire and Nation: Selected Essays 1985–2005* (Ranikhet: Permanent Black, 2010, and New York: Columbia University Press, 2010), pp. 1–20.

[12] Stuart Corbridge, Glyn Williams, Manoj Srivastava, and René Veron, *Seeing the State: Governance and Governmentality in India* (Cambridge: Cambridge University Press, 2005).

expanding the associational life of civil society.[13] They suggest that instead of relegating some people to the negatively marked zone of political society, the attempt should be to extend civil society to include all collective forms of social life, including tribal-communal forms. Legality, for them, "is a sleight of hand, the pen of the legislator or the judgment of a court," and sustained political pressure can often bring about changes in the law or its interpretation that better implement the rule of law and achieve more equal recognition of the property rights of all.

The spirit of legal pluralism championed here is commendable. However, a careful consideration of such proposals shows that the successful pursuit of the project results not in equal but *differentiated* citizenship. The theoretical problem was enunciated many years ago by Marx in "The Jewish Question" and has been recognized by contemporary political theorists such as James Tully writing on Canada or Rogers Smith on the United States.[14] To anticipate some of the terms I will define in later chapters, the attempt to mark the domain of equal citizenship with elements that derive from the heterogeneity of social forms results in a multiplication of exceptions to the norm of equal application of the law. In India, the elements of differentiated citizenship were incorporated into the body of the constitution itself by the exceptional provisions for scheduled castes and tribes and for the minority religious communities, validated to this day as temporary provisions to be revoked in the future, the differentiating criteria being specifically listed in the schedules of the constitution. The differential entitlements have proliferated through a variety of state legislations, not only in relation to the category of "other backward classes" but by extending such entitlements according to a host of other criteria such as mother tongue, domicile, period of residence in the state, etc. The technique of declaring the exception has extended from constitutional

[13] For instance, Sanjeeb Mukherjee, "Civil Society in the East and the Prospects of Political Society," *Economic and Political Weekly*, 45, 5 (January 30, 2010), pp. 57–63; Amita Baviskar and Nandini Sundar, "Democracy versus Economic Transformation," *Economic and Political Weekly*, 43, 46, pp. 87–9.

[14] James Tully, *Public Philosophy in a New Key, Vol. 1: Public Philosophy and Civic Freedom* (Cambridge: Cambridge University Press, 2009); Rogers M. Smith, *Civic Ideals: Conflicting Visions of Citizenship in U.S. History* (New Haven: Yale University Press, 1997).

and legal provisions to virtually the entire corpus of administrative regulations put in place by governmental authorities, all the way down to local levels of administration. This proliferation has resulted in the creation, as I see it, of two opposed tendencies. One is informed by the project of using legislation or legal interpretation to further include the differential demands of plural groups within the recognized domain of rights. But the demand, on grounds of equality, for recognition of yet another exceptional right by citing one that is already recognized can always be countered, also on grounds of equality, by pointing to those who must abide by the universal norm while others enjoy an illegitimate exception. In other words, the legal instrument is equally open to both tendencies. On one side, forces from political society try to use the legal institutions to extend the field of exceptions on the moral ground of securing greater equality. On the other side, those upholding the norms of civil society as the space of equal citizenship resist, also on the ground of equality, the proliferation of exceptions. Given the extraordinary powers, unknown in any other liberal constitutional system in the world, of judicial review that the Indian courts have come to assume, this has indeed become a major field of contest between the two tendencies. I do not see that the advantage lies with those who would like to use the law courts to further extend the recognized space of plural rights. If anything, I see that possibility to be far more effective in the governmental spaces inhabited by political society.

It is also pertinent to mention here the proposal made by Nivedita Menon to think of struggles in political society as aimed not so much at governmental benefits or welfare but as struggles *against* governmentality.[15] She sees this perspective as better suited to capture the radical potential in political society. Once again, with all my sympathy for radicalizing democracy, I am not at all sure that a move against governmentality is the dominant tendency in popular struggles in India since the 1990s, as Menon seems to believe. If there is one overwhelming fact about rural politics in India that I have learnt since the early 1970s, when I first began to study it, it is the steady widening and deepening of the web of governmentality, not merely as technology but as practices of everyday life among rural people. Contrary to

[15] Menon, "Introduction," in Chatterjee, *Empire and Nation*.

those who argue that the state, in its recent neoliberal heartlessness, has withdrawn from the welfare role it played in the days of Nehru and Indira Gandhi, I believe that its arms, bearing the instruments of coercion as well as of looking after populations, are now able to reach more corners of the territory and more sections of the people than any formal governmental structure has ever done in Indian history. India has never been more governed than it is today. As I will explain later, if one sees elements of insurgency in the struggles in political society, that would be nothing new, because insurgency has been a familiar feature of popular resistance to oppressive state orders in Indian history. But popular actions, even those involving prolonged violence, that seek an exceptional place within the order of governmentality are, I believe, a new feature of Indian democratic politics. Insurgent Nandigram in West Bengal, after rebelling against a governmental regime dominated by one political party in 2007, has now settled back into the same governmental regime, but now dominated by another political party. And there are numerous reports from areas of more or less permanent insurgency in many districts of central India of rebel groups negotiating, albeit provisional and unstable, arrangements with local state agencies to distribute governmental benefits. There was undoubtedly a strong force against governmentality that motivated peasant resistance in an earlier era, even in the middle of the twentieth century; I see very little of it today.

5

Tagore's Non-Nation

Tagore on the Nation

In this chapter, we will encounter a somewhat different and far more complex Tagore than the young poet we met in the previous chapter.

Rabindranath Tagore (1860–1941), poet, novelist, dramatist, essayist, composer, and painter, was a towering figure in modern India's intellectual and cultural life. His was perhaps the single most influential contribution to the modern national literary and artistic culture of Bengal. Following the award of the Nobel Prize for literature in 1913, Tagore was, for some time, a noted presence in literary circles in Europe and the United States. His influence on the cultural life of Bengal and India has been far more enduring. For instance, the national anthems of India and Bangladesh are both adapted from songs written and composed by Tagore.

Despite his massive contribution to the construction of the modern national culture of his country, Rabindranath was a consistent critic of nationalism.[1] In his earliest writings on the subject, he drew a sharp distinction between the conditions that produced nationalism in Europe and the absence of those conditions in India. India, he argued, was not, and did not need to become, a nation. In 1901, Rabindranath wrote an article in the journal *Bangadarśan* discussing Ernest Renan's famous essay from the late nineteenth century in which Renan

---

[1] I have discussed Tagore's writings on the nation extensively in my book *Prajā o tantra* (Calcutta: Anustup, 2005), chs 4 and 5. This chapter is, for the most part, my translation of the earlier Bengali essays.

attempted to define the attributes that made up a nation.[2] Rabindranath began by saying:

> We will use the word *jāti* as a synonym for the English word "race," and call the nation *neśan*. If the words "nation" and "national" are adopted in the Bengali language, we would be able to avoid many confusions of meaning. . . . I do not hesitate at all in using the word "nation" in its original form. We have received the idea from the English; we should be prepared to acknowledge our debt by retaining the language too.[3]

Rabindranath then quotes Renan's definition to show that neither race nor language nor material interests nor religious unity nor geographical location was a sufficient condition for the creation of a nation. The nation was a living entity, an object of consciousness. It consisted of two elements. One was situated in the past, the other in the present. The past element comprised the ancient memories of the common people, the heroic and noble achievements of their past. The present element consisted of their desire to appropriately preserve that inheritance and to collectively agree to live together.

> The memory of a glorious past and an ideal future consistent with that memory—those are the important things. . . . The feeling of having collectively shared the burden of suffering and sacrifices in the past and of being prepared to do so once again in the future produces among the people a sentiment of unity and closeness—that is the nation. Although its past forms the background, its perceptible mark can be seen in its present. This is nothing other than a general consent, a clearly articulated desire of all to collectively live the same life.[4]

Rabindranath also adds that the nation is not a timeless entity; it is the creation of human history. "Nations are not eternal. Each had a beginning; they will all come to an end. Perhaps in the course of the

---

[2] Ernest Renan, *Qu'est-ce qu'une nation?: conférence faite en Sorbonne, le 11 mars 1882* (Paris: Calmann Lévy, 1882).

[3] "Neśan ki" (1901–2), in *RR*, vol. 12, p. 675. *RR* refers to *Rabīndra racanābalī*, 15 vols (Calcutta: Government of West Bengal, 1961–8). The year of publication of the original work by Rabindranath is indicated in parentheses.

[4] Ibid., pp. 677–8.

transformation of nations, there will emerge one day a European community. But we do not see signs of it yet."[5]

The same issue of *Bangadarśan* in 1901–2 contained another essay by Rabindranath entitled "Hindutva." In it he applied Renan's definition to find out if the unity of the Hindus could be said to be that of a nation. His answer was that the unity of the European nation was quite different from the unity of the Hindus. "After much warfare and bloodshed, the peoples that European civilization has bound together into a nation are *savarṇa* [of the same *varṇa* or caste]. Once they adopted a common language and manner of dress, there were no other distinctions to be seen among them." Just as it is necessary for a nation to have a common memory, so is it necessary to agree to forget. Those who have come within the nation have had to forget that they were once bitter foes. If one is able to erase that memory, there are no impediments to the desire to live together. "Where the two sides have the same language and the same *varṇa*, it is easy to forget their differences: it is only natural for them to live collectively and mingle into the same entity." On the other hand, "after much warfare, those that the Hindu civilization had brought together were *asavarṇa* [of different castes]. They were by nature not the same. It was impossible to immediately forget their difference with those of the Aryan *jāti* [race, according to Rabindranath's definition]."[6] Hence, it was not possible for Hindu society to unify the many castes and races into a nation in the European style. It had to forge a different kind of unity. This unity was not built around the state, but around the *samāj*.

> . . . In our country, the *samāj* stands above all else. Elsewhere, the nation has preserved itself through many revolutions and emerged victorious. In our country, the *samāj* has protected itself against all dangers for a much longer time. The fact that we have not, despite a thousand years of revolution, oppression and servitude, sunk to the lowest depths of degeneration . . . is only because of the strength of our ancient *samāj*.[7]

Rabindranath thus argued that the political solidarity of the nation could never bring about the common unity of *asavarṇa* peoples. When

[5] Ibid., p. 678.
[6] "Bhāratbarṣīya samāj" (1901–2), *RR*, vol. 12, p. 679.
[7] Ibid., pp. 680–1.

European nations conquered other countries, they never attempted to include the conquered people within the community of the nation. On the contrary, they kept them separate, and in some cases, as with the American or Australian peoples, exterminated them. But Hindu civilization allotted a specific place for such *jāti*, whether non-Aryan or mixed or foreign, within the *samāj* and thereby sought to bring about harmony and unity. One cannot find similar instances of the creation of social harmony in the history of Europe.

Thus, even though he began with Renan's definition, what Rabindranath understood as the foundation of the nation was the biological idea of "race" (in its nineteenth-century sense), which he translated into Bengali as *varṇa* or *jāti*. Today, we may use more recent social scientific language and call it "ethnicity" or "ethnic identity." That is what Rabindranath took to be the necessary basis of the nation. He argued on numerous occasions that the nation could become so powerful in Europe because it contained no differences of race. Everyone within a nation was of the same colour, the same blood. Things were quite the opposite in India. Hence, it was futile to try to build a nation by relying on the political unity of the state. Rather, one would have to turn to the ancient ideal of social harmony constructed by Hindu civilization in which differences of caste or race were not denied but a method devised by which all could live together in peace. This argument does not appear in Rabindranath's writings only in that particular period immediately prior to the Swadeshi movement of 1905–11 when he spoke most enthusiastically about Hindu civilization. As early as 1898, he wrote in an article published in the journal *Bhāratī*:

> The Hindu *jāti* is something of a unique example in the world. It can qualify as a particular *jāti* and also fail to do so. . . . In Europe, the principal element in the formation of the nation is political unity. But the fact that Hindus have never had political unity is not reason enough to conclude that they do not have any sort of unity. . . . Those who have found a place within the great structure [of the Hindu *samāj*] are not all of the same descent. From the Dravidas of the South to the Nepalis of the Himalayas, a variety of *jāti* have, over the ages, come together within the Hindu *samāj*.[8]

---

[8] "Hindur aikya" (1898–9), *RR*, vol. 13, p. 29.

Rabindranath's argument was that the word Hindu did not mean a particular religious group; it was the name of a huge social system consisting of many racial and religious groups. "Musalman is the name of a specific religion, but Hindu is not a particular religion at all. Hindu is a racial summation of Indian history."[9] Many have been born Hindu but have become Christian. "They remain Hindu by *jāti*, but have become Christian by religion."

> There are thousands of Muslims in Bengal to whom Hindus say day and night, "You are not Hindu." They too keep telling themselves, "We are not Hindu." But in reality they are all Hindu–Muslims. It is by no means impossible to imagine a Hindu family in which one brother is Christian, another a Muslim, another a Vaishnava, and all of them living under the care of the same parents; indeed, it is only natural to imagine this, because it represents the real truth, and is therefore auspicious and beautiful.[10]

Again, several years later, when he wrote his lectures on *Nationalism* during World War I, at which time he no longer appealed to any of the moral virtues of the nation as described by Renan, Rabindranath Tagore can still be found saying repeatedly that the European nation represented a "homogeneous race." Even for the much discussed "multinational" case of Switzerland, he argued that the people of that country were of the same blood.[11] On the other hand, the greatest difficulty encountered by India was its "race problem": its society had made a place for many different "races," and now the challenge was to respect the distinctness of each and find a way to maintain unity. "Races ethnologically different have in this country come into close contact. This fact has been and still continues to be the most important one in our history."[12] The attempt to find a solution—through the caste system—was not wholly successful. "In spite of our great difficulty, however, India has done something. She has tried to make

[9] "Ātmaparicay" (1912–13), *RR*, vol. 12, p. 175.

[10] Ibid., pp. 174–5.

[11] ". . . remember that in Switzerland the races can mingle, they can intermarry, because they are of the same blood." "Nationalism in India" (1917), in *The English Writings of Rabindranath Tagore*, ed. Sisir Kumar Das, vol. 2 (New Delhi: Sahitya Akademi, 1996), p. 463.

[12] "Nationalism in the West" (1917), in *English Writings*, vol. 2, p. 419.

an adjustment of races, to acknowledge the real differences between them where these exist, and yet seek for some basis of unity."[13] In these lectures, delivered in 1917, Tagore expressed not even the slightest doubt that India's path to salvation did not lie in trying to become a nation. "India has never had a real sense of nationalism . . . it is my conviction that my countrymen will truly gain their India by fighting against the education which teaches them that a country is greater than the ideals of humanity."[14]

Community, not the State

Not nation, but *samāj*. Not political unity, but the unity of the *samāj*. If there is a thread that binds the political thought of Rabindranath Tagore, this idea is entwined in it. But what is this distinct social system of Hindu civilization that can maintain harmony among the different castes and races? Tagore provided a description of this system in several of his writings. The most extended discussion is in his famous essay "Svadeśī samāj," written at the beginning of the Swadeshi movement in 1905. Rabindranath begins with a sharp distinction: "Let foreigners fulfil those of our needs that foreigners have created, and indeed continue to create, for us. Curzon Saheb is energetically seeking to produce among Indians, desperately short of supplies of rice, a new thirst for tea. Fair enough; let Andrew Yule and Co. fill our tea cups. . . . But the thirst for water is authentically indigenous."[15] Rabindranath's argument was this: before the English arrived in India, the *samāj* would carry out through its own initiative all the beneficial works necessary to meet people's needs. It did not look to the state to perform those functions. Kings would go to war, or hunt, and some would even forsake all princely duties for pleasure and entertainment. But the *samāj* did not necessarily suffer on this account. The duties of the *samāj* were allocated among different persons by the *samāj* itself. The arrangement by which this was done was called dharma.

> That which is called "the state" in English is now called, in our modern languages, the *sarkār*. The *sarkār* has always existed in India in the form

<hr>

[13] "Nationalism in India" (1917), in *English Writings*, vol. 2, p. 453.
[14] Ibid., p. 456.
[15] "Svadeśī samāj" (1904–5), *RR*, vol. 12, p. 683.

of the royal or sovereign power. But there was a difference between the power of the state in Britain with the power of the king in our country. Britain has entrusted the entire responsibility of looking after the welfare of the country to the state. In India, the state only had a partial responsibility. . . . From giving alms to the destitute to teaching the principles of religion and morality to the common people, everything in Britain depends on the state. In our country, such activities are founded on the system of dharma among the people. Thus, the English are happy when the state is alive and well; we are relieved when we can preserve our system of dharma.[16]

But even if it is true that we never had a universally benevolent sovereign power in the past, could we not through our own efforts build such a state now? Rabindranath's answer is clear: "No, we cannot." He says: "We must understand this: the state in Britain is indissolubly founded on the general consent of the entire society; it has emerged out of a process that is natural to that country. We cannot have it here simply by the force of argument. Even if it is inherently of outstanding quality, it will still remain beyond our reach."[17]

An issue that needs our attention here, in order to facilitate the next part of the discussion, is that Tagore's writings on society frequently contain expressions such as "natural principles," "natural process," "natural *niyam* [regulation, law]," etc. What do they mean? We know that, at the end of the nineteenth century, Bengali discussions on social topics carried the strong impress of both French positivism and British Social Darwinism founded by Spencer and Huxley. Bhabatosh Datta says that Tagore's thought contains the idea of a universal law or regulating principle which, when exceeded or disrupted, brings about a disturbance in harmony. Datta thinks that there are shadows of positivism and Herbert Spencer on this idea in Tagore.[18] Perhaps it is in that sense that Rabindranath speaks so often of the "natural" process of development of human society, independent of individual actions, or of the specific process of evolution of a specific civilization or nation. It could also be that Edmund Burke's well-known discussion

---

[16] Ibid., pp. 684–5.

[17] Ibid., pp. 685–6.

[18] Bhabatosh Datta, *Aitihya o rabīndranāth* (Santiniketan: Viswabharati, 1996), pp. 135–6.

on the ancient constitution of each nation, and the specific tradition that is supposed to bind together the way of life of a people with its moral principles and values, had an influence on Rabindranath's thinking. More generally, we know that Rabindranath was greatly influenced by the religious views propounded by Rammohan Roy and by the idea, described in the Upanishads and the *Gītā*, of a principle of universal harmony governing all creation. Discussing Tagore's philosophy, Sachin Ganguly has argued that harmony is the central idea in Tagore's thought, the key to all his arguments and theories.[19] In his English writings, Tagore variously called this the principle of "harmony," "fundamental harmony," and "universal harmony."[20] Hence, Tagore's claim about the preservation of harmony as the particular and fundamental characteristic of Indian social organization was consistent with his overall philosophical position.

Whatever the source, the idea is quite firmly implanted in Rabindranath that each civilization has its own unique character which it must follow in the course of its progression through history. Society does change, but only those changes last that are consistent with its natural character. Innovations that do not naturally merge with the prevailing forms of life become discordant impositions and are in the end rejected by the *samāj*.

European civilization seeks to create unity by keeping differences at bay, or by destroying difference and bringing about homogeneity. On the other hand, Indian civilization does not deny differences, but, by recognizing them and demarcating the relation of each group with all the others, tries to find a place for all in society. "That the bringing together of the diverse into one, of making the stranger into one's own, is not the same as turning everything into a homogeneous mass—do we, in this country, have to shout this truth from the rooftops?"[21] The arrangement by which social unity was sought, even as differences were recognized, is the Indian caste system. In the Swadeshi period,

[19] Sachindranath Gangopadhyay, Pabitrakumar Ray, and Nripendranath Bandyopadhyay, *Rabīndradarśan* (Santiniketan: Centre of Advanced Study in Philosophy, 1969).

[20] For example, in the English works *Sadhana* (1914), *Creative Unity* (1922), and, most elaborately, *The Religion of Man* (1913). See *The English Writings*, vols 2 and 3.

[21] Appendix to "Svadeśī samāj" (1904–5), *RR*, vol. 12, p. 706.

Rabindranath even claimed that had the ancient makers of the *śāstra* known of the Muslim and Christian inhabitants of the country, they would not have restricted their rules to only the Hindu castes but "would have defined the claims of all of these alien groups with the Hindu *samāj* in such a way that there would not have been frequent conflicts between them."[22] In 1911–12, when he was thoroughly disillusioned by the politics of the Swadeshi movement, Rabindranath was still writing, in the context of the history of caste conflicts in India: "It is not in India's nature to scatter itself among the many. India seeks unity, which is why it strives to contain diversity within the bounds of unity."[23] Later, in his *Nationalism* lectures, he says much the same thing about the caste system in India, and reminds his American audience that unlike the European conquerors of the Americas, the Aryans did not try to annihilate the non-Aryan peoples of India but instead sought to include them within society while recognizing their differences. Of course, by 1917 Tagore was far more conscious and articulate than before about the rigidity, and consequent injustices, of the caste system: "In her caste regulations, India recognized differences, but not the mutability which is the law of life. In trying to avoid collisions she set up boundaries of immovable walls, thus giving to her numerous races the negative benefit of peace and order but not the positive opportunity of expansion and movement."[24] Yet Tagore insisted at the same time that "India tolerated difference of races from the first, and that spirit of toleration has acted all through her history. Her caste system is the outcome of this spirit of toleration."[25] He had no doubt at this time that India's ideal was "neither the colourless vagueness of cosmopolitanism, nor the fierce self-idolatry of nation-worship,"[26] but social unity through recognition of the mutual differences of races and communities.

Rabindranath's understanding of the significance and ideals of the Indian caste system was quite in accordance with the views of European Orientalists and modern Indian commentators. The most

[22] Ibid., pp. 704–5.
[23] "Bhāratbarśe itihāser dhārā" (1911–12), *RR*, vol. 13, p. 164.
[24] "Nationalism in India" (1917), in *English Writings*, vol. 2, p. 460.
[25] Ibid., vol. 2, p. 459.
[26] "Nationalism in the West" (1917), in *English Writings*, vol. 2, p. 419.

sophisticated version of this interpretation was to appear in twentieth-century sociology in the writings of the French scholar Louis Dumont.[27] The point to be made here is this: the criticisms that are now familiar to us in the twenty-first century of not only the practices of caste discrimination but also of its supposed ideal of social harmony were entirely absent in learned discussions in Tagore's time. His opinions on the ideal of harmony in Indian society were neither unfamiliar nor unacceptable to his readers and listeners in the Swadeshi age.

One's Own Country

Let us return to Tagore. Not the nation, but *samāj*. Not the political unity of the state, but the social harmony of the *samāj*. In that case, what is the correct meaning of the term *svadeś* (literally, one's own country) that recurs frequently in Rabindranath's writings, not only in the Swadeshi period but even much later? He directly addressed the subject in an essay written at the time of the Non-cooperation movement of 1920–1, a critical moment of transition in nationalist politics in India.

> That the English are in India is an external fact; that there is a *deś* is something we know within ourselves. This truth within ourselves is the eternal truth; the external fact is mere appearance—*māyā*. . . . The event called the rise of the English in India can take many forms. Today it shows itself in the form of the English; tomorrow it can take an even more terrible form in the shape of another foreign power. If we try to chase away this monster of subjection from the outside with bow and arrow, it will simply change its colours and frustrate our efforts. But that I have my *deś* is the truth. Once we realise this truth, the *māyā* of external appearance will vanish of itself.[28]

That I have my *deś* is the truth. It is stated here as a self-evident proposition. What does it mean? Do I have my *deś* because I have been born in a particular geographical territory? Or do I have my *deś*

---

[27] Especially in Louis Dumont, *Homo Hierarchicus: The Caste System and Its Implications*, tr. Mark Sainsbury, Louis Dumont, and Basia Gulati (1970; rpntd Delhi: Oxford University Press, 1998).

[28] "Satyer ahvān" (1921–2), *RR*, vol. 13, p. 293.

because I have been raised in a particular geographical-cultural environment? No, those are not the reasons.

> The certain knowledge that I have a *deś* comes out of a quest. Those who think that the country is theirs simply because they have been born in it are creatures besotted by the external things of the world. But, since the true character of the human being lies in his or her inner nature imbued with the force of self-making (*ātmaśakti*), only that country can be one's *svadeś* that is created by one's own knowledge, intelligence, love and effort.[29]

I believe the key to Tagore's thinking on the nation is hidden in the above statement. My *svadeś* is not something that has merely occupied a patch of territory on the surface of the earth from time immemorial. It does not consist only of its geography or natural resources. It does not even comprise the collection of groups, communities, and peoples that have, through the ages, settled on its land. In other words, my *svadeś* is not simply an inheritance I have acquired by birth. My *svadeś* is something that I, along with others, create by virtue of our knowledge, intelligence, love, and effort. My *svadeś* is the product of our imagination, the object of our quest—it is something we must earn.

Rabindranath has here travelled far from Renan's definition, his starting point. In the Swadeshi period, he had firmly declared that there was no nation in India and that it was futile to try to import it, because the social systems and historical nature of Europe and India were quite different. Instead of looking for the nation, we must revive and reconstruct the *svadeśī samāj*, establish the collective power of self-making or *ātmaśakti*. The relation of every inhabitant of the country with the *svadeś* must be personal and quotidian. But such close personal relations of everyday community life are possible only in a small village. How can such relations develop across an entire country?

> We can only make a small village directly our own and assume the full burden of all its responsibilities. But as we widen the perimeter, we feel the need for machinery (*kal*). We can never visualize the country on the same scale as the village. Which is why one cannot serve the country in an unmediated way; one must seek the help of a machine. We have never

---

[29] Ibid., p. 293.

possessed this machinery, because of which we must now import it from abroad. The machine will not run unless we set up the full range of instruments and procedures that go with it.[30]

By machinery, Rabindranath meant the organization of the modern state—political associations, representative bodies, campaigns for membership, elections, etc. He did not deny that these organizational forms were needed even for the construction of the *svadeśī samāj*. It is not out of place here to point out that Tagore, at the time of the Swadeshi movement in Bengal in 1905–6, even prepared a constitution of the *svadeśī samāj*. What was meant by *samāj* there was not some traditional Indian form of community life but "society" in the full modern Western sense of an association: "We have resolved to jointly set up a *samāj*." One could become a member of that association: "Any Bengali may join this *samāj*." One could also leave the association at will. This *svadeśī samāj* was meant to have a cabinet of ministers, a council of members, elections, and decision-making by majority vote.[31] This was its machinery. In the essay "Svadeśī samāj" Rabindranath gave this alternative to the nation the name *samāj-rājtantra*, literally "sociocracy" or the rule of society.

> We must install the machinery. And regardless of which country its operating procedures come from, we must accept them as well, for otherwise all will be in vain. Yet, fully accepting that requirement, we must also say that India cannot run by machinery alone: unless we can directly experience the individual feelings of our hearts, our true selves will not be drawn to such a thing. You may call this good or bad; you may curse it or praise it; but that is the truth.[32]

Even during the Swadeshi period, Rabindranath did not deny the need for "machinery," i.e. political organization, even though he frequently reminded his audience and readers that mere machinery would not suffice. The crucial shortcoming was that this machine was imported from elsewhere; it was not the product of our natural selves. An example could be found in our political conferences, where

[30] "Svadeśī samāj" (1904–5), *RR*, vol. 12, p. 693.
[31] "Svadeśī samāj sambidhān" (1904–5), *RR*, vol. 12, pp. 744–8.
[32] "Svadeśī samāj" (1904–5), *RR*, vol. 12, p. 693.

there was more idle talk than real business, but that was entirely in accordance with our nature.

> As if we are the groom's party at a wedding: such is the excess of expectations as well as of offerings of food, travel, leisure, and entertainment that it is utterly beyond the resources of the organizers. If they had asked, "You are here to serve your country, not to oblige us; so why should we have to supply you with food and drink, and places to sleep, and lemonades and soda water, and horses and carriages?"—it would have been a very fair question indeed. But it is not in our nature to avoid these obligations by claiming that they are not our business. . . . We prefer not to dissociate our work from the affections of the heart.[33]

With the passage of time, however, this conviction regarding the necessity of establishing the machinery of political organization became clouded by doubt. Sumit Sarkar, in his history of the Swadeshi movement, has described the significance of Tagore's enthusiastic entry into the movement and his withdrawal from it after a very short time.[34] In an article in *Subaltern Studies*, Ranajit Guha has shown that Tagore regarded certain episodes in the Swadeshi movement, such as the social boycott of those who opposed it, especially Muslims, as signs of its fundamental failure. This failure, in turn, Guha argues, could be ascribed to the inability of India's nationalist movement to achieve a position of social hegemony: the degree of coercion there far exceeded that of consent.[35]

That Rabindranath came to see this failure as the inevitable consequence of the political organization of the nation is clear from many of his later writings. In his *Nationalism* lectures, he defines the nation as a collection of people "organized for a mechanical purpose." In the printed version of the lectures, he refers to "the Nation" with a capital N and accuses it of two shortcomings: one, it is an organization or a machine, and two, it is designed for the achievement of narrow and selfish goals. According to him, a true society does not have any

[33] Ibid., p. 691.

[34] Sumit Sarkar, *The Swadeshi Movement in Bengal 1903–1908* (1973; rpntd Ranikhet: Permanent Black, 2010).

[35] Ranajit Guha, "Discipline and Mobilize," in Partha Chatterjee and Gyanendra Pandey, eds, *Subaltern Studies VII* (Delhi: Oxford University Press, 1992), pp. 69–120.

ulterior goals or objectives. It is merely a "natural" arrangement for regulating the innate urge of self-expression of each person through his or her relations with others. A relatively minor aspect of this arrangement is security, which in turn gives rise to statecraft. But statecraft concerns the practices and techniques of material power; there is no possibility there of pursuing the spiritual ideals of human life. Unfortunately, Europe discovered one day that, with the help of science and organization, it could extend the force of material power to such extremes that the entire globe could come under its sway, giving it access to unlimited riches from every part of the world. Thus began the race between nations for greater military power and material wealth, as a consequence of which humanity was presented with the horrors of imperialism and a world war.[36] A political organization or "machine" solely in pursuit of the material interests of the nation can never achieve the overall well being of people and was, instead, more likely to cause overall harm.

> Even if the whole world proclaims that material results are the ultimate end of human life, let India never accept it: that is the boon I seek from the maker of our destiny. After that, if we achieve political freedom, well and good. If not, let us not block the path to a greater freedom with the rubbish of polluted politics.[37]
>
> Some of our young men, drunk on the political liquor sent from foreign distilleries, have now taken to fighting among themselves. Seeing them, I often think that while we have enough indigenous crimes of our own, those who import these foreign ones are making the burden of our sins even more unbearable.[38]
>
> We have been begging for our liberty from a West that is itself in the throes of death. What can this dying creature give us? A new state system in place of the old state system? . . . We will never gain our freedom from a gift of charity—no, never. Freedom belongs to our inner selves.[39]

It hardly needs to be said that Rabindranath's critique of the nation as a Western state organization did not emanate from some nativist pride of Hindu greatness. It is true that he often talked about the ideal

---

[36] "Nationalism in the West", in *English Writings*, vol. 2, p. 421.
[37] "Choṭo o baḍo" (1917–18), *RR*, vol. 13, p. 258.
[38] "Bātāyaniker patra" (1919–20), *RR*, vol. 13, p. 281.
[39] "Svādhikārpramattaḥ" (1917–18), *RR*, vol. 13, p. 269.

of dharma that he believed was the moral foundation of the Aryan civilization in India. He frequently referred to this as the natural property of Indian civilization or the unique historical path that India must follow. But even there, what prevailed in his thinking was the universality of that ideal—the eagerness to make one's own that which was different and new but a force for the good. This urge for universality is what impelled him to condemn in the strongest possible terms the orthodox ritualism of the Hindu religion or its oppressive discriminations of caste. It is the same urge that made him claim that his idea of *svadeś* should not be restricted to any particular nation but should instead encompass the world. On the other hand, Rabindranath's critique of the mechanical pursuit of self-interest embodied in the social organization of the modern West cannot be equated with a socialist or Marxist critique. Then what is the appropriate framework for evaluating Tagore's political thinking?

It has been sometimes suggested that Tagore's idea of *svadeś* is close to Gandhi's idea of *svarāj*. But, as a matter of fact, there is more difference than similarity. Despite the mutual respect and friendliness between them, they were involved in some fierce and well-known political debates which several scholars have discussed.[40] I wish to point to one difference that has not been sufficiently commented upon.

The general consensus among social scientists today is that, regardless of its claims to historical ancientness or to ethnic identity based on race, language, or religion, the nation is a very modern idea. In fact, the nation is an imagined political community produced in the course of the history of the last two hundred years or so. "Imagined" does not mean "imaginary" or "false." Rather, it means the imputation, through certain specific material processes and social institutions, of an imagined bond of kinship to a large mass of people. The nation is not a gift of nature; it has to be constructed. Benedict Anderson has shown that the real medium of the construction of national communities is the coming together of capitalism with the technology of print.[41]

[40] The most recent discussion is in Sabyasachi Bhattacharya, ed., *The Mahatma and the Poet: Letters and Debates between Gandhi and Tagore 1915–1941* (New Delhi: National Book Trust, 1997).

[41] Benedict Anderson, *Imagined Communities: Reflections on the Origins and Spread of Nationalism* (London: Verso, 1983).

Newspapers, novels, textbooks, maps, censuses, thousands of official and unofficial notifications and directives—the medium of print enables the circulation of such material to create a huge space of national public life and enmesh the daily lives of millions. In the twentieth century, print was supplemented by the radio, cinema, gramophone records, and television. This made it possible for a political event in one corner of the country, or a popular film or television serial, or the success or failure of a football or cricket team, to become a part of the lived personal experience of millions of men and women. Despite being separated in their personal spheres, the shared fact of experiencing at once the same national events could create an unseen but deep bond of imagined kinship that seemingly tied them together. This relates not merely to their exterior public lives. It is striking how much of our personal and even intimate lives—our habits and desires—are shaped by the literature, art, music, or advertising produced within the imagined community of the nation. It seems somewhat unreasonable to condemn or dismiss them as "mechanical" or "interest-driven."

So the question arises: did Tagore not see the nation from a rather narrow and limited angle? Was not his project of creating the *svadeś* in fact similar to that of constructing the nation? From several of his comments made in the Swadeshi period, it does seem that Rabindranath identified quite correctly some of the processes of constructing the nation:

> Literature in our country is becoming stronger and livelier by the day and is slowly spreading from the upper layers of society to the lower ones. . . . In this way, the thoughts, sorrows and ambitions of the whole country are gradually being expressed as one. Words that were once learnt by heart in foreign schools are now daily becoming the words of our own *svadeś*, said in our own language in our own literature.[42]

Or:

> The right of self-government is lying in front of us—no one has taken it away, nor can anyone ever take it from us. We can improve education, health, and roads in our villages and neighbourhoods all by ourselves—if we so desire, and if we unite for it.[43]

[42] "Saphalatār sadupāy" (1904–5), *RR*, vol. 12, p. 709.
[43] Ibid., p. 719.

Or think of Rabindranath's invitation to university students to collect, under the direction of the Bangiya Sahitya Parishat (the newly established national literary academy of Bengal), the material relating to the dialects, folk religions, festivals, rituals, stories, songs, nursery rhymes, etc. of the country. Rabindranath was here proposing a very familiar national project.[44] Are we then to say that even though he apparently rejected the nation, his thinking on *svadeś*-creation, at least in the Swadeshi period, was actually not too far from the idea of nation-construction? Did the idea of *svadeś* emerge as a distinct and coherent concept only at a later stage in his thinking? We may find an answer to this question if we consider the complex problem of Tagore's relation to the Gandhian movement.

Tagore and Gandhi

I have referred earlier to Rabindranath's essay "Satyerāhvān" (The Call of Truth) written at the time of the Non-cooperation movement in 1921. In this essay, he described Gandhi's emergence on the national political scene as representing the struggle of truth against the politics of tactical manipulation.

> At this time, Mahatma Gandhi appeared at the door of millions of India's poor— dressed like them, speaking to them in their language. This figure possessed a quality of truth that had nothing to do with the evidence of books. That is why the name that has been given to him— "Mahatma," the great soul—is a true name. Who else has made so many Indians his own kin? . . . The politics that depends on cunning is a barren politics: we should have learnt this lesson a long time ago. The Mahatma has now clearly shown us the enormous strength of truth. Cunning is the natural dharma of the cowardly and the weak. To destroy it, one has to cut through its skin. That is why many clever men in our country still prefer to see the efforts of the Mahatma as akin to the covert moves of a political game of dice. Their minds, corrupted by falsehood, cannot bear to admit that the love that is now sweeping through the heart of the country is not an irrelevant thing—that this indeed is freedom, the *deś* finding itself. Whether the English are still here or not hardly matters. This love is self-revelation . . . this is what I call the liberation of my *deś*. Revelation is freedom.[45]

---

[44] "Chātrader prati sambhāṣaṇ" (1905–6), *RR*, vol. 12, pp. 728–9.
[45] "Satyer āhvān" (1921–2), *RR*, vol. 13, pp. 297–8.

We should note that, in Tagore's view, the manner in which Gandhi had become the kin of millions of Indians had nothing to do with the truth contained in books. It was the truth of love, of the heart. To mix such love with the tactical cunning of politics was to show contempt for it. Yet, to his dismay the Gandhian movement, in its struggle to attain Swaraj, soon took the path of political cunning and organizational discipline.

> I see a huge weight pressing down on the country's mind. An external force seems to compel everyone to say and do the same things. . . . Why this compulsion? . . . The country is being assured that it will get a very coveted thing—very soon and very cheap. . . . Is it not immensely worrying that most people in the country have happily accepted, without debate, and indeed forcibly suppressing all debate, that Swaraj will come on a particular day of a not-too-distant month—that is to say, that they have surrendered the freedom of their own judgement and robbed the same freedom of others? Is it not to rid ourselves of this evil spirit that we look for the shaman? But when the shaman himself shows up as the evil spirit, there is no end to our troubles.[46]

Tagore's regret becomes sharper if we reverse the statement. It was to rid the country of the politics of cunning that the people had chosen Gandhi as their shaman. Now Gandhi himself was imposing the demon of tactical cunning and organizational discipline on the people. Not only that, he was forcing them to adopt such a narrow programme of action that their minds would be, on the one hand, imprisoned within the dull monotony of endlessly turning the spinning wheel and, on the other, intoxicated by the frenzy of the boycott.

> A penance imposed through forcible compulsion cannot rid us of our sins. I have said many times before, and will say it again, that the lure of material gain must not be allowed to destroy our minds. If the Mahatma wants to fight against that machine which oppresses the whole world, we are on his side. But we cannot join this struggle by relying on that besotted, entranced, blind force of obedience that is at the root of all the miseries and indignities in this country. Our main battle is against that force. If we can drive it away, only then will we get *svarāj*, both within and outside us.[47]

---

[46] Ibid., pp. 298–9.
[47] Ibid., p. 303.

The grounds of difference are clear. The people had unhesitatingly accepted the truth that Gandhi had revealed before them because that truth was above politics—unconfined by the machinery of organization, untouched by the tactical deceit of political cunning. But the promise of obtaining swaraj within a year or the programme of spinning and boycott had brought back the same organizational politics of tactical cunning. "The quest for Swaraj is a very easy quest; it proceeds along one or two very narrow paths."[48]

> There is no end to the troubles we create because of our penchant for confusing the religion of ritual with the religion of eternal truth. It is the force of this old ingrained habit that made it possible for the spinning wheel and hand-spun khadi to parade menacingly as the principal religious duty of Swaraj; no one was even surprised by it. . . . The reason why the Mahatma did not shrink from calling Rammohan [Roy] a pygmy—the same Rammohan whom I regard as the greatest person of the modern era—reflects an inner cast of mind that has pulled the Mahatma's activities in a direction that my sense of dharma cannot accept as my own.[49]

There is no doubt that it is the compulsion of organizational politics, frequently referred to by Rabindranath as "the machine," which is his principal ground for differing with Gandhi. Tagore had unhesitatingly accepted the Mahatma as the country's leader because he represented a truth above the clever artifice of politics and outside the arguments of books. In India, people longed to see the full image of their *svadeś* in the person of a leader: this was something Tagore had pointed out as far back as the Swadeshi movement. "We wish to perceive our *svadeś* in a specific person. We need a person who will be the image of our entire *samāj*. Through him, we will worship and serve our great *svadeśī samāj*. By staying in touch with him, we can stay in touch with every member of the *samāj*. . . . At this time, we need a leader of our *samāj*. . . . We need a centre that can provide direction to our many individual efforts."[50] Defending his proposal, Rabindranath maintained that this was not merely part of the culture of India, it

[48] "Svarājsādhan" (1925–6), *RR*, vol. 13, p. 336.
[49] "Carkā" (1925–6), *RR*, vol. 13, pp. 335–6.
[50] "Svadeśī samāj" (1904–5), *RR*, vol. 13, pp. 693–4.

was the character of the East. The reason why Japanese soldiers were giving sleepless nights to Western generals was because they had "gone beyond the machine. . . . They were each related to the Mikado, and through him with the whole country. They had dedicated themselves to this relationship. . . . Japan is showing how the machine can be made consistent with the heart."[51]

Tagore's notion of "the leader" remains somewhat obscure. While, on the one hand, he could not accept the mechanical organization of modern political institutions, he did, on the other hand, recognize the need for solidarities of people that were larger than those of the village or the locality and that could be called *svadeś* in the modern sense. But how were personal relations of kinship to be established between individuals within this large community of the *svadeś*? We have seen that Rabindranath did not bring into his discussion the well-known cultural technologies of imagining and constructing the nation— newspapers, novels, school texts, maps, bureaucratic notifications. I believe that the apparatus of the spinning wheel, khadi and the Gandhi cap, and the various rituals, ceremonies, and emotions associated with them, played an enormous role in the imagination of the Indian nation. But Tagore suspected them to be the disciplinary instruments of a large political machine and sought to avoid them. Instead, he seems to have looked towards a leader who, by his personal character and idealism, would earn the love of everyone and provide the centre of an extensive network of imputed kinship. The intimate bonds of solidarity of the people of the country would be reflected in his person.

But the *svadeś* is not merely a receptacle of imagined kinship. To be a *samāj*, it must perform certain regular and daily services. Gandhi said, "Spin the *charkha*. That is the best way to serve the country." Tagore disagreed. Interestingly, a major reason for his disagreement was that there was no scientific argument in favour of continuing with the spinning wheel.

I am prepared to burn [foreign-made] cloth, but not on the strength of a slogan. Let those who have specialized knowledge collect sufficient evidence in the proper way and explain to us with proper arguments which economic policies will rectify the economic errors the country

[51] Ibid., pp. 690, 695.

has committed in the matter of clothing. . . . Building Swaraj requires extensive knowledge; its methods are difficult and prolonged. They call for not only desire and passion, but also investigation of facts and judgement. They need the combined thoughts and efforts of economists, technologists, educationists and political theorists.[52]

The question is: will not this economic system of true swaraj that Tagore speaks of, built on information and science, have to run according to the logic of the machine? Do we know any other science that uses some other logic? Then what is the significance of pitting science against the spinning wheel? Whatever the answer to that question, I do not think there is any room here to claim that Tagore's idea of *svadeś* and Gandhi's idea of swaraj resembled each other. Ashis Nandy has argued that Tagore relied on the high classical tradition of Indian civilization to reject the nation, while Gandhi put his faith in the little traditions of folk culture to build a critique of the nation within the politics of nationalism. But both reached the same destination—an anti-statist ideal that had a place for patriotism but not for nationalism.[53] My reading of Tagore tells me that his criticism of Gandhi's movement was that because of its reliance on organization and political artifice, it was tarnished by statism. On the other hand, when he invokes information and science to criticize the programme of hand-spinning, he is stepping into the same statist frame of thought. It is not true to say that Tagore did not recognize the need for the state. On several important subjects, he specifically talked about the role of the modern state. For instance, on universal schooling: "If the state does not [through education] open up the minds and imagination [of the common people], then the efforts of philanthropists to start night schools will be like trying to douse a fire with teardrops. This is because the ability to read and write is useful only when it becomes universal in the country."[54] So I don't agree that Tagore and Gandhi were equally, and in the same sense, opposed to the modern state.

As an alternative to the Gandhi programmes, Rabindranath proposed the establishment of cooperatives. The history of the cooperative

---

[52] "Satyer āhvān" (1921–2), *RR*, vol. 13, pp. 303, 300.

[53] Ashis Nandy, *The Illegitimacy of Nationalism: Rabindranath Tagore and the Politics of Self* (Delhi: Oxford University Press, 1994).

[54] "Lokahit" (1914–15), *RR*, vol. 13, p. 228.

movement within the European socialist and radical democratic tradition is long and complex. Tagore himself was directly inspired by the example of cooperatives in Ireland. I do not have the space here to discuss this important aspect of Tagore's thinking, and of his experiments with his own cooperative at Sriniketan. But one point needs to be noted. Tagore's objection to Gandhi's swaraj programme was that it was too narrow; it did not have an adequately comprehensive ideal of the variety of human life.

> For this reason, I believe that if we have to inspire the country in the true quest for Swaraj, we must make the full image of Swaraj directly visible to all. This image may not be very extensive at this time, but we must insist that it be comprehensive and true. ... I consider it essential that we do not restrict the duty of the *svades* merely to the spinning of thread, but spread it across the country in many small and localized efforts. The well being of all is a combination of many things. ... If the inhabitants of even one village can, by their efforts of self-making, make the entire village their own, then the work of finding the *svades* can begin there.[55]

Once again, the ideal space for constructing swaraj becomes restricted to a single village. It is not difficult to suggest that the example of one village may be replicated by others. But how the ideal of comprehensiveness can be so replicated across the country without the use of "the machine" is not explained in Rabindranath's proposal.[56] Gandhi's swaraj programme, on the other hand, did offer a definite solution to the problem of replicability, which is why the Gandhian movement, with all its limitations and contradictions, and irrespective of Gandhi's

[55] "Svarājsādhan" (1925–6), *RR*, vol. 13, pp. 341–2.

[56] Pradyumna Bhattacharya, in his essay "Markser dike" [Towards Marx], has argued that Tagore's idea of *ātmaśakti* or "self-energy" contains a notion of modern community similar to that of the late Marx. Pradyumna Bhattacharya, *Ṭīkā ṭippaṇī* (Calcutta: Papyrus, 1998), pp. 173–202. There is no doubt that Tagore has a notion of community. But the scale of that community is so limited that it is not comparable to Marx's imagining of a regenerated peasant commune in Russia or Gandhi's vision of Swaraj. If one is to think of novels, the possibility of lateral extension of the scale of peasant community that we see in Tarasankar Bandyopadhyay's *Gaṇadebatā* or Satinath Bhaduri's *Ḍhorāi-carit-mānas* is completely absent in Tagore's *Gorā* and *Ghare bāire*.

own personal views on the subject, has become part of the Indian nation, of Indian democracy and popular political culture. The specific techniques of Gandhian satyagraha have been used as instruments of struggle in numerous movements in the United States, South Africa, Palestine, and elsewhere. By comparison, Tagore's ideas on the cooperative are largely forgotten.

One's Own Country in a Single Village

However, in his efforts to build the rural cooperative, Tagore did pose the central question of the community under modern conditions of social and economic life, and the specific form of the nation as a community. As Asok Sen has pointed out, Rabindranath was perfectly aware of the material means of nation-formation such as the circulation of printed literature, textbooks, printed visual images, etc., and himself made copious use of such technologies.[57] In fact, if the question is about the effective use made by Tagore of the cultural technologies of imagining the nation, as described by Benedict Anderson, the answer is so obvious as to need hardly any elaboration at all. There is probably no comparable example anywhere in the world of the construction by a single individual of such an immense range of national cultural resources for so many millions of people, from language to poetry to fiction to drama to music to painting and so much else. Tagore is probably the world's foremost builder of national culture over the past two centuries.

That fact rightly elicits our wonder but does not pose any particular problem requiring explanation. What does pose a serious problem, however, is Tagore's own clear, forceful, and repeatedly expressed opposition to the idea of the modern nation. How are we to explain the paradoxical fact that a major builder of national culture was at the same time one of the most vociferous critics of nationalism? Sen tries to wish away the paradox by claiming that Rabindranath was not really against the nation as such but only against that form of nationalism which is competitive, power-hungry, and dedicated to the pursuit of self-interest. But surely the entire thrust of Tagore's

---

[57] Asok Sen, "Rājnītir pāṭhakrame rabīndranāth," *Bangadarśan*, 11 (July–December 2006), p. 100.

arguments in his *Nationalism* lectures, and in everything that he wrote on the subject subsequently, was to warn his country and the world that nationalism in the West had achieved, through the powers of science and capitalism, a global sway that left nothing outside its reach. He argued that nationalism in Japan, for instance, was seeking, with feverish zeal, to become as aggressive and arrogant as it was in the West, and even in India the same tendency was threatening to overwhelm everything else. Nationalism, as the modern ideology of the nation-state, was for Tagore the full-blown expression of all that was wrong with his contemporary world. To claim that Tagore was really a nationalist who wanted a non-competitive, non-aggressive nation in which the will to power would be dissolved by the juices of cooperation—that he was, as it were, a benign, friendly, non-violent nationalist, is, I feel, to make a mockery of his ideas. Tagore, the trenchant critic of nationalism, must be taken more seriously.

As Sen himself acknowledges, and carefully documents, Rabindranath did try assiduously to think about the political form of a large community that would not be like the modern nation-state. This quest began with "Svadeśi samāj" in 1905. We know that in spite of an idealized invocation of traditional dharma as the moral glue that could bind together a large community straddling thousands of villages, Rabindranath's detailing of the actual constitution of the *samāj* largely followed fairly well-established liberal principles of voluntary membership, elections, councils, committees, etc. But with the passage of time, and the experience of constitutional politics in India and elsewhere, his approval of the procedures of electoral representation definitely waned. He would probably have conceded the instrumental value of such forms of representation as the necessary apparatus or "machinery" of modern political life. But he would have certainly disagreed with those liberal theorists who argue that the heart of democracy lies in ensuring just and fair procedures of representation and not in prejudging the goodness of outcomes; for Tagore, the good outcome was probably of greater importance. With the emergence of Gandhi's mass movements, Tagore was hopeful that a new political form of community along the lines of *svadeśi samāj* would emerge. His hopes were dashed.

Rabindranath then turned to the construction of an alternative community "in two or three villages." Sen, quite appropriately, highlights the importance of this experiment for our evaluation of Tagore's political ideas, but does not, I feel, appreciate the significant differences that underlie the methods that Tagore adopts from those cultural technologies that are familiar to us from the story of nation-construction. Tagore criticized Gandhi's Non-cooperation programme as narrow, one-sided, inflexible and even coercive. He wanted the creative building of a new community that would encompass the full range of human life and respect its immense variety. Thus, although localized, his attempt to build a community based on mutual coopera-tion sought to be total and comprehensive. What was needed was exemplary and dedicated leadership, direct personal bonds of ascribed kinship with every member of the community, sympathy, and concrete and planned activities for solving local problems in a spirit of coopera-tion. Sen recalls the localized success in the Sriniketan area of such efforts at fighting malaria in 1940.[58] But these methods, appropriate for community-building in the locality, were most definitely not those that have been used so influentially for building the imagined national community of millions.

The point is important not merely for our understanding of what was distinctive about Tagore's attempt to think out a political form alternative to that of the nation, but of many similar experiments throughout the twentieth century at creating in a microcosmic locality the forms of the large political community, whether of the nation or of socialism or something else. The distinctive feature of the local experiment is always that it retains the immediacy of the face-to-face community, and uses its vast resources of deep and dense interpersonal memories to invoke trust and innovate subtle solutions. Not only Tagore, but from Gandhi himself and scores of Gandhians to innu-merable others inspired by various communitarian dreams, many people have, through the last century, carried out hundreds of such local community-building efforts in villages all over India. Some may have been motivated by a feeling of nostalgia for some lost idyllic arcadia. It is also a remarkable, though not quite well explained, fact of modern Indian intellectual history that most such builders of rural cooperative communities were city-bred middle-class activists who saw their calling in discovering the future forms of the modern Indian

[58] Ibid., p. 80.

village rather than those of the Indian city—but that is not the relevant point here. In a century of growing violence and conflict between politically mobilized groups, it is undoubtedly true that the face-to-face local community offered many cultural resources to accommodate diversity, even deviance and some degree of contained violence, within the familiar limits of shared trust and tolerance. This is what most activists and thinkers looked to when they chose to focus on the local community. The point has been forcefully made by Ashis Nandy in the context of interreligious communal violence in India.[59]

The crucial question is: how does this new local community multiply itself? How can it succeed in producing the macrocosmic political community in its own image? There are two possible answers to this question. One is to take the local variations seriously and argue that each local community, embodying a specific configuration of social relations and a distinct tradition of local memories, is unique. The particular form of community institutions and practices that works at one place need not work at others. Hence, one form developed in one village must not be simply transported to and copied by other villages; each village must develop its own suitable and unique form of community. Arguing from this position, it is hard to see how a large political community of the same order of magnitude as the nation can ever be imagined. Clearly, the nation as a community cannot be produced by the additive aggregate of thousands of distinct villages; its sense of community must be produced imaginatively in its fulness as a single construct, all its parts existing synchronically and simultaneously on a single plane. That is precisely what the cultural technologies of nation-construction enable. The face-to-face methods of local community construction can never achieve that task. The qualities of everyday familiarity, sympathy, or the ability to inventively use local resources for local solutions, which were of such crucial importance in the local sphere, have little import in nation-construction.

One could get around this problem by introducing a series of mediations—by state institutions, for instance, or by political parties, or by large and organized political movements that aspire to become

---

[59] Ashis Nandy *et al., Creating a Nationality: The Ramjanmabhumi Movement and Fear of the Self* (Delhi: Oxford University Press, 1997).

the state. That was the idea pursued by the Gandhian Congress, and by many other movements of varying national and regional influence. The distinct autonomy of local community building may be allowed, even encouraged, but only within certain larger parameters set by "national" institutions. The mediating institutions between the local and the national thus perform the tasks of direction and command, of setting norms of conduct and rules of discipline. The autonomy of the local then necessarily becomes a subordinate moment of the independently produced "national."

Following his interrogation of the Gandhian movement, Tagore no longer felt inclined to approve of these supervening state or party institutions. He saw them as leading the creative energies of the local into the familiar forms of the Western nation-state based on command, discipline, and competitive self-aggrandizement. Thus, the distinctive feature of Rabindranath's thinking in its late phase was its insistence on building the new local community, with its rich diversity and creativity, all the time hoping that it might become an exemplary instance for the whole country, but without conceding any directing role to any superordinate homogenizing state or state-like political institutions. Unlike the forms of thinking that led, in the late 1930s, to efforts like those of the National Planning Committee led by the younger left-wing leaders of the Congress such as Jawaharlal Nehru and Subhas Chandra Bose, Tagore would have preferred the multiplication of local initiatives, retaining the immediacy of the face-to-face community. To take the example of the fight against malaria, the nationalist state leadership would have thought of a countrywide campaign, using the full complement of scientific methods, national cultural technologies, and the commanding power of the state (which, incidentally, is how malaria was in fact eradicated from India in the 1950s and 1960s). Tagore, the political thinker, was not a votary of this method of imagining the national community.

There is a second answer to the question of how the results of local experiments may be replicated on a wider scale. Here, the local initiative does not attempt to be total and comprehensive; it does not seek to refashion the community in its wholeness. Rather, it seeks to develop specific practices with appropriate institutions. When successfully developed in a local context, these could acquire the form of a set of techniques which may be transported elsewhere after being released from their local constraints. There are many examples of such experiments first carried out in local communities that have now become technologies, widely used in many different contexts and replicated on a national, even global scale. To mention an example from Bengal, think of the initiative of a young university lecturer in Chittagong soon after the birth of the new nation-state of Bangladesh. Moved by sympathy, dedication, and the urge to do something to alleviate the desperate poverty all around him, he brought together a few associates, raised a small fund, and began a project of offering tiny amounts of credit to rural women to supplement their incomes. The most interesting feature of the experiment was that it built on the element of mutual trust and dependence characteristic of the face-to-face community but did not seek to embrace or transform the local community itself. As is now well known, the little initiatives of Mohammed Yunus ultimately produced the techniques of the micro-credit movement that are now being replicated in many parts of the world. Judged by its impact, it is probably the most influential local community initiative carried out in Bengal in the twentieth century. As technology, its practices have been appropriated within the circuits of capital as well as of governmental power. But since they are techniques, those practices are also in principle open for mobilization by forces resisting capital or governmental power. These questions are very much part and parcel of our contemporary political life.

Once again, if one goes with the thrust of Tagore's criticism of Gandhi's khadi programme—that it narrowly focused on a single item and ignored the variety and complexity of issues affecting social life as a whole—then one must conclude that Tagore would have disapproved of local initiatives aimed at producing replicable economic or political technologies. For him, that would amount to giving priority to the "machinery" of social life over its true spirit—which could only be found in the totality and richness of face-to-face community life. Unless one wishes to throw away what is most original and passionately articulated in Rabindranath's writings, I do not see any other conclusion that can be drawn from them.

There have been many attempts in the twentieth century to build model local communities that were expected to become available for emulation on a countrywide scale. All such local efforts were heavily invested with the intricacies of the face-to-face community and relied on dedicated and continually engaged local leadership. As we have seen, Tagore's was a distinguished example of such thinking, but he was only one of many similar thinkers and activists. I strongly believe that such efforts to bring into existence a new local community can neither contribute nor offer an alternative to the large imagined community of the nation. The moral virtues of the face-to-face community have no relevance to the political world of the nation; ethical conduct in the latter world has to be judged by entirely different criteria. Hence, Tagore's political thinking has, for the purposes of contemporary postcolonial politics, largely become irrelevant.

Tagore and the Moral Aesthetic

I have argued so far that the reading of Rabindranath Tagore as a moderate anti-colonial nationalist standing midway between uncritical westernization and insular traditionalism is mistaken. Tagore, in fact, was a powerful critic of the very idea of the modern nation. In its mature form, this criticism involved a questioning of the political organization of the modern nation-state and its practices of strategic and rhetorical cunning. Tagore's complaint was that modern political organizations imposed a set of disciplinary constraints and collective demands that were too narrow and too coercive to allow for the full range of diversity of human life. This was the ground for his difference with the main course of the Indian nationalist movement represented by the Gandhian Congress. As an alternative, he attempted to build in a small rural locality a new community that would rid itself of the irrationalities and injustices of traditional society but, in producing a modern social form, retain the immediacy of the face-to-face community. The unresolved problem was that this local microcosm could not be reproduced on a countrywide scale without resort to the modern technologies of nation-building. Hence, Tagore's idea of a modern community that could be an alternative to the nation-state found no political support either in his own lifetime or later. However, Tagore's position remains an example of the moral critique of the modern state and its political processes of representation—a moral stance that is primarily aesthetic. This is best illustrated by considering the late Rabindranath.

What are the new elements we get in the political writings of

Rabindranath in the last years of his life? Let us consider some citations.

> The contact with Europe revealed to us, on the one hand, the universal laws of causality that govern the natural world and, on the other, the pure ideals of morality that cannot be constricted by the dictates of scripture or ritual tradition or by the regulations imposed by any caste or class. With all our weaknesses, we have been trying in our recent political life to bring about changes based on these ideals. . . . Yet in our families and neighbourhoods, in our social lives, the ideals of individual autonomy and dignity, or of the equal right to just behaviour irrespective of caste or class, have not fully entered our inner selves.[60]

These words could have been said by anyone believing in the principles of Western liberalism. Here, Tagore does not express any doubts about whether the ideals and practices of equal rights could "naturally" grow in Indian conditions. Yet, just two years before he wrote this essay, we find him making the following comment on relations between Hindu and Muslim communities in India: "We have to come together at the roots; otherwise nothing good will come. In the past, we did have some closeness at the roots. Even as we recognized our differences, we were close to each other." He then adds an astonishing remark: "Most of my tenants are Muslim. . . . [In our estate] there have been no troubles so far. I believe the reason is that my relations with my Muslim tenants are natural and unfettered."[61] There is no place here for liberal equal rights or rule of law. Peace and justice depend on the "natural" personal relations between landlord and tenant.

We then notice, in the last two years of his life, a deep sense of despondency about political action.

> The true springs of popular resistance against injustice have, through long years of neglect, become decrepit. I have lost hope. . . . There was a time when one could fight with the force of arms and bravery. But now there is science, based not only on educated intelligence but also on the immense power of money. Yet we have to fight with empty coffers and a popular mobilization that is not disciplined by the rules of collective work. Its powers either lie unconscious or rush around

---

[60] "Kālāntar" (1933–4), *RR*, vol. 13, pp. 212–13.
[61] "Hindu musalmān" (1931–2), *RR*, vol. 13, pp. 366–7.

blindly. . . . We have seen much amassing of untaught crowds. They may be used to break up the great ceremonies of power, but they do not yield fruits of lasting value. In fact, when confronted by sheer brute force, they break into pieces and scatter.[62]

And finally, there was of course his last cry of despair:

> In the meanwhile the demon of barbarity has given up all pretence and has emerged with unconcealed fangs, ready to tear up humanity in an orgy of devastation. From one end of the world to the other the poisonous fumes of hatred darken the atmosphere. The spirit of violence which perhaps lay dormant in the psychology of the West, has at last roused itself and desecrates the spirit of Man. . . . I had at one time believed that the springs of civilization would issue out of the heart of Europe. But today when I am about to quit the world that faith has gone bankrupt altogether. As I look around I see the crumbling ruins of a proud civilization strewn like a vast heap of futility.[63]

Should we then say that the eternal ideals of goodness in human life, of harmony and self-creation, that had guided Tagore's social and historical thinking all his life were abandoned in the last years? Did his faith in the possibility of lasting human well being through a vibrant *samāj*, ethical political mobilization and patriotism, collapse entirely? Or did a much worse and shocking thought about the inevitable evil in modern life enter his mind at this time?

Several years ago, Abu Sayeed Ayub attempted to show that the sense of evil that is supposed to characterize the moment of modernism in Western literature and art was clearly present in Tagore's late poetry. What was absent was the surrender to this sense of evil.[64] Ayub firmly believed that Tagore quite rightly rejected aesthetic modernism, because it was, in Ayub's words, "the currently circulating falsehood of our present." I find it hard to accept this judgement. Rather, I find far more persuasive Sankha Ghosh's conclusion that Tagore was largely uninterested in the main styles of modernism in literature and art in

---

[62] "Kongres" (1939–40), *RR*, vol. 13, pp. 384–5.

[63] "Crisis in Civilization" (1941), in *English Writings*, vol. 3, pp. 722–6.

[64] Abu Sayeed Ayub, *Ādhunikatā o rabīndranāth* (Calcutta: Dey's, 1968; enlarged edition 1971).

the period after World War I, and did not seriously try to understand their concerns and efforts.[65] Ghosh points to a distinction that Tagore himself employs between construction and creation and reminds us that Tagore always thought creation, not construction, the more important and true expression of the human spirit.[66] Rabindranath's distinction was, of course, a familiar one. Construction is the making of something with an eye to a tangible result; it is functional or utilitarian. Creation is to make something without any specific goal; it is made merely out of the joy of creation. The distinction is fundamental to romantic aesthetics. Rabindranath uses the distinction to argue that the modern science of the West is busy with construction, but human life can never find lasting good without creation. That creative task must be done by the people of the East. This is the same argument as that of "the machine" which we have discussed before. Ghosh, of course, argues that after becoming embroiled in the debate over modernism, Rabindranath does indeed introduce several new elements in the poetry and painting of his last years that have become for us post-Tagoreans the first steps to our modernism. The question thus arises: did Tagore introduce into his writings on politics, society, and history in his final years any similar distinctly modernist elements?

The aspect of the modern state that disturbed Tagore most profoundly in his last years was the "scientization" of power, the attempt to reduce the multifarious social exchanges among people to certain rules of technology. This is what he had earlier repeatedly condemned as the dominance of "the machine." In this connection, there is a problem I have mentioned before. This is the problem of extension or spread of the connections of dependence not only beyond the village or neighbourhood but often beyond the nation to many other parts of the world. We may still enjoy the joke about our thirst for tea, but it is an undeniable fact that if the supply of petrol or electricity is for some reason interrupted, the lives of most people in most countries will be thrown out of gear and no force of self-making will restore the supply. The second problem that needs to be pointed out is that even "the machine" can wield powers of persuasion, stake claims to ethical behaviour, and make promises of well being. Rabindranath was not

---

[65] Sankha Ghosh, *Nirmāṇ ār sṛṣṭi* (Santiniketan: Viswabharati, 1982).

[66] "Construction versus Creation," in *English Writings*, vol. 3, pp. 401–9.

prepared to acknowledge this. Indeed, I would go so far as to say that he was largely uninterested in the intricacies of modern technologies of power. To him, they were all mechanical instruments; he did not have the inclination or patience to study them carefully.

Nevertheless, his stance of rejection, on moral grounds, of the politics of mass mobilization, popular representation, and strategic manoeuvre remains attractive to some. For Tagore, a fundamental condition for the efflorescence of free human life was the guarantee of the aesthetic freedom to be creative without any heed to utility or interest. A political process dominated by the pursuit of individual rights, group interests, and the will of the majority is inimical to the requirements of creative freedom. A moral position such as this was, needless to say, unlikely to find a large democratic constituency in twentieth-century India. But in an age dominated by technological rationality and the statistical norm, it remains an attractive moral counterpoint for the intellectual critique of modernity. It is in this politically disengaged sense that Tagore remains relevant for our time.

Recall, for instance, Václav Havel arguing in 1975–7 that the traditional forms of parliamentary politics "can offer no fundamental opposition to the automatism of technological civilization," and that exemplary and inspirational dissidence was the only effective form of resistance to the totalitarian state. This was an early moment of the invocation of universal humanity for a new politics of human rights that has mobilized in the last three decades many idealists disillusioned with traditional forms of political organization. As Samuel Moyn has shown, the human rights movement today is grounded in a moral stance that abjures politics but valorizes the individual act of conscience. It is also premised on the rejection of the emancipatory claims of the postcolonial state.[67] The movement's recourse to legalism as a mode of action does not sit well with Tagore's distaste for "machinery," but his aesthetically grounded critique of the nation certainly resonates with many of the recent invocations of universal humanity. Once again, Tagore in his late years may have anticipated a strand in our contemporary global culture today.

[67] Samuel Moyn, *The Last Utopia: Human Rights in History* (Cambridge, Mass.: Cambridge University Press, 2010). Moyn discusses Havel's open letters on pp. 160–6.

II
Popular Reason

6

The People in Utopian and
Real Time

I*magined Communities* was, without doubt, one of the most influential books of the late twentieth century.[1] In the years since it was published, nationalism unexpectedly came to be regarded as an increasingly messy and often dangerous "problem" in world affairs, and over this time Benedict Anderson has continued to analyse and reflect on the subject, adding two brilliant chapters to his highly acclaimed book and writing several new essays and lectures.[2] Some of these were brought together in 1998, along with a series of essays on the history and politics of Southeast Asia, in *The Spectre of Comparisons*.[3]

Nation and Ethnicity

Theoretically, the most significant addition that Anderson has made to his analysis in *Imagined Communities* is the attempt to distinguish between nationalism and the politics of ethnicity. He does this by identifying two kinds of seriality that are produced by the modern imaginings of community. One is the unbound seriality of the everyday universals of modern social thought—nations, citizens, revolutionaries, bureaucrats, workers, intellectuals, etc. The other is the bound seriality of governmentality—the finite totals of enumerable

---

[1] Benedict Anderson, *Imagined Communities: Reflections on the Origin and Spread of Nationalism* (London: Verso, 1983).

[2] In *Imagined Communities*, revised edition (London: Verso, 1991).

[3] *The Spectre of Comparisons: Nationalism, Southeast Asia and the World* (London: Verso, 1998).

classes of population produced by the modern census and electoral systems. Unbound serialities are typically imagined and narrated by means of the classic instruments of print-capitalism, namely, the newspaper and the novel. They afford the opportunity for individuals to imagine themselves as members of larger than face-to-face solidarities, to choose to act on behalf of those solidarities, and to transcend by an act of political imagination the limits imposed by traditional practices. Unbound serialities are potentially liberating. As Anderson quotes from the novelist Pramodeya Ananta Toer describing such a moment of emancipation experienced by one of his characters:

> By now, Is knew the society she was entering. She had found a circle of acquaintances far wider than the circle of her brothers, sisters and parents. She now occupied a defined position in that society: as a woman, as a typist in a government office, as a free individual. She had become a new human being, with new understanding, new tales to tell, new perspectives, new attitudes, new interests—newnesses that she managed to pluck and assemble from her acquaintances.[4]

Bound serialities, by contrast, can only operate with integers. This implies that for each category of classification, an individual can only count as one or zero, never as a fraction, which in turn means that all partial or mixed affiliations to a category are ruled out. One can only be Black or not Black, Muslim or not Muslim, tribal or not tribal, never only partially or contextually so. Bound serialities, Anderson suggests, are constricting, and perhaps inherently conflictual. They produce the tools of ethnic politics.

I am not sure that the distinction between bound and unbound serialities, despite its appearance of mathematical precision, is the appropriate way to describe the differences in political modalities that Anderson wants to demarcate. It is not clear why the "unbound" serialities of the nationalist imagination cannot, under specific conditions, produce finite and countable classes. Explaining unbound seriality, Anderson says it is that which "makes the United Nations a normal, wholly unparadoxical institution."[5] But surely, at any given

[4] Quoted in *Spectre*, p. 41.
[5] *Spectre*, p. 29.

time, the United Nations can have only a finite number of members. And that is because, with explicitly laid-down procedures and criteria of membership, the imagining of nationhood has been reduced here to the institutional grid of governmentality. Again, if by revolutionaries we mean those who are members of revolutionary political parties, then the number of revolutionaries in a country, or even in the whole world, will also be finite and countable (assuming, of course, that there are transparent and unambiguous rules of membership of such parties), in the same way that the census claims to provide a figure for, let us say, the number of Hindus in India. It is also not clear in what sense the serialities of governmentality are "bound." The series for Christians or English speakers in the world is, in principle, without end, since to every total that we count today one more could be added tomorrow. But, of course, the series is denumerable, exactly like, say, the series of positive integers, even though at any given point of time such a set of Christians or English speakers will contain a finite number of members.

Some years ago, Anderson asked me what I thought of Hegel's idea of the "wrong infinity." I must say that I was stumped by the suggestion that a somewhat quaint remark by the long-dead German philosopher might call for some sort of moral response from me. After carefully reading Anderson's "logic of seriality," I can now see what he was asking me. The denumerable but infinite series, such as the sequence of positive integers which is the basic form of counting used by governmental systems like the census, is, for Anderson, of the same dubious philosophical status as it was for Hegel. To describe change or "becoming" by means of a sequence of finite quantities, which is what the statistical logic of governmentality would prescribe, is not to transcend the finite at all, but merely to set one finite against its other. One finite merely reappears in another finite. "The progression of infinity never gets further than a statement of the contradiction involved in the finite, viz. that it is somewhat as well as somewhat else. It sets up with endless iteration the alternation between these two terms, each of which calls up the other."[6] This is the "wrong or negative infinity." Hegel makes a withering comment on those who try to grasp the

---

[6] G.W.F. Hegel, *Encyclopaedia of the Philosophical Sciences*, Part 1, tr. William Wallace (Oxford: Clarendon Press, 1975), p. 137.

infinite character of, say, space or time by following in this way the endless progression of finite quantities:

> In the attempt to contemplate such an infinite, our thought, we are commonly informed, must sink exhausted. It is true indeed that we must abandon the unending contemplation, not however because the occupation is too sublime, but because it is too tedious. It is tedious to expatiate in the contemplation of this infinite progression, because the same thing is constantly recurring. We lay down a limit: then we pass it: next we have a limit once more, and so on for ever. All this is but superficial alternation, which never leaves the region of the finite behind.[7]

The "genuine infinity," by contrast, does not simply negate one finite by its other, but also negates that other. By doing so, it "returns to itself," becomes self-related. The true infinity does not set up an abyss between a finite this-world and an infinite other-world. Rather, it expresses the truth of the finite, which, for Hegel, is its ideality. It encapsulates in its ideality the infinite variability of the finite.

I have not brought up this abstruse Hegelian point merely to obscure the distinction between unbound and bound serialities on which Anderson hangs his argument about the residual goodness of nationalism and the unrelieved nastiness of ethnic politics. On the contrary, I think Hegel's idea of the true infinity is an example of the kind of universalist critical thought characteristic of the Enlightenment that Anderson is keen to preserve. It is the mark of what is genuinely ethical and indeed—I use this word in sincere admiration—noble in his work.

Hegel's true infinity, as I said, is only an example. One finds similar examples in Kant and (at least in the standard readings) in Marx. Faced with the indubitable facts of historical conflict and change, the aspiration here is to affirm an ethical universal that does not deny the variability of human wants and values or cast them aside as unworthy or ephemeral, but rather encompasses and integrates them as the real historical ground on which that ethical universal must be established.

---

[7] Ibid., p. 138. Hegel makes specific use of his distinction between the true and the false infinity to criticize Fichte's arguments about the legal and moral validity of a contract. Hegel, *Philosophy of Right*, tr. T.M. Knox (London: Oxford University Press, 1967), p. 61.

Much philosophical blood was spilt in the nineteenth century over the question of whether there was an idealist and a materialist version of this aspiration and, if so, which was the more truthful. Few take those debates seriously any more. But as the sciences and technologies of governmentality have spread their tentacles throughout the populated world in the twentieth century, the critical philosophical mind has been torn by the question of ethical universalism and cultural relativism. The growing strength of anti-colonial nationalist politics in the middle decades of this century contributed greatly to the recognition of this problem, even though the very successes of nationalism may also have led to the chimerical hope that the cultural conflicts were merely the superficial signs of the production of a richer, more universal, modernity. Decolonization, however, was soon followed by the crisis of the postcolonial state and the culture wars became identified with chauvinism, ethnic hatred, and cynically manipulative and corrupt regimes. To all intents and purposes, nationalism became incurably contaminated by ethnic politics.

Anderson has refused to accept this diagnosis. He continues to believe that the politics of nationalism and that of ethnicity arise on different sites, grow on different nutriments, travel through different networks, mobilize on different sentiments, and fight for different causes. But unlike many in the Western academy, he has refused to soothe the liberal bad conscience with the balm of multiculturalism. He has also remained an outspoken critic of the hard-headed developmentalist of the "realist" school whose recipes for third world countries flow out of a cynical double standard that says "ethics for us, economics for them." Anderson closes *The Spectre of Comparisons* with an evocative listing of some of the ideals and affective moments of nationalism and remarks: "There is something of value in all of this—strange as it may seem. . . . Each in a different but related way shows why, no matter what crimes a nation's government commits and its passing citizenry endorses, My Country is ultimately Good. In these straitened millennial times, can such Goodness be profitably discarded?"[8]

Idealist? I think the question is quite meaningless, especially since we know that Anderson, more than anyone else in recent years, has

[8] *Spectre*, p. 368.

inspired the study of the material instruments of literary and cultural production that made possible the imagining of modern political communities in virtually every region of the world. Romantic? Perhaps, but then much that is good and noble in modern social thinking has been propelled by romantic impulses. Utopian? Yes. And there lies, I think, a major theoretical and political problem, which is also the chief source of my disagreement with Anderson.

Time: Utopian and Real

The dominant strand of modern historical thinking imagines the social space of modernity as distributed in empty homogeneous time. A Marxist could call this the time of capital. Anderson explicitly adopts the formulation from Walter Benjamin, using it to brilliant effect in *Imagined Communities* to show the material possibilities of large anonymous socialities being formed by the simultaneous experience of reading the daily newspaper or following the private lives of popular fictional characters. It is the same simultaneity experienced in empty homogeneous time that allows us to speak of the reality of such categories of political economy as prices, wages, markets, etc. Empty homogeneous time is the time of capital. Within its domain, capital allows for no resistances to its free movement. When it encounters an impediment, it thinks it has encountered another time—something out of pre-capital, something that belongs to the pre-modern. Such resistances to capital (or to modernity) are always thought of as coming out of humanity's past, something people should have left behind but somehow haven't. But by imagining capital (or modernity) as an attribute of time itself, this view succeeds not only in branding the resistances to it as archaic and backward, but also in securing for capital and modernity their ultimate triumph, regardless of what some people believe or hope, because after all, as everyone knows, time does not stand still.

It would be tiresome to pile on examples of this sort of progressive historicist thinking because they are strewn all over the historical and sociological literature of at least the last century and a half. Let me cite here one example from a Marxist historian who was justifiably celebrated for his anti-reductionist view of historical agency and who once led a bitter attack against the Althusserian project of writing "history without a subject." In a famous essay on time and work-discipline in the era of industrial capitalism, E. P. Thompson spoke of the inevitability of workers everywhere having to shed their pre-capitalist work habits: "Without time-discipline we could not have the insistent energies of the industrial man; and whether this discipline comes in the form of Methodism, or of Stalinism, or of nationalism, it will come to the developing world."[9]

I believe Anderson has a similar view of modern politics, as something that belongs to the very character of the time in which we now live. It is futile to participate in, or sympathize with, or even to give credence to efforts to resist its sway. In *Imagined Communities*, he wrote of the modular forms of nationalism developed in the Americas, in Europe, and in Russia which then became available for copy by the anti-colonial nationalisms of Asia and Africa. In *The Spectre* he speaks often of "the remarkable planetary spread, not merely of nationalism, but of a profoundly standardized conception of politics, in part by reflecting on the everyday practices, rooted in industrial material civilization, that have displaced the cosmos to make way for the world."[10] Such a conception of politics requires an understanding of the world as *one*, so that a common activity called politics can be seen to be going on *everywhere*. Politics, in this sense, inhabits the empty homogeneous time of modernity.

I disagree. My reason was explicated in Chapter One of this book and I will now restate it in different words. I believe this view of modernity, or indeed of capital, is mistaken because it is one-sided. It looks at only one dimension of the time-space of modern life. People can only imagine themselves in empty homogeneous time; they do not live in it. Empty homogeneous time is the utopian time of capital. It linearly connects past, present, and future, creating the possibility for all those historicist imaginings of identity, nationhood, progress, etc. that Anderson, along with others, has made familiar to us. But empty homogeneous time is not located anywhere in real space—it is utopian. The real space of modern life exists in heterogeneous time: space here is unevenly dense. Here, even industrial workers do not all

[9] "Time, Work-discipline and Industrial Capitalism," in E. P. Thompson, *Customs in Common* (London: Penguin, 1991), pp. 352–403.

[10] *Spectre*, p. 29.

internalize the work-discipline of capitalism, and more curiously, even when they do, they do not do so in the same way. Politics here does not mean the same thing to all people. To ignore this is, I believe, to discard the real for the utopian.

Obviously, I can make my case more persuasively by picking examples from the postcolonial world. For it is there more than anywhere else in the modern world that one could show, with almost the immediacy of the palpable, the presence of a dense and heterogeneous time. To call this the co-presence of several times—the time of the modern and the times of the pre-modern—is only to endorse the utopianism of Western modernity. I prefer to call it the heterogeneous time of modernity. And to push my polemical point a little further, I will add that the postcolonial world outside Western Europe and North America actually constitutes *most* of the populated modern world.

Let me clarify my argument with a brief reference to Karl Marx. In *Capital*, volume 1, Marx emphasizes repeatedly that abstract labour, or labour-power, is an *average*; its value is measured by the *average* labour-time socially necessary for its reproduction. He adds that "in a given country in a given period, the average amount of the means of subsistence necessary for the worker is a known *datum*."[11] As we now know, Marx was making one of the earliest, and most insightful, attempts to enunciate a method of discovering law-like generalizations about social phenomena in an age when science still meant a corpus of laws about a deterministic world. He was doing this by bringing the uncertainties of social events (in this case, what he called the accidental form of value) under scientific control through the formulation of statistical laws. The philosopher Ian Hacking has, among others, shown how in the nineteenth century inherently chance-laden events such as mortality, crime, bankruptcy, suicide, etc. were made the objects of policy (by the police, public health officials, accountants, insurance companies, etc.) by bringing them under the umbrella of abstract statistical concepts such as the mean, the normal distribution, and the law of large numbers.[12] Marx did the same for the analysis of the chance-ridden world of commodities by defining the concept of

[11] Karl Marx, *Capital*, vol. 1, tr. Ben Fowkes (London: Penguin, 1990), ch. 6, p. 275.

[12] Ian Hacking, *The Taming of Chance* (Cambridge: Cambridge University Press, 1990).

abstract labour as an abstract statistical average that did not correspond to any singular or concrete act of labour but that nevertheless had real effects. The critic of political economy could work with abstract categories such as wages, prices, savings rates, growth rates, etc. as if those formed the basis on which real economic agents acted, without the critic for once forgetting that these were abstract statistical categories representing the social average. As Marx put it: "in the midst of the accidental and ever-fluctuating exchange relations between the products, the labour-time socially necessary to produce them asserts itself as a regulative law of nature."[13]

Marx also said that when actual buyers and sellers in the market behaved as if values were the natural attributes of the things that appeared before them as commodities, they were practising fetishism. I do not wish to open here the long and tangled history of the idea of false consciousness, but I don't read Marx as asserting in *Capital* that the scientific discovery of the real social relations underlying the value of commodities would clear up the mystifying ideologies of fetishism that clouded the perceptions of ordinary people. In fact, he says quite clearly: "Something which is only valid for this particular form of production, the production of commodities, . . . appears to those caught up in the relations of commodity production (and this is true both before and after the above-mentioned scientific discovery) to be just as ultimately valid as the fact that the scientific dissection of the air into its component parts left the atmosphere itself unaltered in its physical configuration."[14] There are just two further points I wish to make on this subject. First, given the domination in the course of the twentieth century of statistical reasoning in all of the scientific disciplines as well as in the public discourse of everyday life, I am not sure that the strong distinction many Marxists have drawn between the fetishism of ideology and the truth of science is all that sustainable. Economic science (or bourgeois political economy) has increasingly incorporated within itself, through cyborg mechanisms such as the feedback loop, the statistical estimation of expectations and the techniques of self-adjustment, the allegedly ideology-driven and fetishized behaviour of economic agents as *data* for policy-making. Second, as we also know from the history of centralized state planning and market

[13] Marx, *Capital*, vol. 1, ch. 1.4, p. 168.
[14] Ibid., p. 169.

regulations in the twentieth century, the "as if" behaviour of economic agents does not spring naturally out of Mother Earth: it has to be brought into existence, even in the so-called market economies, by the force, often the coercive force, of new economic institutions backed by the regulative and legal powers of the modern state. That is where my distinction between civil and political society becomes relevant to the classical Marxist categories.

Political forms such as the passive revolution (which we will talk about in a later chapter) become relevant only in contexts that can be distinguished in some meaningful way from those of bourgeois hegemony. If we were convinced that the Indian republic, for instance, was for all intents and purposes indistinguishable from liberal capitalist democracies, we would not have been talking of political society as distinct from civil society. Since we are not so convinced, we must describe the differences in the way ruling groups wield power in India from the way capitalists exercise power in Western democracies. The key difference lies in the social forms of labour. Even though we might claim that a certain sway of generalized commodity production has come to prevail over most of Indian society, the discerning observer, whether capitalist or bureaucrat or politician, cannot and does not assume that all economic agents act as if they were abstract subjects behaving in accordance with the requirements of abstract labour. The facts are plain to see. Economic agents producing the same goods or services in, let us say, the formal and informal sectors operate under such drastically different conditions that it is impossible to claim that an average amount of labour-time socially necessary for the reproduction of labour-power actually prevails across the different segments of the social forms of labour. Units in the so-called informal sector may reproduce themselves by not paying taxes, or violating safety or health regulations, or exploiting family labour. If the state were to uniformly enforce the same regulating conditions of production on all economic units, many or most informal units would cease to exist. But, as is well known, governmental agencies in India do not impose the same regulations on everyone. Some are treated as exceptions to the general rule. Being treated as exceptions is the result, I have suggested, of a political process of negotiation. The field where the norm is expected to prevail is civil society. The field of exception is where the norm is suspended; it is dealt with as political society.

Having said this, let me return to Anderson's distinction between nationalism and the politics of ethnicity. He agrees that the "bound serialities" of governmentality can create a sense of community, which is precisely what the politics of ethnic identity feeds on. But this sense of community is illusory. In these real and imagined censuses, "thanks to capitalism, state machineries, and mathematics, integral bodies become identical, and thus serially aggregable as phantom communities."[15] By contrast, the "unbound serialities" of nationalism do not, one presumes, need to turn the free individual members of the national community into integers. It can imagine the nation as having existed in identical form from the dawn of historical time to the present without requiring a census-like verification of its identity. It can also experience the simultaneity of the imagined collective life of the nation without imposing rigid and arbitrary criteria of membership. Can such "unbound serialities" exist anywhere except in utopian space?

To endorse these "unbound serialities" while rejecting the "bound" ones is, in fact, to imagine nationalism without modern governmentality. What modern politics can we have that has no truck with capitalism, state machineries, or mathematics? The historical moment Anderson seems keen to preserve is the moment of classical nationalism. Referring to today's politics of ethnicity in the United States and other old nation-states, he calls it (perhaps overlooking the deep moral ambivalence of Dostoyevski's characterizations) "a bastard Smerdyakov to classical nationalism's Dmitri Karamazov."[16] He chastises the "long-distance nationalism" of Irish-Americans for being so out of touch with the "real" Ireland, ignoring the fact that "Ireland" here truly exists only in utopian space, since the real space of this politics is the heterogeneous one of contemporary American social life.

Anderson's positing of an opposition between nationalism and ethnicity can be traced, therefore, to the distinction between popular sovereignty, enshrined in classical nationalism's equation of the people with the nation, and the governmentality which really came into its own in the second half of the twentieth century. But how are we to understand this opposition? As an opposition between the good and

[15] *Spectre*, p. 44.
[16] Ibid., p. 71.

the bad? Between something that should be preserved and something else to be abjured? Or should we say, following the course of capitalist modernity in the twentieth century, that the opposition between popular sovereignty and governmentality expresses a new set of contradictions in a capitalist order that now has to maintain class rule under the general conditions of mass democracy?

Popular Reason

This is the place to confront another concept of modern politics in real time. The concept is that of populism. It has not yet made its entry into the hallowed portals of political theory and is still regarded as fit only for empirical discussions of sociology. However, considerations of contemporary democratic politics cannot avoid taking account of populism, especially because its practices constitute much of what is known today as ethnic politics, and because these overlap with the politics of nationalism. It would be useful, therefore, to consider here the analysis of populism offered by Ernesto Laclau.[17]

Laclau discusses populism as a continuation of his earlier Gramsci-inspired analysis of hegemony.[18] He takes seriously the necessary entanglement of rhetoric with the activities of democratic politics. But populism, in particular, he refuses to dismiss merely on the ground that populism is vague and empty, or that it tries to mean everything to everybody. On the contrary, "instead of starting with a model of political rationality which sees populism in terms of what it lacks—its vagueness, its ideological emptiness, its anti-intellectualism, its transitory character," Laclau proceeds "to enlarge the model of rationality in terms of a generalized rhetoric (what . . . can be called 'hegemony') so that populism appears as a distinctive and always present possibility of structuration of political life."[19] Indeed, I will go so far as to say that populism *is* the *effective* form of democratic politics in the contemporary world. Needless to say, there are specific reasons of contemporary history that have produced this condition. Those reasons have a great deal to do with capitalism and governmentality.

[17] Ernesto Laclau, *On Populist Reason* (London: Verso, 2005).
[18] Ernesto Laclau and Chantal Mouffe, *Hegemony and Socialist Strategy* (London: Verso, 1985).
[19] Laclau, *Populist Reason*, p. 13.

The key move that Laclau makes is to acknowledge the sheer heterogeneity of demands in a modern democratic polity and then distinguish between differential and equivalent demands. In the former case, each demand is considered in isolation from the others and is either pressed or satisfied in a differential way. In the latter case, equivalences are sought to be established between several demands. The former, says Laclau, can be considered democratic demands, but it is only in the latter form that we get *popular* demands.

I have elsewhere pointed out the distinction between the homogeneous conception of the nation based on undivided popular sovereignty and the heterogeneous conception of the social based on a congeries of populations. The connection between the two is established by contemporary political regimes through the instruments of governmentality.[20] One of the key features of modern governmental techniques is the flexibility they provide in the domain of policy—the ability to break up large agglomerations of demands and to isolate specific groups of benefit-seekers from others. This, we could say following Laclau, is the differential mode of responding to democratic demands. But the politics of the governed has taken other forms in contemporary democracies. It has sought to establish equivalences among various democratic demands and bring them together into the form of a popular claim. It does this, Laclau says, through rhetorical and performative political acts that establish chains of equivalences over different demands. There is frequently no common substantive content to these equivalences; that is to say, it is not necessary for the various demands to substantively overlap with one another in order to assert their equivalence. Rather, the relation of equivalence is derived from the *negative* fact that they are all unfulfilled demands directed at an unresponsive governmental authority.

This rhetorical-performative operation in turn produces the second condition for effective populism, namely, the creation of an internal antagonistic border separating "the people" from those identified with the institutions of power. As the chain of equivalences builds up into the form of a common popular demand, the commonness comes to be emphasized by the fact that the demands are all aimed at a common target, namely, the wielders of power, and is exemplified

[20] Chatterjee, *The Politics of the Governed*, pp. 27–41.

by the identification of such agents of power as the antagonists of the people. In the recent history of populist politics around the world, this internal antagonistic division has been drawn along lines of class or ethnicity or identification with a political regime or party.

Laclau emphasizes that the negative content of the relations of equivalence produces a vague and imprecise articulation of demands, and that the assertion of "the people" as the outcome of the chain of equivalences is indeed in the nature of an empty signifier. But that is precisely the strength of populism as a form of democratic politics. "The 'people,' in this case, is something less than the members of the community: it is a partial component which nevertheless aspires to be conceived as the only legitimate totality."[21] Not only that, the partial character of the notion of "the people" may in fact produce the sense, even within the populist movement, of a deficient community— deficient because of the failures of the agents of power—and could project "the people" as a fulness to be achieved as the horizon of political possibility rather than its immediate ground. This is what frequently produces the affective force that congeals and pushes forward a populist movement based on an apparently transitory mobilization of diverse, ill-assorted, and partial social components. The basic condition is that, despite their utmost sophistication, the technologies of modern governmentality can never satisfy all the differential demands which arise in a heterogeneous social space. "If a society managed to achieve an institutional order of such a nature that all demands were satisfied within its own immanent mechanisms, there would be no populism but, for obvious reasons, there would be no politics either."[22] Precisely, therefore, populism is the effective form of contemporary democratic politics.

> Only in an impossible world in which politics would have been entirely replaced by administration, in which piecemeal engineering in dealing with particularized differences would have totally done away with antagonistic dichotomies, would we find that "imprecision" and "simplification" would really have been eradicated from the public sphere. In that case, however, the trademark of populism would be just the

[21] Laclau, *Populist Reason*, p. 81.
[22] Ibid., p. 116.

special emphasis on a political logic which, as such, is a necessary ingredient of politics *tout court*.[23]

Populism, then, according to Laclau, consists of the following: (1) the unification of a plurality of demands in an equivalential chain; (2) the constitution of an internal frontier dividing society into two camps; and (3) the constitution of a popular identity which is something qualitatively more than the simple summation of the equivalential links.[24] Needless to say, the emergence of such a populist formation can take place only through acts of politics—that is to say, through rhetoric, mobilization, and performative action. Not every attempt at populist mobilization succeeds. In fact, many fail, and most others succeed only briefly. But the three features described above summarize the typical form of the politics of bound serialities criticized by Anderson.

These features run contrary to the accepted normative values of representative democracy. They do not respect any principle of correspondence between specific demands and their representative articulation. The alliances they produce are based on vague and arbitrary associations. They create deep and potentially dangerous antagonisms between a self-righteously constituted "people" and their supposed enemies. It is perhaps not surprising, therefore, that political theorists generally have been hostile to populism as a form of democratic politics, in the same way that Anderson has been hostile to ethnic politics and the politics spawned by governmentality. Pierre Rosanvallon, who has observed the emergence of new democratic practices such as the public overseeing of government performance, the prevention by public resistance of controversial government projects, and the subjection of government functionaries to non-judicial trial by the public, has nonetheless condemned populism as the absolute counter-democracy. Populism, he says, takes the democratic function of public vigilance to the extreme and "becomes a compulsive and permanent stigmatization of the ruling authorities, to the point where these authorities are seen as radically alien enemy powers."[25] Indeed,

---

[23] Ibid., p. 18.

[24] Ibid., p. 77.

[25] Pierre Rosanvallon, *Counter-democracy: Politics in an Age of Distrust* (Cambridge: Cambridge University Press, 2008), p. 268.

for Rosanvallon populism is a pathology "in which the democratic project is totally swallowed up and taken over by counter-democracy. . . . Populism is an acute manifestation of contemporary political disarray and a tragic expression of our inability to overcome it."[26]

Part of the reason why populism appears to be the absolute counter-democracy is that it is not seen as a strategic politics in the field of governmentality that could be used by demand-makers as well as by those who hold governmental power. I have already mentioned that one response of government agencies to attempts to set up popular chains of equivalent demands is to deal with those demands differentially. By such deployment possible combinations leading to the formation of a popular bloc antagonistic to governmental authority can be broken up. However, as the Gramscian perspective on hegemony reminds us, those in power also need to seek the consent of the people. In an electoral democracy, they have to secure the support of their constituents every few years. To do that, governmental authorities too could resort to populist politics by forging chains of equivalent demands and setting up a popular combination that is opposed by some putative enemy. The contemporary politics of nationalism often functions this way, by identifying some foreign enemy and its internal agents as the antagonists of the people as nation. The key point made by Laclau is that the popular "community" is always deficient, just as it is never possible for any government to satisfy all democratic demands. Hence, within the strategic field of the politics of governmentality, there is always a tussle between the differential and equivalential modes, setting a limit to the scope of populism. Without dismissing the dangerous anti-democratic potential contained within populist politics, the reasonable conclusion appears to be that the field of governmentality itself has the dynamic resources to restrain populism from becoming the absolute counter-democracy.

The Common Sense of Governmentality

It would be useful to return here to a theme introduced in Chapter One of this book. The relation between the utopian and real time of capital,

---

[26] Ibid., p. 273.

or that between unbound and bound serialities, largely coincides with the two senses of the norm and the relation that is then implied between the normative and the empirical. How is this relation specified in the domain of modern democratic politics? There is, of course, the old liberal paradigm of civic pedagogy which asserts the universal moral validity of individual liberty, rule of law, and representative government, and recommends that those who do not as yet espouse those values must first be educated in them before they can be fully incorporated into the world of free self-governing citizens. A different, more strategic, political perspective was provided within Marxist discourse by Gramsci's concept of hegemony, which suggested that the modern capitalist state was not simply an apparatus of force used to perpetuate the domination of the bourgeoisie but was indeed a constituent element of an entire field of social institutions mobilized to secure the consent of the dominated classes. Since then, especially in the second half of the twentieth century, the idea of popular sovereignty as well as the technologies of governmentality have been thoroughly universalized, so that it could safely be asserted today that, irrespective of political regimes or ideologies, the normative standing of those two concepts, in either one of the two senses of the norm, is unassailable. Thus, even military dictators and one-party regimes must claim today to rule on behalf of the people. Similarly, even stateless persons, or indeed the most primitive communities uninitiated into the ways of the modern world, are not outside governmentality, since some authority or the other must claim responsibility for providing them with the basic needs of human subsistence. Curiously, then, while there could always be principled exclusions from civil society on the ground of the lack of adequate civic qualifications, the web of governmentality today is in principle coextensive with humanity itself, even though in practice its reach may not be equally effective everywhere.

The reason for this, some might claim, is the universal validity of the concept of human rights. However, human rights are by no means accepted everywhere or by everybody and are often challenged as a Western or Christian idea. In comparison, the valorization of "the people" as a foundational term of political legitimacy is virtually universal today. As the locus of sovereignty, this is endorsed everywhere in the concept of popular sovereignty as the foundation of modern nation-states. But the influence of this normative idea appears to have travelled well beyond its theoretically approved domain to provide the moral justification for a plethora of demands and movements in the empirical domain of democratic politics. Such demands, as I have noted before, are not restricted only to the domain of the nation-state but go beyond its boundaries. This has prepared the ground for contemporary populism.

There is an interesting relation between the normative domain of unbound seriality, located in utopian time, and the empirical domain of bound seriality, grounded in real time, suggested by Gramsci's notion of "common sense." We may describe common sense as the empirically prevailing states of consciousness of ordinary people. For Gramsci, common sense is not the same as religion, because religion is only fragmented common sense, partial and one-sided. The same ordinary people who claim to have faith in religion will be found to frequently hold beliefs and engage in practices that are contrary to that religion. Indeed, one of Gramsci's most powerful insights into popular Catholicism is the contradictory character of subaltern consciousness which can affiliate with the religion while at the same time engaging in a critique of the orthodoxy of the church. But common sense is also not the same thing as philosophy which, Gramsci says, aims to be systematic and unitary.

Yet Gramsci also makes the intriguing remark that "everyone is a philosopher."[27] One might take this as a radical-sounding slogan without any serious content. But it is possible to construct out of this comment a more complex Gramscian argument that has more profound implications for our discussion of the place of popular reason in contemporary democracy. If we accept that the foundation of the modern state is the sovereignty of the people and that every governmental regime needs to seek some kind of consent for its rule from the people, then the question arises of how that consent is to be verified. In capitalist democracies where the hegemony of the bourgeoisie prevails, consent is sought through the mechanism of electoral representation in which the normal rule is that each individual member of "the people" has one vote. In this democratic space of popular

---

[27] Antonio Gramsci, *Selections from the Prison Notebooks*, tr. Quintin Hoare and Geoffrey Nowell-Smith (New York: International Publishers, 1971), p. 330.

judgement, there is no difference between the value that must be put on the opinion of a philosopher and that of a peasant. Each counts for one. If that be the case, it is perfectly valid to argue that everyone is a philosopher, because every person must be assumed to have the same capacity for rational judgement in political matters.

This is the ground, linking the normative to the empirical, that, I suggest, provides the site for the politics surrounding governmentality. This politics can be strategic, allowing governments to deal with demands in a differential way, just as it allows the governed to establish chains of equivalence in order to invoke "the people." When it is successful in responding to demands differentially, governmentality approaches the pure model of administration. But governmentality can also create the ground for popular politics to endow itself with high rhetoric and moral passion. Such is the range of contemporary democratic politics in real time. Modern democracies are always, without exception, oligarchies of property and expertise; the domain of political society, infused by popular mobilizations, acts as a constant reminder of democracy's abstract foundation in popular sovereignty.

From this, we also get a clue to solving a familiar puzzle of postcolonial politics: why is it the case that, faced with a dominant nationalist formation, the common form of oppositional politics is the assertion of ethnic identities based on governmental classifications frequently dating back to colonial times? Just as nationalism has assiduously denied all substantive heterogeneity among the people as a colonial fiction, opposition movements have turned governmental classifications of populations into *political* categories by mining the statistical and ethnographic resources of colonial knowledge and building chains of equivalence to mark out deep faultlines between an ethnic "people" and its oppressors who wield power in the postcolonial nation-state. The moral contrast between Anderson's unbound and bound serialities as "good" and "bad" only turns the puzzle into an aporia.

Political Society as Resistance

I have earlier introduced the concept of political society to explain the new forms of mobilization that take place over the politics of governmentality. One complaint against my use of political society is that it appears to empty the political actions of poor and exploited people of any concerted or sustained resistance to an oppressive and corrupt state machinery. Instead, it seems to focus exclusively on the negotiated transactions between government agencies and target population groups over the distribution of governmental benefits. This, my critics have complained, is merely dwelling on the administration of so-called welfare; where is the politics in it?

It is true that political society does not offer a transformational narrative threatening the course of capitalist development. It is not a concept of revolutionary politics. Rather, it is a response to the new technologies of government which, by the end of the twentieth century, have developed their own flexible instruments to break up the class-based political solidarities of the high industrial age and create the myriad and changing grids within which population groups could make their demands. Political society represents an altered, even though emergent and often inchoate, response to changed conditions of governmentality.

Consequently, one needs to be wary of imposing a singular conception of the political subject derived from older traditions of revolutionary politics. Far from denying that violent actions do indeed take place in the domain of popular politics in India, I have specifically mentioned them as strategic acts that are often resorted to by agents in political society when dealing with governmental power. But one must resist the essentializing move that elevates such acts as the only ones that are quintessentially political. I do not know that there is any one singularly describable political subject in India today. I am often reminded, for instance, of the destitute woman I once met in a village in West Bengal whose daily business it was to go from the panchayat office of the local government to the office of the ruling political party to that of the opposition party to that of the block development officer, making her plea for some help. She would do this routinely every day, until once every few days she would get something—perhaps a food ration, a sari, or a blanket, or perhaps even some cash, which she would receive after someone had filled out the forms and she had inked her thumb and pressed it on the official piece of paper. This woman survived by daily manipulating the local levers of an utterly banal political machine, but I find it unconscionable to exclude her from the domain of political subjectivity. I will voice my full-throated support for a political order that will bring destitution of this kind to an end or arrange that unfortunate persons like her find guaranteed shelter and care, but I cannot blame her for not having the subjectivity to will such an order into existence, since those who claim to be such subjects have not thus far found a way to bring it about.

Most scholars find everyday politics excruciatingly boring. This may be the result of our habit of following politics through the news headlines where only the extraordinary, the spectacular, and the sensational find a place. Further, those who set store by the political subject engaging in the heroic politics of the street can never fail to find it if they regularly follow the headlines. Yesterday, the political subject was on hunger strike in Manipur, protesting against the atrocities of the army. Today, he is digging up roads in Nandigram to prevent the police from coming in. Tomorrow, when Nandigram calms down, she will be throwing stones at the police in Kashmir. But in any one of those places, after the extraordinary act of resistance ceases either because it is repressed by force or runs out of steam or, as sometimes happens, wins its immediate demands, does the political subject vacate the scene when everyday politics is resumed? Or does she pursue a different mode of political action? It is the latter activity that I find analytically interesting, because it generally receives little attention. I do not deny the transformative role that critical events have often played in history. But those are precisely the heroic events that have drawn the attention of historians and political analysts. In looking at political society as a condition of un-heroic everyday politics, I am trying to find that which is new in the quotidian. The destitute woman in a West Bengal village in the 1960s would have probably sat outside the landlord's house or begged in the bazaar; today she goes to the panchayat or party office. I think that difference deserves not to be brushed aside.

The point came up earlier in the course of debates over *Subaltern Studies*. As is well known, that project began in the early 1980s by drawing attention to the moment of rebellion as the window into peasant consciousness. In ordinary times of subordination, the peasant appears submissive and fatalistic, incapable of resisting the conditions of oppression that daily weigh him down. But at the moment of insurgency, the peasant becomes a subject in his own right. This valuable insight that led to a critique of the elitist assumptions of both colonial and nationalist histories of peasant movements was, however, magnified into a new political theory, as it were, where, instead of the sovereign colonial or nationalist subject, the subaltern was held up as the new sovereign subject of history. Whatever its merits as a romantic literary trope, it was not a good theory of history because it reduced to matters of little consequence the everyday struggles of the subordinated peasant to make a livelihood, sustain a social world, and nourish a moral community of some worth and dignity. We thus came to recognize that while insurgency is undoubtedly a crucial and revealing moment in subaltern history, it is nonetheless an extraordinary moment which, while throwing light on the daily life of ordinary existence, cannot ever fully explain it.[28]

I think the idea of political society followed, at least in part, from this recognition. There is resistance in political society, sometimes even of a spectacular kind. But more often than not, it is resistance that tests rather than overtly violates the limits of conventional political practice. In so doing, it sometimes manages to induce responses from governmental agencies that change the familiar forms of the conventional.

Popular Politics and the Barriers to Capital

I do not believe anything is to be gained any more by merely reasserting the utopian and revolutionary politics of classical nationalism. Or rather, I do not believe it is an option available for a theorist from the postcolonial world. Let me end by commenting briefly on Anderson's perspective on comparisons.

Anderson begins *The Spectre of Comparisons* with a report on his experience in 1963 of acting as an impromptu interpreter of a speech by Sukarno in which the Indonesian president praised Hitler for being so "clever" in arousing the patriotic feelings of Germans by depicting the ideals of nationalism. Anderson

> felt a kind of vertigo. For the first time in my young life I had been invited to see my Europe as through an inverted telescope. Sukarno . . . was perfectly aware of the horrors of Hitler's rule. But he seemed to regard

---

[28] I have reviewed this intellectual transition in "A Brief History of *Subaltern Studies*," in Partha Chatterjee, *Empire and Nation*, pp. 289–301.

these horrors . . . with the brisk distance from which my schoolteachers had spoken of Genghiz Khan, the Inquisition, Nero, or Pizarro. It was going to be difficult from now on to think of "my" Hitler in the old way. (p. 2)

This "doubled vision," looking "as through an inverted telescope, is what Anderson, borrowing from José Rizal, so felicitously calls "the spectre of comparisons." It forced him to look at "his" Europe and "his" Hitler through the eyes and mind of Sukarno, just as Sukarno himself had learnt to look at Europe through the eyes and minds of his Dutch teachers. This is the critical anthropologist's vision, which does not shy away from having to come to terms with a fundamental relativism of worldviews. Anderson's work is a wonderful example of the struggle to grapple with this doubled vision, carried out in his case with acute analytical skill and outstanding intellectual and political integrity.

What Anderson does not seem to recognize is that as comparativists looking upon the world in the twentieth century, the perspective of the Indonesian can never be symmetrical with that of the Irishman. One's comparative vision is not the mirror image of the other's. To put it plainly, the universalism that is available to Anderson to be refined and enriched through his anthropological practice could never have been available to Sukarno, regardless of the political power the latter may have wielded as leader of a major postcolonial nation. The universalist ideal that belongs to Anderson as part of the same inheritance that allows him to say "my Europe" can continue *to encompass* its others as it moves from older national rigidities to newer cosmopolitan life-styles. For those who cannot say "my Europe," the choice seems to be to allow oneself *to be encompassed* within global cosmopolitan hybridities or to relapse into hateful ethnic particularities. For Anderson, and others like him, upholding the universalism of classical nationalism is still an ethically legitimate privilege. For those who now live in the postcolonial nations founded by the Bandung generation, charting a course that steers away from both global cosmopolitanism and ethnic chauvinism means necessarily to dirty one's hands in the complicated business of the politics of governmentality. The asymmetries produced and legitimized by the universalisms of classical nationalism have not left room for any ethically neat choice. Even the patriotic absurdities of diasporic communities, which Anderson so dislikes, will seem, by this reckoning, less the examples of perverse nationalism and more those of a failed cosmopolitanism.

At a recent meeting in an Indian research institute, after a distinguished panel of academics and policy-makers had bemoaned the decline of universalist ideals and moral values in national life, a Dalit activist from the audience asked why it was the case that liberal and leftist intellectuals were so pessimistic about where history was moving at the beginning of the twenty-first century. As far as he could see, the latter half of the twentieth century had been the brightest period in the entire history of the Dalits, since they had got rid of the worst social forms of untouchability, mobilized themselves politically as a community, and were now making strategic alliances with other oppressed groups in order to get a share of governmental power. All this could happen because the conditions of mass democracy had thrown open the bastions of caste privilege to attack from the representatives of oppressed groups organized into electoral majorities. The panellists were silenced by this impassioned intervention, although one or two could be heard muttering something about the inevitable recurrence of the Tocquevillean problem of the dominance of mediocrity under conditions of democracy. I came away persuaded once more that it was morally illegitimate to uphold the universalist ideals of nationalism without simultaneously demanding that the politics engendered by governmentality be recognized as an equally legitimate part of the real time-space of the modern political life of the nation. Without it, governmental technologies will continue to proliferate and serve as manipulable instruments of class rule in a global capitalist order. By seeking to find real ethical spaces for their operation, the incipient resistances to that order may be allowed to invent new terms of political justice. As the counterpoint to what I believe is a one-sided view of capitalist modernity held by Anderson, I continue to adhere to Marx's methodological premise:

> [C]apital drives beyond national barriers and prejudices as much as beyond nature worship, as well as all traditional, confined, complacent, encrusted satisfactions of present needs, and reproductions of old ways of life. . . .
>
> But from the fact that capital posits every such limit as a barrier and hence gets *ideally* beyond it, it does not by any means follow that it has

really overcome it, and, since every such barrier contradicts its character, its production moves in contradictions which are constantly overcome but just as constantly posited. Furthermore. The universality towards which it irresistibly strives encounters barriers in its own nature, which will, at a certain stage of its development, allow it to be recognized as being itself the greatest barrier to this tendency, and hence will drive towards its own suspension.[29]

In the remaining chapters of this book, I will follow the effects of popular reason in two domains of contemporary political life. One is that of popular culture, shaped by the operation of capital in various forms of cultural community. The other is that of the project of bourgeois hegemony in postcolonial democracy. Both trajectories will involve further elaborations on the themes of unbound and bound serialities, capital and community, and civil and political society.

[29] Karl Marx, *Grundrisse*, tr. Martin Nicolaus (Harmondsworth: Penguin, 1973), p. 410. I am indebted to Dipesh Chakrabarty's "Two Histories of Capital" which reminded me of this apt citation from Marx as well as of the article by E.P. Thompson cited earlier. See Chakrabarty, *Provincializing Europe: Postcolonial Thought and Historical Difference* (Princeton: Princeton University Press, 2000).

7

The Sacred Circulation of National Images

In 1962, India went to war with China over a piece of disputed territory up in the Himalayas. I was in high school at the time and impressionable enough to be swept away by the patriotic fervour. Our cause was right, we believed, because the territory in question was clearly ours: wasn't there a MacMahon line, drawn on a map solemnly signed in 1914 by representatives of the governments of British India and Republican China? What greater proof did one need to support our claim? Of course, the military campaign went disastrously for India and, along with millions of my compatriots, I smarted under the national humiliation. Later, when the scales of adolescence fell off my eyes, I realized we had been fighting not over territory—after all, the land in question was up in the mountains and completely uninhabited—but over its representation. We had been fighting over maps. The image wielded far greater power over our imaginations and passions than the real thing.

It is the same story everywhere with national images. What is interesting is the special way in which a particular national culture turns an image into an icon, to be reproduced, distributed, displayed, and sacralized. Sumathi Ramaswamy has given us a fascinating history of how the map of India itself has been iconized in the feminine and divine form of Bharat Mata or Mother India, with its own characteristic iconographic marks.[1] What is it about an image that allows it to be multiplied and disseminated as a national icon while fully retaining

[1] Sumathi Ramaswamy, *Goddess and the Nation: Mapping Mother India* (Durham, N.C.: Duke University Press, 2010).

its quality of sacredness? Let me pursue this question by looking at the way national monuments have been displayed in school textbooks in Bengal. I cannot claim deep familiarity with textbooks from other parts of India, but I would be surprised if they turned out to be radically different.

My choice of sources is deliberate. I will be talking about official nationalism, produced as an ideological ensemble within the institutional ambit of a nation-state regime. Most elements in this ensemble can be traced back genealogically to earlier formations in colonial and sometimes even pre-colonial histories. But they are reconstituted into a new discursive order by the official nationalism of the postcolonial nation-state. This ideological function, while it is supervised and directed by the state, is not necessarily confined only to formal state institutions. When successful, the official ideology proliferates in the practices of non-state institutions such as schools, clubs, professional associations, cultural organizations, media, etc. Most secondary schools have been run in Bengal as private trusts, sometimes with government grants but often without. Textbooks were provided by private publishers in accordance with syllabi laid down by a public school board.

Official nationalism has a performative as well as a pedagogical function.[2] In the performative mode, it must display the unity and singularity of the nation and the equal place within it of all citizens. In the pedagogical mode, however, official nationalism must reckon with the fact that all citizens cannot be treated equally, because all are not yet "proper" citizens; they must be educated into full membership of the "true" body of national citizens. Under official nationalism, schools become a crucial site for both functions. In the performative mode, schoolchildren frequently participate in events that play out the simultaneous and equal participation in the national space of diverse groups of Indians: the "unity in diversity" theme is the most common trope for performing the national. Here the school largely replicates practices that are more effectively played out on other sites, such as the parades on Republic Day, and in cinema and television.[3] In the other

---

[2] The distinction has been made by Homi Bhabha, "DissemiNation," in Bhabha, ed., *Nation and Narration* (New York: Routledge, 1990), pp. 291–322.

[3] For extended discussions on the Republic Day parade and official newsfilms in India, see Srirupa Roy, *Beyond Belief: India and the Politics of Postcolonial*

mode, however, the school, with its curriculum, its texts, and its expository and disciplinary regime, is the place where the pedagogical function of official nationalism can be observed in its purest form. It is not surprising that the content of school textbooks has been so often the bone of political contention in contemporary India.

Before Nationalism

Bibidhārtha saṃgraha (literally, Collection of Diverse Knowledges), founded in 1851 and edited by the polymath Rajendralal Mitra, was the first illustrated Bengali journal that regularly published articles on places of archaeological and historical interest. Besides being a leading figure in the Asiatic Society of Bengal, the most prominent editor in his day of Sanskrit manuscripts, and a leading historian of art and architecture, Mitra was also a pioneer in the publication of Bengali maps and the founder of the Photographic Society of India. Both the engraved illustrations and the historical articles in *Bibidhārtha saṃgraha* were drawn from current English publications on the subject. The illustrations of monuments have the same picturesque quality that was the hallmark of colonial illustrative art and of early colonial photography.[4] (Figures 1 and 2) The age of nationalism was yet to appear in Bengal.

When the gods Brahma, Indra, Narayana, and Shiva visited Delhi in 1879, after catching the train from Saharanpur, they were taken on a tour through the city by the rain-god Varun who, judging by the account of the visit, had probably memorized Baedeker's or Thomas Cook's guide to India (the former guide was first published in the 1850s and the latter in the 1860s).[5] He knew, for instance, that the

---

Nationalism (Durham, N.C. and New Delhi: Duke University Press and Permanent Black, 2007).

[4] The connection between the picturesque and the scientific in early colonial representations of Indian monuments has been discussed in Tapati Guha-Thakurta, *Monuments, Objects, Histories: Institutions of Art in Colonial and Postcolonial India* (New York: Columbia University Press, 2004), ch. 1.

[5] Durgacharan Ray, *Debgaṇer martye āgaman* (1880; reprint Calcutta: Dey's, 1984), pp. 45–57. This is one of the first travel guides in Bengali, written as an account of a visit by the gods keen to find out how their creation was faring under British rule.

great mosque of the city was 201 feet long and 120 feet wide and that the Red Fort was spread across two and a half miles. Objective knowledge was colonial knowledge; the objective gaze was the colonial gaze. Few among the new English-educated Indians were questioning these truisms of the times.

School textbooks of history in nineteenth-century Bengal rarely carried illustrations. Metal engraving, lithography, and halftone printing were still expensive and textbooks had to be cheap. Halftone printing was patented in France in 1857 and was commercially used in Europe and the United States by the 1880s. The first halftone press was set up in Calcutta in the 1900s, but some publishers were getting halftone blocks made for them in Europe. Wood engravings were, of course, both cheap and widely used, but they were rarely employed in textbooks, possibly because of their association with the pulp literature of the bazaar. We have to move forward to the 1920s to find illustrated history books for schoolchildren. By then nationalism was, of course, well set on its journey in Bengal. On the one hand, revolutionary groups were carrying out daring attacks on British officials; when revolutionaries were tried and hanged, they became national martyrs. On the other hand the Congress, under the leadership of C.R. Das, launched a very successful mass campaign of non-cooperation with the colonial government. In literature, theatre, art, and music the nationalist agenda was being pushed vigorously.

The school curriculum was, of course, still under official colonial control and no hint of disloyalty was tolerated in the pages of textbooks. Flipping the pages of a widely read textbook from 1924 on Indian history, we find engraved illustrations of rulers and monuments—exactly the engravings we would have found in older colonial histories and travel accounts.[6] The monuments have the same picturesque quality and some of the engraved blocks look well worn from repeated use. (Figure 3) If national icons were being produced at this time, their mass circulation in school textbooks had not yet happened. This particular book, however, established one pattern for historical illustrations that would be henceforth repeated: ancient India (called the "Hindu period") would be represented by Hindu and Buddhist religious architecture, and medieval India (called the "Muslim

---

[6] Bijaychandra Majumdar, *Bhāratbarṣer itihās* (Calcutta: Sen Brothers, 1924).

period") by forts, victory towers, and royal tombs. (The exception for ancient India was the headless statue, lodged in the Mathura museum, of the Kushana ruler Kanishka, a source of endless mirth for generations of schoolchildren.) Interestingly, the modern or "British period" was illustrated not by monuments but by portraits of viceroys.

Nationalist Transformations

There is a moment soon after Indian independence in 1947 that appears to be something like a nodal point in this story. One is unsure here which way the plot will move. Official nationalism was still being constituted. Ultimately, the plot does, of course, move in one particular direction.

The textbooks of the early 1950s show one important change as far as illustrations are concerned. Engravings are replaced by photographs printed from halftone zinc blocks. A textbook of 1950 written by the well-known historian Kalidas Nag, a specialist on the art and architecture of South East Asia, is copiously illustrated by photographs.[7] These have one curious feature. The picturesque quality has disappeared. There are no trees or images reflected on water or stray human figures in the foreground. (Figure 4) Images of historical monuments are acquiring an iconic quality. What else can one say about the photographed image of the Taj, obviously printed from a metal block that has long outlived its aesthetic appeal?

The contrast is brought out sharply by comparing this textbook with another publication of the same time that was also meant for children but not as a prescribed school text. *Biśva paricay*, brought out by one of the largest publishers of children's books, was meant as an upmarket publication, printed on glossy paper with photographs on every page, to be bought as a gift or a prize.[8] The photographs here have a self-consciously artistic quality about them; they are not intended to serve any iconic function. Notice, for example, the photograph of the Qutb tower shot through a ruined gateway or that of the Taj Mahal from the bank of the River Jamuna. (Figures 3 and 5) These images would not get into officially prescribed textbooks intended for the first generation of Indian children born after Independence.

[7] Kalidas Nag, *Svadeś o sabhyatā* (Calcutta: Modern Book Agency, 1950).
[8] *Biśva paricay* (Calcutta: Deb Sahitya Kutir, 1953).

What happens next is inexplicable in terms of any theory of modernization or development. Technologically, it is a reversal, a throwback. But it is not caused by any technological gap or absence. From the late 1950s or early 1960s, photographs disappear from history textbooks, to be replaced by images that look like etchings or engravings but which are actually drawings by pen and ink made to look like engravings and transferred photographically on to metal blocks. But they are definitely not artist's sketches: there is not the slightest trace of an individualized aesthetic gaze. These are representations of historical monuments that do not have a significant indexical function—they do not refer to something real out there in real space and time; rather, they are icons.

Let me present some random selections, because almost any textbook published in the last forty years will do. Take the picture of the temple at Tanjore (Figure 6) or of the Qutb Minar or the Taj (Figure 7).[9] They are clearly drawn from photographic images—the angle of vision, the perspective, the framing, all suggest this. But they are not photographs; they are drawings. Even Kanishka, the "headless monarch," is drawn as a copy of his museum statue. (Figure 8) What can be the reason for this strange denial of the advantages of photographic reproduction?

I suggest that the answer lies in the way in which the effect of sacredness is produced in the national icon. There is an economy of this iconicity that requires that the image be cleansed of all traces of a self-conscious artistic aesthetic. There must be no hint of the picturesque or the painterly, no tricks of the camera angle, no staging of the unexpected or the exotic. The image must also be shorn of all redundancy: any element lacking a specific place within the narrative economy of this national iconography must be removed from the image. Hence, no superfluous foliage or shimmering reflections on water, no lazy dog sleeping in the shade or stray passersby going about their daily business. The "artistic" has no place within the visual domain of the sacred.

---

[9] The Tanjore image is from Dilip Kumar Ghosh, *Bhārat o bhāratbāsi* (Calcutta: New Book Stall, 1974), p. 103. The Taj picture is from Dineschandra Sarkar and Kalipada Hore, *Bhārat-itihāser rūprekhā* (Calcutta: Vidyoday, 1973), pp. 70, 112.

The sacredness of national icons plays a curious role within the pedagogical apparatus of history. It is well known, for instance, that a common trope in the narration of history is the romantic one of imaginatively inhabiting a past era. The effort here is to close the distance in time by travelling back into another period and, in a sense, participating in the experience of another time and another people. The historical romance—in the form of novels, ballads, or drama—is the most obvious literary genre in which this imaginative anachronism is practised. But it is also a common pedagogical tool employed by history teachers and is not infrequently, or so at least I suspect, a powerful affective impulse that drives the work of many professional historians. This romantic attitude towards the historical object encourages proximity; it invites the reader or viewer to enter the world to which the object belonged. The attitude is the same as that which impels modern-day travel, as distinct from traditional pilgrimage. Not surprisingly, it promotes a visual language that emphasizes not just vividness or a lifelike quality but also the exotic and the picturesque.

The attitude of sacredness I am talking about is exactly opposed to that of the romantic. It is founded on a reverential distance of the viewer from the object. But this distance cannot be one of time, because then the object would be consigned irretrievably to some lost period peopled by others. To enter the sacred domain of "our" national treasures, the object must be recovered for "our" worshipful gaze. I suggest that this is effectively done by the iconic image of the monument. An iconic image, as I understand it, is not merely an easily recognized or conventional logo. It is the representation of a sacred object in which the image itself partakes of the sacred quality of the original. To imagine, as it were, a treasure-house of national monuments, the schoolchild must be presented with a gallery of iconic images that are situated in no particular place or time but in fact belong to the whole of the national space and to all time. After all, as the nationalist will remind us, has not the nation existed from time immemorial? In contrast with the imaginative anachronism of the romantic trope, the iconic image produces a visual anachronism in which the real object is taken out of its context in a specific place and time, and located in an abstract and timeless space. The image now becomes the pure and sacred original, compared to which the real object can only be observed (by the tourist, for example) in its corrupt and utterly profane real-life context. The iconic image is not indexical.

Judith Mara Gutman has argued about Indian photographs that, unlike the Western realist aesthetic, they reflect a completely different and distinctly Indian conception of reality.[10] The painted photograph is the most commonly cited example to show how, in this case, paint is used not to supplement but in fact to hide the technologically produced likeness to the real object. It has been, of course, correctly pointed out that Gutman's claim of a radically different Indian aesthetic is hugely simplistic and overstated.[11] But her argument that in Indian photographs everything within the picture field happens at once, as though in an idealized and timeless space, appears to hold especially for the iconic images of national monuments I have been talking about. And to achieve this effect, the photograph itself is avoided, for its very lifelike quality threatens to introduce into the image those indexical elements that suggest a specific time and context within which the monument actually exists. The iconic drawing allows for much greater control, so that all that is redundant to the sacred economy of the image can be carefully eliminated.

Consider, for instance, a picture of the Red Fort in Delhi from a textbook published in 1987.[12] (Figure 9) The Mughal fort, once the seat of imperial sovereignty, entered the sacred geography of Indian nationalism when officers of Subhas Chandra Bose's Indian National Army were tried there for treason and cruelty to prisoners by the colonial government in the last days of British rule. Those convicted as traitors by the British were regarded as national heroes by Indians. Since India became independent in 1947, it has become an annual ritual for the prime minister to address the nation from the fort's ramparts on Independence Day. On that day, the national flag flies from the flagstaff on top of the fort. The picture of the Red Fort freezes this moment and elevates it into an abstract ideality by eliminating

[10] Judith Mara Gutman, *Through Indian Eyes: Nineteenth and Early Twentieth Century Photography from India* (New York: Oxford University Press, 1982).

[11] For instance, by Christopher Pinney, *Camera Indica: The Social Life of Indian Photographs* (Chicago: University of Chicago Press, 1997), pp. 95–6.

[12] Sobhakar Chattopadhyay, *Bhārater itihās* (Calcutta: Narmada Publication, 1987), p. 182.

everything from the picture field except for the bare architectural façade and the national flag flying from an impossibly high flagstaff. Such is the process by which the sacred iconicity of the monument is produced. No photograph could have achieved the effect with such controlled economy.

I should add that two other categories of images in history textbooks are also reproduced, virtually without exception, as line drawings: the maps, always redrawn by artists from unacknowledged originals, and the portraits of national leaders that fill up the pages of the "modern period;" here too photographs are almost never used, even though they often form the basis for the artist's line drawings.

It might be supposed that there are economic or technological reasons for preferring line drawings to photographs. Are they cheaper to print? Not really, because both are printed from zinc blocks produced by the same photographic process. It is sometimes argued that line blocks produce better prints on inferior quality paper than halftone blocks. There is some substance in this argument. But if there was a clear pedagogical or aesthetic case to be made for the representational superiority of the photographic image, then there is no reason to believe that it would not have been used in textbooks, even if it meant a slightly higher price. In fact, the use of the line drawing is so ubiquitous that block-makers manufacture and sell readymade blocks of historical monuments for use in history textbooks. (Figure 10) It seems to me that the pedagogical purpose of nationalist education is believed to be served far more effectively by such idealized drawings than by the suspiciously profane realism of photographs.

I should emphasize that we are talking about a professional practice within a pedagogical regime that has acquired the consensual form of a convention. When we try to decode the underlying order of meanings, we do not imply that the artists or publishers or teachers participating in the practice are conscious of that underlying structure or even curious about it. Such is the commonsensical obviousness of every conventional practice.

My argument would be clinched if I could show that even after the latest technological revolution in the Bengali textbook industry— namely, the rapid introduction of phototypesetting and offset printing in the last two decades—historical illustrations continue to follow the

Fig. 1: The Delhi fort (showing the chosen residence of the
Empress Nurjahan), engraving (source: *Bibidhārtha saṃgraha*, 1854)

Fig. 2: The riverfront at Benares, engraving
(source: *Bibidhārtha saṃgraha*, 1852)

Fig. 3: Taj Mahal, engraving (source: Majumdar, *Bhāratbarṣer itihās*, 1924)

Fig. 4: The Shiva temple at Tanjore, photograph
(source: Kalidas Nag, *Svadeś o sabhyatā*, 1950)

Fig. 5: The Qutb Minar, photograph (source: *Biśva paricay*, 1953)

Fig. 6: The temple at Tanjore, line drawing
(source: Dilip Kumar Ghosh, *Bhārat o bhāratbāsī,* 1974)

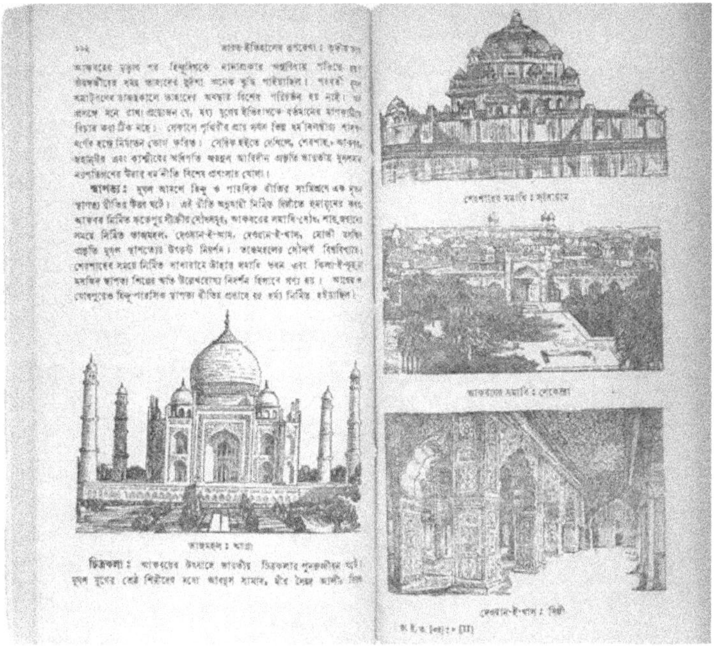

Fig. 7: Taj Mahal, line drawing (source: Sarkar and Hore, *Bhārat-itihāser rūprekhā*, 1973).

Fig. 8: The headless statue of Kanishka, line drawing (source: Ghosh, *Bhārat o bhāratbāsī*, 1974)

Fig. 9: The Red Fort, Delhi, line drawing (source: Sobhakar Chattopadhyay, *Bhārater itihās*, 1987)

7176 Rs. 3·00

Fig. 10: The Red Fort, metal block for sale, advertised in the catalogue of Dass Brothers, Calcutta, 1960

Fig. 11: The Red Fort, Delhi, photograph (source: Atulchandra Ray, *Bhārater itihās*, 2001). Notice the parked bicycle and people sitting under the tree in the foreground

pattern I have described. The evidence on this point is, however, still somewhat ambiguous. Most history textbooks I have seen published in the last ten years do, in fact, contain the same line drawings, even when their texts are phototypeset and the books printed by the photo offset process.[13] One significant novelty is the introduction of glossy colour photographs of monuments on the covers. One textbook has a bunch of colour photographs printed on glossy art paper stuck in the middle of the book: the photos of the Sanchi stupa or the Taj Mahal are those we would find on picture postcards.

But I also found a book that appears to have broken the convention by abandoning line drawings and reintroducing photographs—after half a century since the early days of the Indian republic.[14] This book has a sheaf of colour photos—once again, picture postcard quality— and maps in colour. It also has black and white photographs of monuments strewn across its pages, many with a deliberately vivid and picturesque quality that suggests proximity and indexical familiarity rather than abstract remoteness and sacred iconicity. (Figure 11) Does this mark a new trend? It is too early to tell. It is possible that there is a recognition that, with the proliferation of colour magazines, cinema, and television, even schoolchildren in small towns and villages are now exposed to a visual language that makes the iconic drawing seem archaic and jaded. Perhaps new pedagogical techniques, enabled by the most recent technologies of mechanical reproduction, will be fashioned to create the effect of sacredness by which alone an imagined national space, dotted by timeless images, can exist in its spectral purity, purer even than the real-life original.

Or could it be that that iconic space is being desacralized? Perhaps the romantic trope has finally won the day, making room for those familiar techniques of historical reconstruction by which an object can be imaginatively grasped in the here-and-now while, at the same time, locating it in a specific time and place in the past? I see no reason to

[13] Among popular textbooks today that continue to use line drawings instead of photographs are Nisith Ranjan Ray, *Bhārat paricay* (Calcutta: Allied Book Agency, 2001); Jiban Mukhopadhyay, *Svadeś paricay* (Calcutta: Nababharati, 2002); Prabhatangshu Maiti, *Bhārater itihās* (Calcutta: Sridhar Prakashani, 2001).

[14] Atulchandra Ray, *Bhārater itihās* (Calcutta: Prantik, 2001).

believe that this is the case. If the artistic photograph finds a place in history textbooks, my guess would be that sacred images would be produced and circulated by other means. What they might be, I cannot tell. At the moment, I see that the old images have still not yielded their place on the pages of Bengal's school textbooks. And in any case, I see that Indians, like many other people, are still prepared to fight over maps.

8

Critique of Popular Culture

The Criticism of Culture

In 1992, at a conference to mark a decade of cultural studies carried out by the Birmingham school, Stuart Hall spoke very critically of "the theoretical fluency of cultural studies in the United States." He was not, he said, demanding that American cultural studies become more like British cultural studies. The problem was not that American cultural studies was unable to theorize power in the field of culture or that it had formalized out of existence the relations of history and politics to culture. On the contrary. "There is no moment now, in American cultural studies," he said, "when we are *not* able, extensively and without end, to theorize power—politics, race, class and gender, subjugation, domination, exclusion, marginality, Otherness, etc. There is hardly anything in cultural studies which isn't so theorized." But by carrying out this task through an "overwhelming textualization" of the material it studied, cultural studies was in danger of "constituting power and politics as exclusively matters of language and textuality itself." This allowed no room for cultural studies to become "a practice which always thinks about its intervention in a world in which it would make some difference, in which it would have some effect." Hall then went on to propose that Antonio Gramsci's "organic intellectual" and Michel Foucault's "specific intellectual" were alternative ways of thinking how the student of culture might intervene in the real world of culture. In any case, whatever the particular method by which this was done, Hall's plea was to "return the project of cultural studies from the clean air of meaning and textuality and theory to the something nasty down below." I take Stuart Hall to mean by this that cultural studies should not avoid making moral, aesthetic, or political judgements about the world of culture that it claimed to study.[1]

But how did it come to be that a field of study that promised to investigate the production, consumption, and valorization of culture by connecting it to relations and practices of power found itself unable to make judgements about good and bad culture? Why did the scholar of culture have to restrict herself to locating specific cultural acts within complex structures of power but refrain from becoming a cultural critic? Let me approach this question by making a quick review of the study of popular visual culture as it has developed in India in the last three or four decades.

To take the case of cinema first: there is a framing debate, going back to at least the early 1960s, about the relation between cinema and the viewing culture of the public in India. On one side is the argument that the mass audience of the Indian cinema, steeped in traditional beliefs and practices and raised for generations in pre-modern viewing cultures, is simply incapable of understanding or appreciating the rational-realist cinema. As a result, not only has serious art cinema failed to take root in India's modern aesthetic life, but the film industry too has routinely churned out mythological and melodramatic rubbish that is cinematically infantile and ideologically retrograde. As Chidananda Das Gupta, one of the most articulate proponents of this view, claimed, the audience of the popular Indian cinema was unable to distinguish between fact and myth. This was shown by the political deification of film stars in Tamil Nadu and Andhra Pradesh and the persistence over half a century of Hindu mythological themes in the popular Hindi cinema. He also pointed out that unlike folk art that is produced organically within communities, the popular cinema is industrially produced and "vast manipulative forces" are at work.[2] Reasserting the importance of taking a stand on social values, Das Gupta rejected the trend of uncritically endorsing the popular cinema as popular culture. Culture could not be allowed to go uncriticized, he seemed to be saying, simply because it was popular.

[1] Stuart Hall, "Cultural Studies and its Theoretical Legacies," in Lawrence Grossberg, Cary Nelson, and Paula Treichler, eds, *Cultural Studies* (London: Routledge, 1992), pp. 277–94.

[2] Chidananda Das Gupta, *The Painted Face: Studies in India's Popular Cinema* (New Delhi: Roli Books, 1991), pp. 256–7.

On the other side was the provocative argument offered by Ashis Nandy who insisted that the non-modernity of the popular Indian cinema and its audience was a sign of the resilience of a tradition of viewing practices that still refused to cave in before the global onslaught of a culture of modern technological and commercial rationality. The alleged failure of Indian cinemagoers to appreciate realist cinematic narrative was in fact a rejection of the cultural values of modern industrial life and an endorsement of the inherited virtues of tradition, faith, and community. Indeed, Nandy even insisted that the popular Indian cinema, though industrially produced, had "a built-in plurality that tends to subvert mass culture even when seemingly adapting to it passively."[3] It was neither classical nor folk, and yet, "now that modernity has become the dominant principle in Indian public life . . . it is the commercial cinema which, if only by default, has been . . . more protective towards nonmodern categories."[4]

This is a difference in viewpoints that still persists, at least in the public domain in India. There is no hesitation here in making aesthetic, moral, or political judgements about the cinema, whether high or popular. In the scholarly domain, however, things are quite different. As Ravi Vasudevan has reminded us in his survey of the analytical literature on the Indian cinema, the extreme terms of the debate between Das Gupta and Nandy have been largely superseded by the profusion of empirically rich and theoretically sophisticated studies that have appeared in the field of Indian film studies in the last decade and a half.[5] Both sides in that old debate had assumed a certain pre-given and fixed structure of the viewing practices of the allegedly pre-modern Indian audience. That structure, both positions assumed, could only confront the modern technology of the cinema on the terms allowed by their own inflexible practices; the structure could not adapt or change to accommodate the new. Most theorists

[3] Ashis Nandy, "Introduction: Indian Popular Cinema as a Slum's Eye View of Politics," in Ashis Nandy, ed., *The Secret Politics of Our Desires: Innocence, Culpability and Indian Popular Cinema* (Delhi: Oxford University Press, 1998), p. 13.

[4] Ashis Nandy, "The Intelligent Film Critic's Guide to Indian Cinema," in Ashis Nandy, *The Savage Freud and Other Essays on Possible and Retrievable Selves* (Delhi: Oxford University Press, 1995), p. 235.

[5] Ravi S. Vasudevan, "Introduction," in Vasudevan, ed., *Making Meaning in Indian Cinema* (Delhi: Oxford University Press, 2000), pp. 1–36.

and historians studying the Indian cinema today will reject this assertion, and hence, reject both of the views represented by Das Gupta and
Nandy. The popular Indian cinema, they will say, has in fact modernized itself as well as its audience by adapting traditionally available
narrative forms and performance techniques and inserting them into
a modern technological medium. In the process, both the cinema and
its audience have been transformed, albeit in complex ways that need
to be documented and understood. This would be the prevailing
common sense among students of Indian cinema today.

I believe this change in the terms of the debate is part of a larger
change that has taken place in the last two decades in cultural disciplines such as anthropology and literary theory as well as in approaches
to the study of cultural history. The older debate was fundamentally
informed by a historical paradigm of modernization, whether Weberian
or Marxian. The model was that of a modern sector, with modern
economic, political, and cultural institutions breaking into and transforming the traditional sector. It was with this model in mind that
one set of scholars, impatient with the slow pace of transformation,
complained of the rigidities of traditional practices and the lack of
initiative, and perhaps even sincerity, within the modern sector to
change the pre-modern. And the same model provoked the rival group
of scholars to bemoan the loss of traditional virtues and celebrate the
traces of resistance to modernization. What has happened in the last
twenty years, on the one hand with the critique of anthropology as a
colonial science, and on the other with the emergence of postcolonial
literary and cultural studies, is a realignment of the terms for the study
of modernity.

I will list just three elements of this realignment that are relevant for
the next part of my discussion. First, it is no longer taken for granted
that there is only one model or version of modernity that must be
adopted by people all round the globe. The study of actual transformations of institutions and practices in different countries of the world
in the modern period have prompted scholars to talk about different
modernities, alternative modernities, and even multiple modernities.
Not only that, the history of Western modernity itself is being
interrogated from this standpoint. It was always known that there were
many counter-currents to the supposedly relentless sweep of modernity in Europe and North America, but the dominant ideologies of

colonial modernization insisted on presenting an image of Western modernity as homogeneous, internally consistent, and universal. Now it is being argued that these counter-currents are not vestiges of some decadent past but integral, even if complexly structured, aspects of Western modernity itself. Further, Western modernity was not necessarily autonomously generated from within the parameters of European history, as all post-Enlightenment thinkers had assumed, but was itself the product of its encounters with non-European cultures, especially through the history of European empires. These arguments seriously complicate the earlier narrative of a modern sector, already formed by European historical processes, transforming through a pedagogical project the traditional structures of pre-modernity all round the world.

Second, it is now clear that even within the modern sector, transformations do not occur in the same way, or even in the same direction, in different institutional spaces. To cite an example I have used before, the spread of modern medicine in India was accompanied by a transformation of the institutions of traditional Ayurvedic and Yunani practices which adopted patented drugs, standardized textbooks, university examinations, and public registration of physicians, but did not thereby seek to become special branches of modern medicine and instead claimed their status as alternative medical practices. But nothing like this happened in the case of Indian chemistry or Indian mathematics.[6] To take an example from the cultural world, while the adoption of modern Western forms such as the novel or proscenium theatre or oil painting led to fundamental transformations of Indian literature, drama, and art, the field of Indian music, even as it adopted instruments such as the harmonium and the violin, or techniques such as notation, or technologies such as the gramophone record, radio, and cinema, or institutions such as the music school, unquestionably

[6] Partha Chatterjee, "The Disciplines in Colonial Bengal," in Partha Chatterjee, ed., *Texts of Power: Emerging Disciplines in Colonial Bengal* (Minneapolis: University of Minnesota Press, 1995), pp. 1–29. For recent studies on the subject, see Seema Alavi, *Islam and Healing: Loss and Recovery of an Indo-Muslim Medical Tradition 1600–1900* (Ranikhet: Permanent Black, 2008); Kavita Sivaramakrishnan, *Old Potions, New Bottles: Recasting Indigenous Medicine in Colonial Punjab 1850–1940* (New Delhi: Orient Longman, 2006); Guy Attewell, *Refiguring Unani Tibb: Plural Healing in Late Colonial India* (New Delhi: Orient Longman, 2007).

retained its character as Indian music, distinguishable in systemic terms from Western music.[7] The dynamics of modernity, then, turn out to have different effective histories in different institutional sites, even in the same historical period and for the same people. This phenomenon cannot be understood as uneven development, because it is not simply a problem of different time-lags or uneven dispersion over space. Rather, it becomes necessary to suspend the totalizing structural contrasts between the modern and the pre-modern and focus instead on localized, contingent, and often transient changes in actual practices.

Third, on the ethical-political question of the use of power—usually the coercive power of the state—to transform pre-modern institutions and practices, there has also been a change. At least in the cultural disciplines, if not in the social sciences as a whole, there is a much greater sensitivity today to the destructive social and cultural effects of large-scale, centralized, state-sponsored projects of modernization. Even in the domain of governance, there is greater emphasis on taking account of the heterogeneity of populations and the micro-management of security and welfare policies to suit local conditions. If there has been a shift from the state to the market as the principal agency of global transformations, this has not resulted in the global homogenization of cultures; ever new localized spaces are being created for the production of cultural difference and the mobilization of identity politics. This has not made the operations of power regimes, or indeed the resistance to them, any more benign, but the ethical questions they raise no longer seem to be susceptible to universally applicable solutions. The political ethics of social change now tend to be evaluated within contextual, contingent, and strategically defined conditions.

This leads me to my final theoretical remark before returning to the subject of Indian visual culture. An important theoretical lineage of

[7] Janaki Bakhle, *Two Men and Music: Nationalism in the Making of an Indian Classical Tradition* (New York: Oxford University Press, and New Delhi: Permanent Black, 2005); Lakshmi Subramanian, *From the Tanjore Court to the Madras Music Academy: A Social History of Music in South India* (Delhi: Oxford University Press, 2006); Amanda J. Weidman, *Singing the Classical, Voicing the Modern: The Postcolonial Politics of Music in South India* (Durham, N.C.: Duke University Press, 2006).

the new cultural studies inaugurated in Britain in the early 1980s went back to the remarkable writings on cultural politics by Gramsci. Hall specifically recalled this in his lecture.[8] Perhaps it is not a coincidence that, almost at the same time, but with no direct connection, the writers assembled under *Subaltern Studies* began their critique of both the colonial and the nationalist historiography of India by drawing from the theoretical insights of Gramsci. I believe I am not wrong in saying that these two strands of recent scholarship have been influential in realigning the terms of debate on modernity, including that in the field of cultural studies. And since Gramsci's writings are a common source for both these strands, I wish to recall one intriguing sentence from the *Prison Notebooks* in which Gramsci speaks of "the philosophy of praxis" as having become "a criticism of 'common sense', basing itself initially, however, on common sense." He goes on to add that "it is not a question of introducing from scratch a scientific form of thought into everyone's individual life, but of renovating and making 'critical' an already existing activity."[9] I believe this sentence states in an aphorism a project that the new cultural disciplines—those that have emerged out of the critiques of theories of modernization—are struggling to formulate. The task is no longer to interrogate popular culture with the fully formed apparatus of a scientific worldview. Rather, it is to begin from the practices of popular culture, to immerse oneself in its forms, in order to develop its critique. The methods of such a critique remain elusive, which is why it is worth investigating those works of cultural production that not merely inhabit and celebrate the modes of popular culture but self-consciously seek to transform them.

Popular Practices of Photography

To illustrate some of these problems of method, let me turn to another field of popular culture in India that is only once removed from the field of cinema, namely, photography. Judith Mara Gutman advanced the initial argument that Indian photographs, although they were products of the same modern Western technology, did not follow the

---

[8] Hall, "Cultural Studies and its Theoretical Legacies."
[9] Antonio Gramsci, *Selections from the Prison Notebooks*, tr. Quintin Hoare and Geoffrey Nowell-Smith (New York: International Publishers, 1971), pp. 330–1.

Western realist aesthetic at all and instead reflected a completely different and distinctly Indian conception of reality.[10] Unlike a Western
photograph where the viewer was carefully led from one part of
the picture to another according to a familiar set of realist-narrative
conventions, in Indian photographs everything within the picture
field seems to happen at once, as though in an idealized and timeless
space. Using the painted photograph as her example, she argued that
early Indian photographic artists used paint not to supplement but in
fact to hide the technologically produced likeness to the real object.

Gutman's claim of a radically different Indian aesthetic was criticized for being hugely simplistic and overstated.[11] But more recent
scholars, such as Christopher Pinney, who have made more careful and
nuanced studies of popular photography, have also tried to define
the elements of the aesthetic conception that governs popular visual
culture in India. For instance, there is the practice of the darshan,
widespread in all parts of India, in which the devotee comes into visual
contact with the image of the deity and secures, by the physical act of
seeing and being seen, the blessings of the divine. The practice has
extended from divine images to men and women with special qualities
of holiness and even into the political field: from emperors to local
chiefs, Hindu and Muslim, as well as modern political leaders like
Gandhi, all granted darshan to those who came to see them in the hope
of gaining merit from visual contact with the holy and the powerful.
Several scholars have argued that the conventions that govern the
representation of divine or powerful figures in popular visual imagery
in India are shaped by this idea of darshan. Pinney has cited the example of a widely available photolithograph of the saintly figure of
Ramakrishna, much revered in Bengal, showing him seated with his
wife Sarada and his disciple Swami Vivekananda in front of the image
of the goddess Kali at the Dakshineswar temple in Calcutta.[12] (Figure
12) The image is a composite one, with photographs of the three
human figures inserted in the foreground of a painted photo of the Kali

[10] Judith Mara Gutman, *Through Indian Eyes: Nineteenth and Early Twentieth
Century Photography from India* (New York: Oxford University Press, 1982).

[11] For instance, by Christopher Pinney, *Camera Indica: The Social Life of Indian
Photographs* (Chicago: University of Chicago Press, 1997), pp. 95–6.

[12] The photolithograph image printed for circulation around 1920 is reproduced in Pinney, *Camera Indica*, p. 105.

idol, completely violating the norms of both narrative realism and historical plausibility (since the three could never have posed for the camera in this fashion). Curiously, however, the Kali idol at Dakshineswar is shown with two strikingly realist adornments: a framed and garlanded photograph of Ramakrishna on one side of the wall and a clock with the hands at nine o'clock on the other. The lithographed image seems to have been composed to give the viewer the chance to obtain a simultaneous darshan of all four powerful figures, divine and human, for, as it were, the price of one.

To take another example: Ashish Rajadhyaksha, in a classic essay on D.G. Phalke, the pioneer of early Indian cinema, showed how Phalke evolved methods such as frontal staging and direct address into the camera, forms that are antithetical to the aesthetic styles of the Western film, by building into the new technology of the cinema prevailing popular conceptions of viewing such as darshan.[13] Arvind Rajagopal has extended the argument to the much more recent phenomenon of the serially televised *Ramayana* where the viewing of the epic was regarded by millions as a weekly darshan of the gods.[14] Similarly, Pinney has given us a fascinating analysis of the visual representation of bhakti or devotion to the god Shiva, whose power is commonly represented in the phallic form of the shivalinga. In a widely available calendar print, Pinney shows: "Within the *ling* Shiv literally encompasses Parvati and hierarchy is denoted spatially. In this image we see the notion that within each consecrated image or *murti* there lives the *pran* [life] of the gods: the external form of the image contains the form of the god who contains the goddess."[15] (Figure 13) It is precisely this image which, Pinney then shows, is cleverly reworked in a photographic montage produced by a small-town studio in central India. (Figure 14) Using complex printing techniques, this "marriage" photograph inserts a full-face portrait of the bride within a profile of the groom and then encloses both of those images within a larger

[13] Ashish Rajadhyaksha, "The Phalke Era: Conflict of Traditional Form and Modern Technology," in Tejaswini Niranjana, P. Sudhir, and Vivek Dhareshwar, eds, *Interrogating Modernity: Culture and Colonialism in India* (Calcutta: Seagull, 1993), pp. 47–82.

[14] Arvind Rajagopal, *Politics After Television: Religious Nationalism and the Reshaping of the Indian Public* (Cambridge: Cambridge University Press, 2001).

[15] Pinney, *Camera Indica*, pp. 116–18.

shadow profile of the groom. "The montage clearly replicates the calendar image of the *shivling . . .*"

It is clear that the modern technologies of print and photography, even as they penetrated deep into the everyday culture of ordinary people, did not mean the adoption of a realist visual aesthetic in the popular domain. Rather, as Pinney suggests with reference to the hugely popular lithograph images that have been produced since the late nineteenth century, the powers of Western realist art were mimicked and subverted into the "xeno-real"—"the form of colonially authorized realism that circulates outside its framework of origination: it is jettisoned into the colony, where it comes (primarily) to signify itself."[16] (Figure 15) As several recent exhibitions and studies of so-called bazaar prints and calendar art have shown, many elements of Western realist art were freely adopted in these popular prints on mythological, historical or social subjects, but emptied of their original meaning; there was no gesture of affiliation to any larger philosophical or aesthetic conception of "realism." (Figure 16) As Pinney explains: "Classicism and mythology supplied a system of references for the forms of their own idealized behaviour, whose translatability was dependent on their vacuity. In the xeno-real there is a double (and doubly productive) emptiness."[17]

Pinney has made one more point about the political significance of popular visual prints that is worth thinking about. The circulation of a large body of nationalist images suggests, he says, a rather different history from that described in the standard accounts of Indian nationalism drawn almost entirely from textual sources. First, the affective intensity of feeling evoked by the abstract idea of the nation seemed to be conveyed most powerfully by the visual representation of the nation as an actualized landscape.[18] Second, the most powerful image of the nationalist political struggle in the popular imagination was the depiction of armed revolutionaries (called "terrorists" by the British)

---

[16] Christopher Pinney, *Photos of the Gods: The Printed Image and Political Struggle in India* (Delhi: Oxford University Press, 2004), p. 31.

[17] Ibid., p. 32.

[18] This is also suggested by Sumathi Ramaswamy in her study of the cartographic representations of an imagined and lost Tamil homeland. Ramaswamy, *Lost Land of Lemuria: Fabulous Geographies, Catastrophic Histories* (Berkeley: University of California Press, 2004).

rather than the leaders of the non-violent mass movement.[19] (Figure 17) It is too early to pronounce on the validity of Pinney's specific hypotheses, but he has raised, it seems to me, a very important issue concerning the appropriate sources for the study of popular politics, especially in a country where most people do not read. Should visual sources be treated merely as providing illustrative supplements to a history constructed on the basis of the written or spoken word, or can they be allowed to rewrite that history?

But to return to the question I raised at the beginning of this chapter: do these photographs or prints qualify as art? Can we make judgements on their aesthetic quality? On what grounds? By which criteria?

Even though such extreme distinctions as that between a modern high aesthetic and non-modern popular tastes, or between Western and Indian ways of seeing, would be considered unacceptable in scholarly circles today, it is nevertheless noticeable that in explaining the distinctive features of popular viewing practices in India, even the most careful scholars tend to fall back upon some conceptual distinction that is supposed to lie behind and thereby explain the differences in practice. For instance, looking at practices of photographic portraiture in India, Pinney has suggested that the Western aesthetic concept that the visible external body is anchored in an invisible internal ground of character does not obtain in the popular domain in India. Rather, "the external body is freed from the constraints with which it is shackled in the Western tradition of painted portraiture."[20] Similarly, there is an influential body of literature on the popular Indian cinema which argues that the dominant conceptual framework that shapes its aesthetic modes is mythic-iconic, in contrast to the realist aesthetic of the Hollywood cinema.[21] Kajri Jain, in her valuable study of the production of calendar art or bazaar images, observes that the artists who design these iconic images of gods for the market themselves regard them as inferior art. But Jain attempts to redeem their aesthetic claim by

[19] Pinney, *Photos of the Gods*.

[20] Pinney, *Camera Indica*, p. 200.

[21] For instance, Ashish Rajadhyaksha, "The Phalke Era: Conflict of Traditional Form and Modern Technology;" Geeta Kapur. "Revelation and Doubt in *Sant Tukaram* and *Devi*," in Geeta Kapur, *When Was Modernism: Essays on Contemporary Cultural Practice in India* (New Delhi: Tulika, 2000), pp. 233–64.

suggesting that calendar images circulate in a different conceptual field of value from that of Western bourgeois art.[22]

The problem with this form of explanation is that popular visual practices are being understood in terms of certain essential conceptual structures that must, in the end, be defined by reference to textual sources, whether it is darshan or the significance of the icon or the notion of the *pran* [life] that inhabits a body or the social valuation of the gift, etc. The assumption is that practices are external manifestations of concepts and beliefs that constitute the system of meanings that define a culture. This view of culture has a hoary lineage in the human sciences, especially in anthropology, and Clifford Geertz is probably its most recent, distinguished, and sophisticated explicator. But I believe this approach inhibits rather than facilitates the critical understanding of contemporary popular culture.

Have recent scholars seriously attempted to make judgements, whether aesthetic or ethical-political, on the products of popular culture they have studied? We may turn to Pinney, whose work I have considered at length in this chapter. Speaking about the plethora of exotic backgrounds, supplied by painted backdrops or clever printing techniques in the studio, against which people choose to be photographed, Pinney says that they are "a space of exploration." There is also "the inventive posing that . . . is concerned with the transcendence and parody of social roles. The photographic studio becomes a place not for solemnization of the social but for the individual exploration of that which does not yet exist in the social world."[23] (Figure 18) Again, speaking of the "wedding collage" compositions of photograph and paint, he speaks of "the compacted and constructed dream world, set free from any arbitrary frame, that this local photographic technology makes possible. Released from its habitual chronotopic imprisonment, these photographic images conflate time and place, so that at least several temporally discrete moments come to coexist within the same fabulous space."[24] (Figure 19) The phrase that is repeated most often here is

---

[22] Kajri Jain, "More Than Meets the Eye: The Circulation of Images and the Embodiment of Value," in Sumathi Ramaswamy, ed., *Beyond Appearances? Visual Practices and Ideologies in Modern India* (New Delhi: Sage, 2003), pp. 33–70.

[23] Pinney, *Camera Indica*, p. 178.

[24] Ibid., p. 134.

"freedom"—freedom to explore, to invent, to subvert, to dream—in contrast to the prison-like confines of the realist conventions that come as a package with the Western technology of photography. This space of creative freedom, defined in contradistinction to the aesthetic norms of Western painting and photography, becomes the ground for making judgements about popular lithographs and photography in India. That is the space where they have recently gained a status as "popular art," as shown by the growing number of collections and exhibitions of such hitherto ignored images.[25]

The question is: are we justified in attributing the quality of art to these products of popular consumption because we have persuaded ourselves that they have been created under conditions of "freedom"? Are we not imposing notions of artistic creativity that have come from very different historical and philosophical lineages that we have, in fact, identified as unrelated and opposed to the aesthetic world of the popular? Is this the only way in which we can claim this domain of popular cultural production as worthy of aesthetic appreciation—by declaring that they are products of the creative freedom of the popular artist? I am reminded here of the passionate intervention by Johannes Fabian, the anthropologist of African popular culture who wrote about popular painting and music in contemporary Zaire (now the Democratic Republic of Congo): "there is no justification for using the concept of freedom quasi-logically, a priori, in distinguishing high from low, elite from popular culture. . . . Not mere exposure to power and oppression, but transformation of experience into communicable expressions, is at the origin of popular culture as resistance to colonial and postcolonial domination. . . . That freedom must exist for cultural creation to take place is, I believe, a position that needs to be maintained even if actual conditions in most postcolonial African countries, certainly in Zaire, seem to make it difficult to credit popular culture with much liberation. . . ."[26] The problems with this position are apparent from the very tortuousness of its formulation. Beginning

---

[25] Tapati Guha-Thakurta has made this point in *The Aesthetics of the Popular Print: Lithographs and Oleographs from 19th and 20th Century India* (Calcutta: Birla Academy of Art and Culture, 2006).

[26] Johannes Fabian, *Moments of Freedom: Anthropology and Popular Culture* (Charlottesville: University Press of Virginia, 1998), p. 18.

with an admirable gesture of refusal to restrict the concept of creative freedom to elite high culture, it ends up by declaring a dogmatic and metaphysical faith in the freedom of the popular artist, even if "actual conditions" indicate otherwise.

I wish to suggest a different method for approaching the question of artistic quality in the production of popular culture. This involves a move away from concepts and ideas to the *practices* of production and consumption. I do not insist that practices are external manifestations of concepts that constitute the structure of meanings that characterize a culture; rather, popular culture *consists* of practices. Of course, practices are shaped by institutional norms. Spaces for "creative freedom" may be available within a specific structure of norms; "freedom" may also lie in resisting those norms. In any case, the question of "freedom" here admits of no universal answer; its relevance and effect depend on specific, institutionally located, sets of practices.

The principal framework within which practices may be described and understood is, I propose, that of a *discipline*. A discipline is that set of authorized practices by which cultural products are made. It is, as Foucault has explained, a genealogically assembled set whose elements may have been drawn from a variety of sources. But within an identifiable institutional space of cultural production and consumption, a discipline will specify authorities and authorized practices, techniques and skills, modes of training, norms of excellence, forms of use of cultural products, and judgements of taste. Disciplines usually invoke a tradition that authorizes, through a memorialization of their origins, whether historical or mythical, the specific practices of cultural production and use. Moreover, as Talal Asad has pointed out with respect to the religious disciplines, the aesthetic or ethical quality of the product is not necessarily a function of the degree of "creative freedom" exercised by the practitioner; on the contrary, the more strict and rigorous the adherence to discipline, the more valued may be the outcome.[27]

The study of discipline in this sense is not unknown, whether in anthropology or in the specialized studies of arts and crafts. However, several features will be different in the study of the disciplines involved

---

[27] Talal Asad, *Genealogies of Religion: Discipline and Power in Christianity and Islam* (Baltimore: Johns Hopkins Press, 1993).

Fig. 12: Photolithograph, *c.*1920 (source: Pinney, *Camera Indica*)

Fig. 13: Calendar photo, 1983 (source: Pinney, *Camera Indica*)

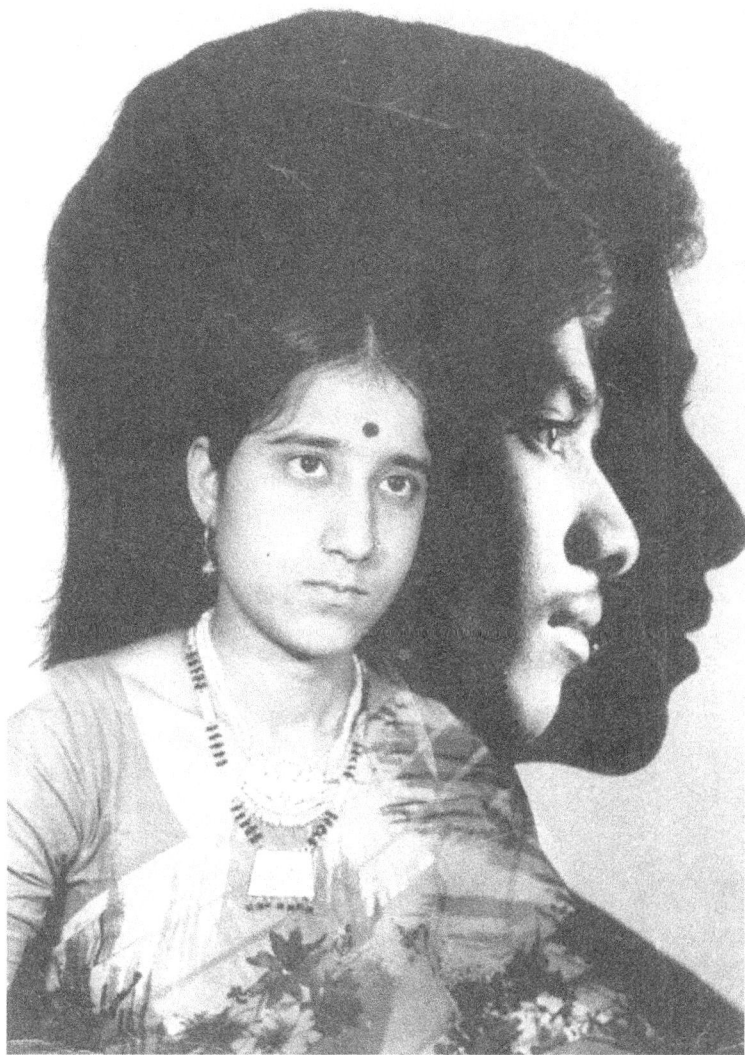

Fig. 14: Photo composition, 1980 (source: Pinney, *Camera Indica*)

Fig. 15: *Madan bhasma*, oleograph, Chorebagan Art Studio, Calcutta, *c.*1890
(source: CSSSC Archive)

Fig. 16: *Shivaji*, lithograph, Bharat Printing Works, Pune, *c.*1890
(source: CSSSC Archive)

शहीद भगत सिंह   ভারত মাতার মুক্তি সাধনায়   Shaheed Bhagat Singh

J. P. Co./R. 106   শহীদ ভগৎ সিং

Fig. 17: *Bhagat Singh, c.*1950, lithograph (source: Pinney, *Photos of the Gods*)

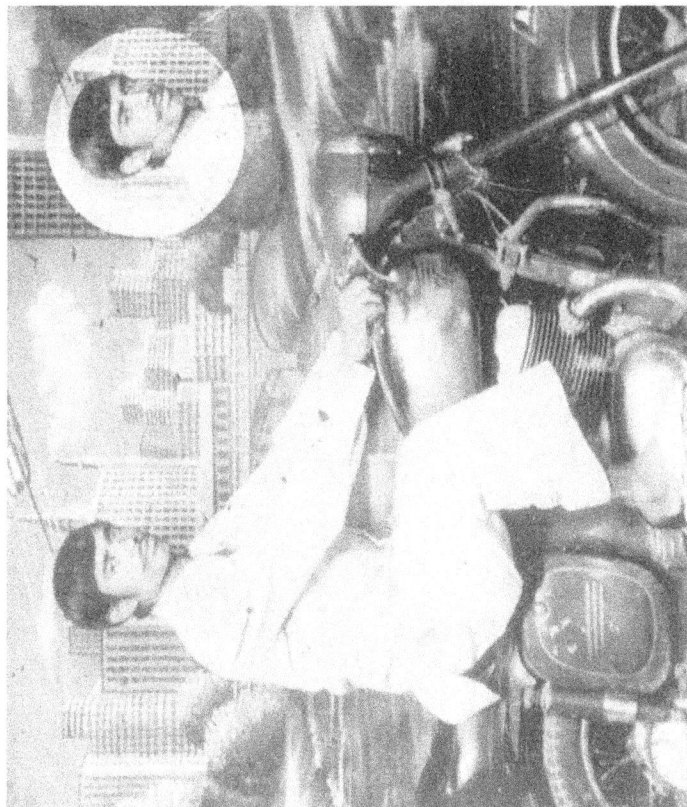

Fig. 18: *Man on a motorcycle, c.1983* (source: Pinney, *Camera Indica*)

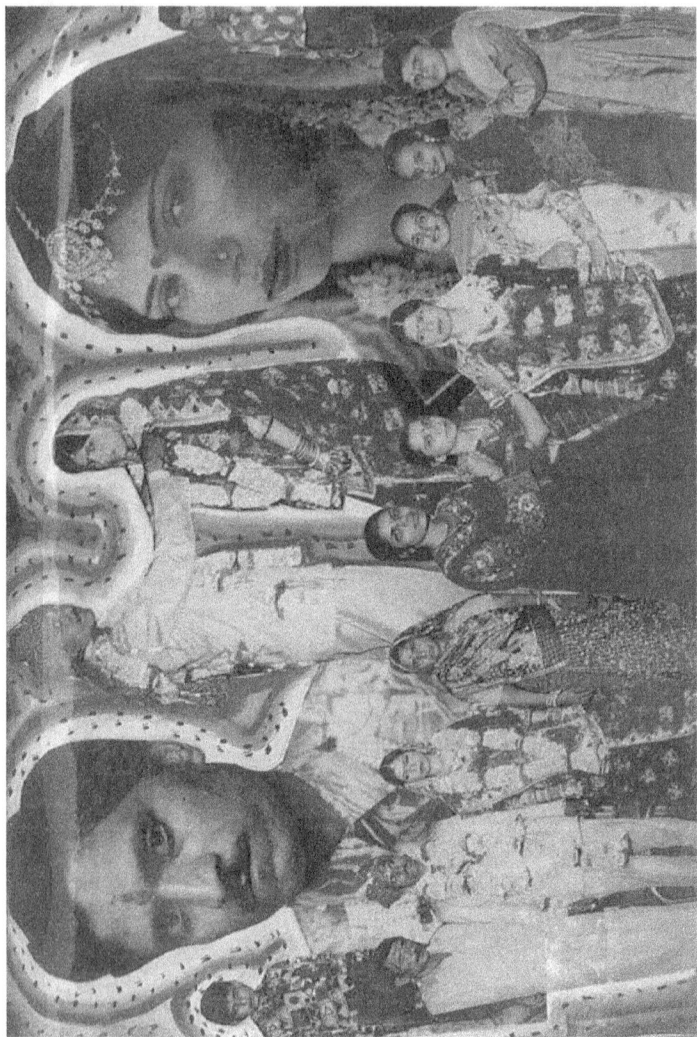

Fig. 19: Vijay Vyas, colour collage, 1996, photos, watercolour and ink (source: Pinney, *Camera Indica*)

Fig. 20: Golden barge at College Square, 2002 (source: CSSSC Archive)

Fig. 21: Temple façade made of broken gramophone records, 2002
(source: CSSSC Archive)

Fig. 22: Madhubani style pandal, 2002 (source: CSSSC Archive)

Fig. 23: Madhubani style Durga image, 2002 (source: CSSSC Archive)

Fig. 24: Titu Mir's fort at Babubagan, 2002 (source: CSSSC Archive)

Fig. 25: Mughal miniature style Durga image, 2002
(source: CSSSC Archive)

Fig. 26: Sanatan Dinda, Durga image in stone idol style, 2002
(source: CSSSC Archive)

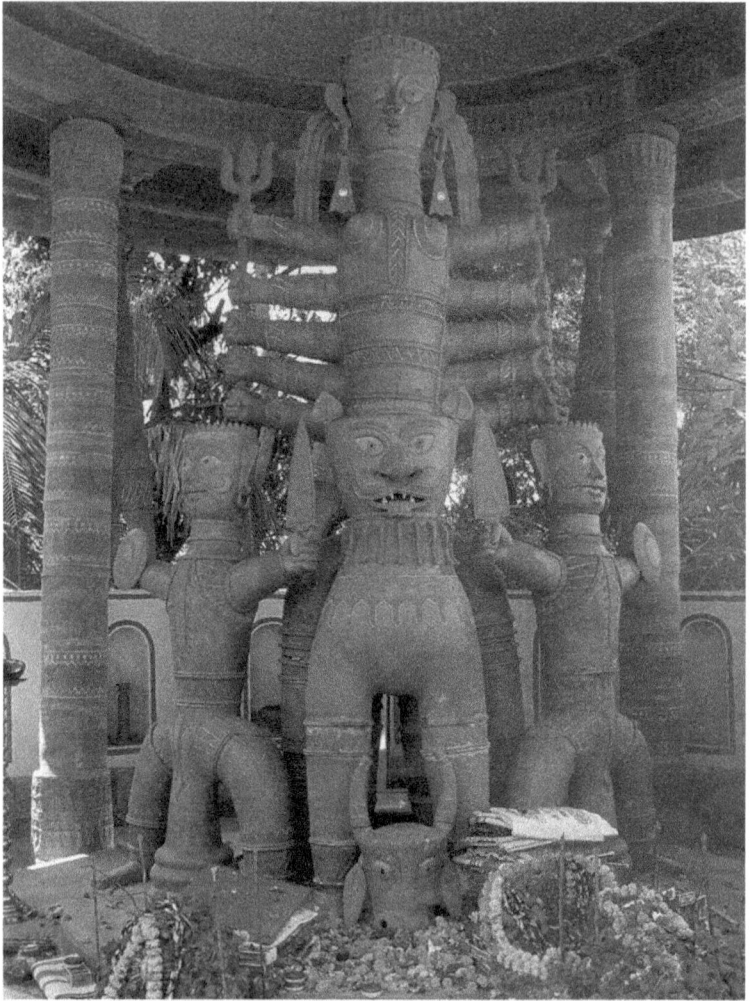

Fig. 27: Bhabatosh Sutar, Durga image in terracotta, 2003
(source: CSSSC Archive)

in contemporary popular cultural production. First, the usual assumption of an organic unity between the disciplines of cultural production and a community of users of culture must be abandoned. One must be prepared to find only a tenuous presence of such a community, or perhaps no community at all. The relation between producers and users of popular culture may be mediated by institutions such as the market or the media. Second, we must, I believe, stay away from the conservationist instinct of preserving the "dying arts and crafts." This effort has its place, and it may even make some difference to the real world of artisans and craftspeople. But it is not, I think, consistent with the method of investigating how disciplines of traditional artistic production have succeeded or failed to reinvent their practices to cope with the changing conditions of popular culture. Third, this must be a study of traditional disciplines in a process of change. The appropriate methods here would not be those of the old anthropology or studies of folk culture. Rather, one has to be more genealogical, identifying why and how specific elements of disciplinary practice are modified or abandoned and new ones adopted. No general framework of tradition versus modernity will work here. The question of the decline of old institutions and authorities and the emergence of new ones, as traditional disciplines innovate and reinvent themselves, will be a major topic of interest of these studies. Fourth, the criteria for making aesthetic judgements are to be found *within* the disciplines. This is unlikely to be a simple matter of identifying the norms and criteria that defined quality or taste in the traditional discipline, even though memories of such a tradition may continue to carry some weight in redefining quality and taste under the new conditions of popular culture. There will be contestations over authorities and norms, varying degrees of value attached to traditional skills and techniques, uncertainty about traditional methods of training, new evaluations of competence and virtuosity, search for new sources of patronage, appeals to a new "public" and, finally, an active engagement with the idea of novelty. All of this will make the field of aesthetic judgement on any particular site of popular cultural production a highly contested one. But that is not to say that distinctions and judgements are not being made on those sites, or that disciplinary practices, even if new ones, are not being imposed on both producers and users. By looking more closely at disciplines, rather than at underlying aesthetic concepts, we may, I am suggesting, find a way of making distinctions among the products of popular culture, and thus of providing a critique of the judgement of popular taste.[28]

Art in Popular Culture

I will use as my final example a range of cultural productions that come out of a single popular festival in the city of Calcutta. It is the annual Durga Puja which is held in autumn on the occasion of the ritual worship of the goddess Durga (let us use the word "worship" for puja, ignoring the difficulties of translation). Through the twentieth century, the Durga Puja has emerged as the single most important cultural festival of Calcutta. Principally, it takes the form of about a thousand community pujas held for five days in September or October in different neighbourhoods of the city. Around the community pujas is a celebration by millions involving clothes, fashion, food, tourism, music, theatre, and, most importantly for our purposes here, the mass viewing of Durga images in their specially constructed pavilions in each neighbourhood.[29] I am here drawing on the recent researches on the festival carried out at the Centre for Studies in Social Sciences, Calcutta, by a team led by the art historian Tapati Guha-Thakurta.[30] The huge variety of cultural productions associated with the Durga Puja gives us a chance to review several of the issues I have raised above concerning traditional disciplines, innovation, the loss and recovery of community, religion and art, the role of the market and the media, the distinction between artisans and artists, and above all the question of making aesthetic judgements in the field of popular culture.

I do not have the space here to elaborate on the religious significance and social history of the Durga Puja in Bengal, except to say that the current form of the urban community puja has developed in

[28] It is hardly necessary to acknowledge that I am here invoking Pierre Bourdieu's investigations into popular taste in *Distinction: A Social Critique of the Judgment of Taste*, tr. Richard Nice (Cambridge, Mass.: Harvard University Press, 1984). Clearly, new methods have to be invented to uncover the disciplinary sources of judgement of popular taste in countries such as India.

[29] Anjan Ghosh, "Durga Puja: A Consuming Passion," *Seminar*, 559 (March 2006).

[30] Tapati Guha-Thakurta, "From Spectacle to 'Art'," *Art India Magazine*, vol. 9, no. 3, pp. 34–56.

Calcutta over the last hundred years or so. It was originally funded by small contributions from residents of a neighbourhood, but in recent years the major funding appears to come from corporate advertisers. Although the religious significance of the worship of Durga is tied with the mythical story of the annihilation of the buffalo demon by the goddess of power, in its popular form it is strongly associated with the idea of the married daughter, accompanied by her children, paying a brief annual visit to her natal home. The traditional Durga idol is made of clay against a scaffolding of bamboo and straw, with clothes and ornaments of silk and tinsel. The idol has to be made anew every year and ritually immersed in water at the end of the four-day period of worship. Moreover, there are a host of specialized disciplines of both craft and performance traditionally associated with different aspects of the Durga puja and its accompanying celebrations, and it is these that have undergone the greatest transformations in recent years.

The most proximate dynamic shaping these changes is the emergence over the last four or five decades of a certain competitive spirit among the neighbourhood pujas in Calcutta. A mass public, consisting of no less than a few million people, both residents and visitors to the city, moving from one pavilion (called pandal) to another at all hours of night and day for four or five days, is the target of this competitive effort. The size of the crowds is the most obvious measure of which pandal is the most popular. But there are also more formal competitions with sponsors announcing awards adjudicated by celebrities. There is much pride attached to the drawing of crowds and winning of awards. The efforts of the organizing committees of the neighbourhood pujas in selecting artists and designers are, not surprisingly, guided by those motives.

The competitive spirit has led, at one level, to a privileging of the spectacle. Familiar street corners and parks are suddenly transformed, albeit only for a few days, into famous historical or archaeological sites, or perhaps into structures that have recently been in the news. Thus, one could find puja pandals that are replicas of an Assyrian palace of Mesopotamia or St Peter's of Rome or the Kremlin, or of the capsized *Titanic* (made in the year when the movie was released), or of the school of wizardry attended by Harry Potter, or (why not?) the burning World Trade Center towers. The sociologist Pradip Bose has described the space of the Durga puja in Calcutta as a perfect example of Foucault's "heterotopia" where the real blends with the impossibly unreal and where several incompatible elements can coexist.[31] (Figure 20) It is spectacle that moves crowds here rather than piety. Of course, Guha-Thakurta has made the point that the spectacle might create its own sacral aura, eliciting an engagement that is as intense as religious devotion. But, precisely because the spectacle produces its effect through the elements of novelty and the uncanny, it is difficult to relate this to our problem of the transformation of traditional disciplines. The matter is further compounded by the frequent resort to gimmicks in using the most unlikely material to erect giant pavilions to house the Durga image. Thus, one has seen pandals made of tea cups, broken gramophone records, biscuits, medicine bottles, and sugarcane fibre. (Figure 21) It is arguable that there is some technical virtuosity involved in using such outlandish material to build structures that are both functional and recognizable. If so, the question of what sorts of disciplinary skills are mobilized to produce these gimmicks might become an interesting topic for research. But as far as I know, no one has yet attempted to answer this question.

The most important part of Guha-Thakurta's work is her study of the so-called "art" or "theme" pujas. These images and pavilions attempt quite self-consciously to achieve a more elevated aesthetic effect. There are several types here. On the one hand, we have designers from middle-class backgrounds, frequently with formal art school training, who conceptualize a theme that defines the stylistic unity of the entire display and direct various craftspeople to execute the separate items. On the other hand, we have a new crop of artists from an artisanal background, usually with training in a traditional craft but with exposure to the world of the modern arts, sometimes even having an art school degree, who may collaborate with an art director or, at times, design and execute the entire display with his own team of craftspeople. For both these types, of course, we have teams of persons having specialized craft skills who work under the direction of the main designing team. The degree to which such craftspeople enjoy independent authority in their own field varies.

Let us look at some of the specific cases that Guha-Thakurta has described. One pandal was designed in the style of the well-known

---

[31] Pradip Kumar Bose, "Pujor kalkātār bikalpalok," *Bāromās* (1997).

Madhubani frescoes of Bihar, with a Durga image built in the traditional clay but matching the Madhubani style. (Figures 22 and 23) To clinch the claim of authenticity, an entire team of Madhubani men and women painters, representing the different caste groups with their distinct styles, was brought over from Bihar to paint the pavilion and indeed to exhibit their methods of work to the crowds during the course of the pujas. The design team for this pandal consisted of an art teacher who worked out the concept and an artist with a crafts background but with an art school degree who supervised the execution and built the Durga image. The traditional crafts theme has become quite popular in recent years.

But it is not only traditional arts and crafts from other places, presented with a claim of authenticity, that constitute new "themes" for the puja pavilions. Popular historical memory could also be invoked to endorse themes of current political interest. A particularly interesting theme a few years ago was that of inter-religious communal harmony, that being the year of the deadly massacres of Muslims in Gujarat. One pandal was designed as the bamboo fortress of Titu Mir, an early-nineteenth-century leader of a peasant rebellion against the British in Bengal. (Figure 24) The choice was particularly striking because Titu Mir was a fiery jihadi Muslim, inspired by the new Wahabi doctrine that had just reached Bengal from Hejaz through Delhi. He was the scourge of Hindu landlords and Muslim preachers accused of not being sufficiently orthodox. No one knows what his bamboo fortress looked like because, apart from a mention in the British official reports, there is no visual trace of it anywhere. But the choice of Titu Mir as the symbol of Hindu–Muslim accord, and the use of his imagined bamboo fortress as the site for the worship of a Hindu goddess, reflects a popular historical mythography in which, recalling Pinney's point, armed anti-colonial resistance trumps everything else. Another pandal that year had the Durga image done in the style of Mughal miniature paintings. (Figure 25) Yet another pavilion was modelled on the recently destroyed Bamiyan Buddhas of Afghanistan with Durga carrying flowers instead of weapons in her hands. The pavilions, we might say—as discussed in a previous chapter—were empty signifiers that could be filled, at that particular political conjuncture, with equivalential chains representing the popular content of inter-religious harmony.

So what is the role of religion here? Many of the familiar accoutrements of the traditional Durga puja have been dispensed with and entirely new elements, dictated by commercial or political motives, allowed entry. And yet there is always a core set of practices, involving the Durga idol and its worship, where prescribed religious ritual is followed. The method appears to be to demarcate a specific set of practices as subject to the exclusive direction of religious authorities, leaving other practices to be determined by other authorities. Thus, there is space available for intense religious piety, in the offering of puja to the goddess, for instance, or watching the ceremonies of arati involving ecstatic chanting, drumming and dance by trained practitioners. Other spaces, however, can be left open for spectacle and art.

One place where religion and art pull in different directions is around the status of the worshipped Durga image. Religious rules require that the idol be ritually thrown into water at the end of the puja. But some images now acquire enough of an aura as an art object to elicit proposals for preserving them in a museum. Sanatan Dinda, who grew up learning the traditional craft of idol-making but then took a degree from art school, is a professional modern artist in his own right. He makes Durga images in a distinctly modernist style but, despite attractive offers from buyers, has refused to sell them, insisting that the worshipped idol must be immersed in the river. (Figure 26) Bhabatosh Sutar, on the other hand, also with a crafts background and art school training, made a striking terracotta Durga image a few years ago which is now permanently displayed on the lawns of a luxury hotel in Calcutta. (Figure 27) There have been proposals to set up a park somewhere in the city to display Durga images that qualify as "art." Such museumization will require another set of debates and contests over the jurisdiction of religious authorities over popular cultural practices.

To return to the question of the traditional disciplines and their ability to adapt and innovate, an interesting example has been provided by Guha-Thakurta's study of two generations of a family of traditional clay-modellers. The father, Mohanbanshi Rudrapal, still operates from Kumartuli, the oldest and largest potter's quarter of Calcutta, using traditional designs and methods. His younger son, Pradip, works with his father but has a degree in fine arts from the prestigious Baroda school and is seeking to enter the "art" puja circuit.

The elder son, Sanatan, has broken off with his father and moved out of Kumartuli to set up his own studio and establish a brand of his own. Two factors seem to be relevant in this account of disciplinary innovation within a structure of inherited skills and training: first, the shift from one generation to the next and, second, exposure to a different disciplinary mode (in this case, art school training).

The crucial question is whether it is possible to make aesthetic distinctions and judgements of taste using criteria drawn from different, and possibly conflicting, disciplinary traditions. The judgements of modernist art will often conflict with the criteria of excellence used by the traditional idol-maker. Yet, as the Durga puja example shows, such conflicting judgements are actually being made in the field of popular cultural practices. The point to be emphasized here is one that the study of popular culture has made repeatedly in the last three decades, namely, that these contests and debates over cultural production are not resolved by disinterested philosophical analysis but by the acts of authorities and practitioners within fields of institutional power. Traditional disciplines have room for debates and change, albeit in varying degrees; whether they will adapt to new conditions or stagnate and die depends on the acts of the various authorities that decide on disciplinary practices. What the Durga puja example shows, I think, is a point I cited from Gramsci: here is a set of traditional popular practices that have become self-critical. They have not done so autonomously. On the contrary, they have innovated by responding to new opportunities and seeking new authorities drawn from very different disciplines.

It is in this context that it needs to be pointed out that the work of academic scholars of popular culture is already one of those new disciplinary authorities that are being invoked to authenticate and authorize these innovations in popular culture. No one can deny today the growing influence of the new work of scholarship on the popular visual arts or on different branches of the popular performing arts in countries like India. Such work is being drawn upon to open new institutional spaces of display and performance and to justify new practices. It is difficult in Western academic contexts to appreciate the weight and significance that is attached to scholarly opinion on these matters in the local vernacular circles of popular artistic production. When associated with scholars located in prestigious national and international institutions, such opinions can catapult local popular artists and their work into the zones of attention of the media and the market, those crucial mediating institutions that foster contemporary popular culture. It is not uncommon for such scholars to suddenly discover, often to their annoyance, that what they had written about some local popular festival or product or artist in a faraway scholarly journal was being quoted, not always faithfully, to advertise the product or to attract tourists. Like it or not, scholars of popular culture are being, and will be, mobilized in the partisan wars over changing aesthetic practices, In this sense, to return to the topic I introduced at the beginning of this chapter, the study of popular culture is already actually making a difference to at least some parts of the real world of culture, even if the effects have not always been intended. My plea is for such studies to become aware of this role and to be both more self-consciously critical and responsible in their engagement with the changing cultures of the people.

III

Democracy

9

Community and Capital

Community in the West

I must confess that when the debate raged in Anglo-American academic circles some thirty years ago between liberal individualists and communitarians, I found little in it to sustain my interest. It seemed to me an utterly provincial debate, repetitious and largely predictable in its arguments, playing out all over again a set of confrontations with which students of Western political philosophy in the rest of the world had been familiar for at least a hundred years. Today, I think I was perhaps a little too impatient. Had I not been so dismissive of the significance of the debate for the future advance of political theory, I might have noticed then, as I do now, that in rehearsing once more the fundamental antinomies of political theory in the West, the debate was in fact pointing to some of the ways in which practices of modern politics in non-Western countries might be theorized and perhaps even institutionalized.

I will not spend time here going over the various arguments and counterarguments of this debate, on which much has been written.[1] Let me come straight to the point most relevant for my discussion. The communitarian attack on liberal individualism had two prongs—one, methodological, and the other, normative. From the methodological angle, the communitarians argued that the image of the individual self as constructed by liberal theorists was false. Individuals were not, as liberals would have it, sovereign subjects, unencumbered by involuntary

---

[1] Two convenient selections that give a fair sampling of these arguments are Michael Sandel, ed., *Liberalism and its Critics* (New York: New York University Press, 1984), and Shlomo Avineri and Avner de-Shalit, eds, *Communitarianism and Individualism* (Oxford: Oxford University Press, 1992).

obligations, freely choosing between available options on the basis of their individual preferences. On the contrary, those preferences were shaped by a network of social attachments into which people were born; not all attachments were freely chosen. The very constitution of the individual self became a false abstraction if it was removed from the actual social circumstances that provided the cultural and moral resources with which individual wills were formed.

Arguing from the normative angle, communitarians charged that by constructing the individual self as one unencumbered by prior social attachments, the liberal theorist had emptied the idea of political obligation of all genuine moral content. If one's ties with the community in which one was born had no intrinsic moral value, how would the liberal individualist explain why people were so often prepared to make sacrifices for their family or kin or ethnic group or country? More generally, communitarians argued, individuals needed the community to give moral meaning to their lives; even personal autonomy was more satisfactorily achieved within the community than outside it. Above all, communitarians were unprepared to accept the liberal premise that the protection of individual freedom required that considerations of right must have priority over questions of the common good. The latter, they insisted, were at the very heart of modern participatory politics, and liberal attempts to constrain and devalue them as something potentially divisive and dangerous had only laid the ground for widespread apathy among citizens and manipulative politics by powerful organized interests in most liberal democracies of the West.

The reply of the liberal individualists to the methodological criticism of the communitarians was that the latter's image of the self as one shaped by the experience of life in a community could well be true, but this was only a particular theoretical position designed to make a particular case about the common good. There were several other contending positions on the common good and so deep were the divisions between them that there could not be any general consensus in society on these questions. The liberal argument was that the only situation in which all these contending views could get an equal and fair chance to represent themselves was one in which the procedures were neutral between individuals. This was the basis for the methodological claims of liberal individualism.

On the moral plane too, the liberal individualists did not altogether reject the importance of community for individual lives. Some agreed that community was a need; others argued that the goals of community could be realized even in a liberal society. Their main concern was that by undermining the liberal system of rights and the liberal policy of neutrality on questions of the common good, communitarians were opening the door to majoritarian intolerance, the perpetuation of conservative beliefs and practices, and a potentially tyrannical insistence on conformism.

One feature of this debate that particularly struck me was the narrow and impoverished concept of community that was being employed on both sides. Some communitarian theorists—Alasdair MacIntyre and Michael Sandel, in particular—talked about family and neighbourhood as primary attachments that served to locate individual selves within the community.[2] But others, both liberals and communitarians, strongly objected to placing so much value on small group attachments that flaunt the banner of "tradition;" these solidarities, they said, were more often than not the means through which socially conservative, patriarchal, and illiberal practices were maintained and transmitted. There have also been movements, in political writing as well as in activism, for community-based participatory politics in local neighbourhoods, both urban and rural, in various countries of Europe and North America. These movements have been inspired by populist or anarchist ideologies of both left and right wing varieties. One of their principal characteristics, however, has been their marginality, often a preferred marginality, to the main institutions and practices of political life in those countries.

Looking back on the liberal–communitarian debate, the only form of the community that seems to have found a large measure of approval was the political community of the nation. Michael Walzer argued that the nation-state was the one community which could give every person within a certain territory the same status as citizen and also satisfy every person's need to participate in the social distribution of goods.[3] This gave rise to charges that, by emphasizing uniform citizenship, Walzer was implicitly arguing against immigration and cultural diversity within the nation. David Miller, who has also attempted to construct a theory of socialist politics in industrially advanced Western democracies, argued,

---

[2] Alasdair MacIntyre, *After Virtue: A Study in Moral Theory* (Notre Dame, Indiana: University of Notre Dame Press, 1984); Michael J. Sandel, *Liberalism and the Limits of Justice* (Cambridge: Cambridge University Press, 1982).

[3] Michael Walzer, *Spheres of Justice* (New York: Basic Books, 1983).

like Walzer, that the aspirations of community were most feasibly satisfied in the citizens' membership of a nation.[4]

It would appear then that Western political theory does not deny the empirical fact that most individuals, even in industrially advanced liberal democracies, lead their lives within an inherited network of social attachments that could be described as community. It also recognizes to a large extent that the community fulfils a certain moral condition for an effective and satisfying sense of participation by people in a social collective. Nevertheless, there is a strong feeling that not all communities are worthy of approval in modern political life. In particular, attachments that seem to emphasize the inherited, the primordial, the parochial, or the traditional are regarded by most theorists as smacking of conservative and intolerant practices and hence as inimical to the values of modern citizenship. The political community that seems to find the largest measure of approval is the modern nation that grants equality and freedom to all citizens irrespective of biological or cultural difference. But in this respect, too, there is a recent spate of criticism that attacks the idea of the nation as inherently intolerant, patriarchal, and suspicious of diversity and which argues that the time has come to develop post-national forms of political solidarity. This is an interesting development, but I will postpone discussion of it to a later chapter.

Community in the East

Turning to the idea of community in the non-Western parts of the world, one notices a similar opposition in most of the theoretical literature between community as the relic of pre-modern tradition and large, universalist, and impersonal political identities as the hallmark of modernity. Guided by this modernizing propensity, much of the recent history of non-Western societies has been written as a progressive narrative of the evolution from small, local, and primordial community attachments to large, secular solidarities such as that of the nation. In the era of colonial rule, colonial writings usually described these societies as a collection of backward *gemeinschaften* lacking the internal dynamic to transform themselves into modern industrial nations. Nationalist thinkers challenged the assumption of historical incapacity but agreed that their own

[4] David Miller, *Market, State and Community* (Oxford: Oxford University Press, 1989).

project was to overcome the numerous community attachments and build up the nation as the most powerful and legitimate claimant for political loyalty.

There is, however, an interesting twist to the way in which this nationalist project of modernity was formulated as one that was different from Western modernity. While non-Western nationalists agreed that many of the traditional institutions and practices in their societies needed to be thoroughly changed for them to become modern, they also insisted that there were several elements in their tradition that were distinctively national, different from the Western, but nevertheless entirely consistent with the modern. Borrowing the categories of Orientalist or colonial thought, they frequently posed this difference as one between Western materialism, individualism, and disregard for traditional values on the one hand, and on the other Eastern spiritualism, community solidarity, and respect for tradition. In doing this, nationalist writers picked out the liberal individualist strand in modern social theory as the one most characteristic of the West and often exaggerated its features to the point of caricature. But in posing the contrast between individualism in the West and communitarian values in the East, and insisting that the latter represented a better, or at least more appropriate, version of modernity for non-Western countries, nationalist thinking in effect played out the same arguments that we encountered in the liberal–communitarian debate. Indeed, one still hears these arguments as part of the official ideologies of many Asian and African states—arguments that are sometimes used with complete cynicism to defend authoritarian regimes and policies. It should be obvious, therefore, that having been born in an intellectual climate in which these arguments were the staple of everyday conversation, I found little in the debate of the 1980s that could hold my attention.

The nationalist posing of the question as one between Western individualism and Eastern communitarianism did not provide any new theoretical answers regarding the place of community in modern political life. On the contrary, just as there were, among non-Western nationalists, advocates of community attachments as the repository of social solidarity, moral value, and national tradition, so were there critics who condemned those attachments as signs of parochial backwardness, feudal and patriarchal bondage, and the failure of the nation to attain the true heights of modern political association. The theoretical terms had been set by the categories of Western social theory; apparently, all that non-Western thinkers could do was fill up those categories with a different cultural content and then play out the same arguments in a different national arena.

I could give many examples from the history of modern political thinking in India. The setting up of the contrast between individualism in the West and community in the East is as old as modern Indian nationalism. When Indian travellers visited England in the late nineteenth century, they marvelled at the achievements of Western science and technology and fervently wished to emulate them in their own countries. But they were also appalled by the conditions in which the poor lived in the industrial cities and were convinced that this could never happen in India, where community ties would ensure that not even the poorest were reduced to such a degraded state. The contrast was present in the more basic dichotomy between Western materialism and Eastern spiritualism which was central to the construction of non-Western nationalist ideology. Western materialism was easily connected to an individualist way of life and criticized for its lack of regard for social obligations, mutual dependence, and the solidarity of the social whole. This limitation of Western modernity was sought to be rectified by what was claimed to be the spiritual aspect of culture in which the Eastern traditions of community life were said to hold out many lessons for the modern world. We encountered some of these arguments in our discussion of Rabindranath Tagore's views on the relevance of the *samāj* for modern India.

In the history of Indian politics, Gandhi's intervention in the 1920s produced one of the most remarkable trends in both political thinking and activism that extended the possibilities of this argument to its limits. In recent years, Ashis Nandy has reworked the Gandhian position with much ingenuity. His principal argument is that, for more than a hundred years, with the advance of nationalism and the institutions of the modern state, there has occurred in countries such as India a tussle between the forces of modern individualism and those of traditional primordialities. What is highlighted in liberal economic and political theory is the bright side of modern individualism with its emphasis on the rapid creation of wealth and general prosperity, and the free flowering of the individual personality. What is ignored is the underside of modern individualism— the callous impersonality and massification of market-driven societies that destroy age-old institutions of sociability and community living without putting anything in their place. Contrary to the beliefs of the modernizers, traditional community structures are not simple and inflexible: primordialities are multilayered, the self is open-ended, adjustment and compromise are ethical norms. Left to themselves, Nandy argues, these traditional community structures have more effective civilizational resources than the institutions of the modern state to resolve disputes, tolerate difference, and allow for the development of a better adjusted and more accommodative personality. The crucial institutions here are those that belong to the "little traditions" of local community life which are the products of many centuries of coping with social change. The difficulty is that the ruling elites in non-Western countries have increasingly surrendered to the intellectual and procedural sway of the modern state and used its capacity for the efficient deployment of force to break down the supposedly retrograde and parochial institutions of traditional community life. At this time, Nandy thinks, the odds are overwhelmingly stacked against the little traditions as the modern nation continues to be built "on the ruins of one's civilizational selfhood;" the community, if not defeated, "is certainly in decline."[5]

The defence of community institutions in Gandhian thinking has had a fair degree of influence on movements of resistance by weak and marginalized sections of the people threatened by the onward march of modernization. In particular, its emphasis on indigenous cultural modes of collective action has encouraged the development of many innovative forms of campaign and mobilization even in the arena of modern political organizations. The mass movements of the Indian National Congress under the leadership of Gandhi in the last three decades of British colonial rule are well-known examples.[6] But similar examples of political mobilization shaped by indigenous cultural forms that are quite different from those made familiar by the history of modern politics in the West

[5] The quoted phrases are from Ashis Nandy *et al.*, *Creating a Nationality: The Ramjanmabhumi Movement and Fear of the Self* (Delhi: Oxford University Press, 1995), pp. xi, 203. I have given here a summary of Nandy's argument insofar as it is relevant for our present discussion. Nandy's writings, proceeding from a "modified Gandhian position," cover a wide variety of subjects. See, for instance, the following: *The Intimate Enemy: Loss and Recovery of Self under Colonialism* (Delhi: Oxford University Press, 1983); *Traditions, Tyranny and Utopias: Essays in the Politics of Awareness* (Delhi: Oxford University Press, 1987); *The Savage Freud and Other Essays on Possible and Retrievable Selves* (Delhi: Oxford University Press, 1995); "The Political Culture of the Indian State," *Daedalus*, 118, 4 (Fall 1989), pp. 1–26.

[6] An early attempt to theorize the Gandhian appeal to "traditional politics" within the history of modern political institutions is Lloyd D. Rudolph and Susanne H. Rudolph, *The Modernity of Tradition: Political Development in India* (Chicago: University of Chicago Press, 1967).

can be found in many countries of Asia and Africa in both colonial and postcolonial periods. These examples constitute essential material for a history of the domestication of the modern state in non-Western societies.

In theoretical terms, however, I am not persuaded that arguments of the Gandhian type, including their recent modified versions such as those proposed by Nandy, can make any contribution that could take the debate between individualism and communitarianism beyond the apparent impasse in which it has found itself in Western political theory. The identification of all modern institutions of state and politics with the ideology of Western individualism and their conflict with the traditional communities of the East collapses the opposition once more into the familiar terms of modernity versus traditionalism, with the exception that this time it is tradition and primordiality which are privileged over modernity. True, the Gandhian position has been able to gain considerable tactical leverage in its struggles against the depredations of the modernizing state by placing itself outside the intellectual and institutional arena of modernity. But since it refuses to acknowledge its own role as a constituent part of the politics engendered and ordered by the presence of the modern state in non-Western societies, it chooses to end every argument with a stubborn gesture of rejecting the modern state altogether. By doing this, it also refuses to make the unique experiences of modern politics in the non-Western world a constituent part of the task of rethinking modern political theory itself.

Capital and Community

That is the task which, I think, faces the non-Western political theorist: to find an adequate conceptual language to describe the non-Western career of the modern state not as a distortion or lack, which is what inevitably happens in a modernization narrative, but as the history of a different sequence of modernity that varies in its consequence from the normative practices and institutions recommended by Western political theory. But before I come to the implications of this task, I need to dwell a little on that other lack—the incomplete universalism of modern political theory.

In an earlier work, I have attempted to state what I think is the main reason for the poor theorization of the concept of community in modern social thought.[7] Western political theory since the Enlightenment has been organized around the idea of the free and equal individual as

[7] Partha Chatterjee, "A Response to Taylor's Modes of Civil Society," *Public*

the locus of productive energy, subjective rights, and cultural creativity in modern society. The power of this abstract idea has been accompanied by the equally powerful historical process of the dismantling of feudal as well as absolutist institutions in Western Europe, and the release of productive capital and productive labour on an unprecedented scale. The conceptual device of abstract liberty and equality which gave shape to the universal rights of the citizen was crucial not only for undermining pre-capitalist practices that restricted individual mobility and choice to traditional confines defined by birth and status but also, as the young Marx noted a hundred and fifty years ago, for separating the abstract domain of Right from the actual domain of life in civil society.[8] In legal-political theory, the rights of the citizen were unrestricted by race, religion, ethnicity or class (by the early twentieth century, the same rights would also be made available to women), but this did not mean the abolition of actual distinctions between men (and women) in civil society. Rather, the universalism of the theory of rights both presupposed and enabled a new ordering of power relations in society based precisely on those distinctions of class, race, religion, gender, etc. At the same time, the emancipatory promise held out by the idea of universal equal rights has acted as a constant source of theoretical critique of actual civil society in the last two centuries and has propelled numerous struggles to change unequal and unjust social differences of race, religion, ethnicity, class, and gender.

In these transactions between theory and actuality, community attachments have been seen as belonging to the mundane lives of actual civil societies—obdurate remnants of their pre-capitalist pasts or practical instruments for managing social differences on the ground. They have been regarded as objects of inquiry by empirical sociologists, not of philosophical speculation by political theorists. In the mirror of theory, community attachments have always appeared as restrictions on universal citizenship as well as on the universality of capital. To the extent that the universality of the state has been limited by the existence of nations (that is to say, the universality of the state and of capital has had to reveal

---

Culture, 3, 1 (Fall 1990), pp. 119–32; *The Nation and Its Fragments: Colonial and Postcolonial Histories* (Princeton: Princeton University Press, 1993), ch. 11.

[8] See, especially, Karl Marx, "On the Jewish Question," (1843) in Karl Marx and Frederick Engels, *Collected Works*, vol. 3 (Moscow: Progress Publishers, 1975), pp. 146–74.

itself in the existence of many nation-states and many national econo-mies), the nation is the only form of community that has sometimes found a place, and that too a fairly marginal one, in the high theory of political obligation.

As a matter of fact, the emergence of mass democracies in the ad-vanced industrial countries of the West in the twentieth century has produced a new distinction between the domain of theory built around the idea of the citizen and the domain of policy inhabited not by citizens but by populations. Unlike the concept of the citizen, as I have explained in an earlier chapter, the concept of population is wholly descriptive and empirical: it does not carry a normative burden. Populations are identi-fiable, classifiable, and describable by empirical or behavioural criteria, and are amenable to statistical techniques such as censuses and sample surveys. Unlike the citizen who carries the ethical connotation of partici-pation in the sovereignty of the state, the concept of population makes available to government functionaries a set of rationally manipulable instruments for reaching large sections of the inhabitants of a country as the targets of their "policies"—economic policy, administrative policy, law, and even political mobilization. Indeed, as Foucault has pointed out, a major characteristic of the contemporary regime of power is a certain "governmentalization of the state."[9] This regime secures legitimacy not by the participation of citizens in matters of state but by claiming to provide for the well being of the population. Its mode of reasoning is not deliberative openness but rather an instrumental notion of costs and benefits. Its apparatus is not the republican assembly but an elaborate network of surveillance through which information is collected on every aspect of the life of the population to be looked after. It is not surprising that, in the course of the present century, ideas of participatory citizenship that were so much a part of the Enlightenment notion of politics have fast retreated before the triumphant advance of governmental technologies promising to deliver more well being to more people at less cost. Indeed, one might say that the actual political history of capital has long spilled over the normative confines of liberal political theory to go out and con-quer the world through its governmental technologies.

In the countries of Asia and Africa, where the career of the modern state

[9] See, in particular, Michel Foucault, "Governmentality," in Foucault, *Power*, ed. James D. Faubion (New York: New Press, 2000), pp. 201–22.

has been foreshortened, ideas of republican citizenship have sometimes accompanied the politics of national liberation. But without exception, they have been overtaken by the developmental state which has promised to end poverty and backwardness by adopting appropriate policies of economic growth and social reform. With varying degrees of success, and in some cases with disastrous failure, postcolonial states have deployed the latest governmental technologies to promote the well being of their populations, often prompted and aided by international and non-governmental organizations. In adopting these technical strategies of modernization and development, communities have often entered the field of knowledge about populations—as convenient descriptive categories for classifying groups of people into suitable targets for administrative, legal, economic, and electoral policy. In many cases, classificatory criteria used by colonial governmental regimes have continued into the postcolonial era, shaping the forms of both political demands and developmental policy. Thus, caste and religion in India, ethnic groups in South East Asia, and tribes in Africa have remained the dominant criteria for identifying communities among the population as objects of policy. So much so that a huge ethnographic survey undertaken by a government agency in India has actually identified and described a total of exactly 4635 communities that are supposed to comprise its population.[10]

I am convinced that the attempt by modern governmental technologies to classify populations into determinate and enumerable communities is a telling sign of the poverty of modern social theory. It is a commonplace in the descriptive ethnography of the non-Western world to find that the community is contextually defined, that its boundaries are fuzzy, that a particular community identification does not exhaust the various layers of selfhood of a person, that it makes little sense to ask a community member how many of them there are in the world.[11] And yet, it is this contextuality and fuzziness that legal-administrative classifications and statistical techniques of enumeration must erase in order to make populations amenable to governmental policy. If a policy is meant

[10] K. Suresh Singh, ed., *People of India*, 43 vols (Calcutta: Anthropological Survey of India, 1995–).

[11] The point has been well made in Sudipta Kaviraj, "The Imaginary Institution of India," in Partha Chatterjee and Gyanendra Pandey, eds, *Subaltern Studies VII* (Delhi: Oxford University Press, 1992), pp. 1–39.

to benefit, let us say, poor people from a backward caste in India, both the criterion of poverty and that of backward-casteness must be unambiguously defined and made evident by governmental verification. What is lost in the process is the richness of meaning and the strategic flexibility afforded by the cultural repertoire of a people to handle social differences. This is the loss that writers such as Nandy bemoan. As I have said before, contemporary technologies of government regard communities as so much demographic material, to be manipulated instrumentally. They are not objects of philosophical or moral inquiry. In theory—to put it, if I may, in a nutshell—capital and community are antithetical.

The contradiction was highlighted in an interesting way in the 1990s' discussions over the work of Robert Putnam and his associates on governmental performance in northern and southern Italy.[12] Two concepts were proposed by Putnam to explain why governments seem to work better in certain regions of northern Italy. These concepts are civic community and social capital. In a civic community, according to Putnam, citizens have equal rights and obligations, participate actively in public affairs as well as in a dense network of civic associations, and bear feelings of respect, trust, and tolerance towards their fellow citizens. Where civic community is strongly rooted, democratic government tends to perform better. Why? Because civic community fosters the creation of social capital. Social capital, says Putnam following a suggestion by James Coleman, consists of organizational features such as trust, norms of reciprocity, and networks of civic engagement that facilitate coordinated social action.[13] Unlike conventional capital which is ordinarily a private good, social capital is a public good. It is not the personal property of those who benefit from it. Social capital, unlike other forms of capital, is mainly produced as a byproduct of other social activities. Thus, the more intensive the network of civic associations engaged in various collective activities and the stronger the norms of reciprocity between the members of these associations, the greater the stock of social capital. Indeed, social capital is inculcated above all through socialization and civic education as well as by collective sanctions.

[12] Robert D. Putnam, Robert Leonardi, and Raffaella Y. Nanetti, *Making Democracy Work: Civic Traditions in Modern Italy* (Princeton: Princeton University Press, 1993).

[13] James S. Coleman, *Foundations of Social Theory* (Cambridge, Mass.: Harvard University Press, 1990).

The examples Putnam cites of the working of social capital are, however, drawn from studies of rotating credit arrangements among peasants or urban workers in Indonesia, Nigeria, and Mexico. The chief characteristic of these institutions is that they are able to create credit mechanisms in situations where conventional credit markets based on capitalist calculations cannot work. This is done, Putnam says, by pledging social capital, i.e. the stock of mutual trust built up through other social interactions and networks. Thus, Javanese peasants operate local mechanisms of mutual help based on traditional but concrete practices of interdependence in the exchange of labour, capital, and goods in a variety of social activities. The urban poor in Mexico City have developed a whole array of credit associations based on reciprocity and mutual trust. These institutions are much more than merely economic; they are mechanisms that strengthen the solidarity of the community.

It seems to me that the concept of community is being invoked here to supply what does not properly belong to the concept of capital. The examples of credit associations are particularly telling. Anyone familiar with the ethnographic literature on non-Western agrarian or nomadic-pastoral societies will immediately recognize how deeply these exchange practices are implicated in the entire structure of material interaction and symbolic meaning that characterize those societies. Such practices would be integral elements of the "traditional" lives of those communities and, more often than not, they are likely to be destroyed by the advance of "modern" institutions of capitalist production and exchange. When they survive, they do so at the margins of the modernized sectors, among populations and in activities that have still not been fully absorbed into the network of capital. Why are these examples that belong to the older communitarian histories of non-Western societies being mobilized here in the cause of political institutions in modern Western democracies?

My answer is that by adding "social" to capital and making that the motive force of "civic" community, capital is being made to do what it has always failed to do, namely, ground the social institutions of a modern capitalist economy in community. The description of the civic community as presented by Putnam is a restatement of the manifold virtues of participatory citizenship to which the communitarian theorists still sing their praises. Putnam's attempt is to show that a culture of active citizenship of this kind is *empirically* associated with well-functioning democratic systems. But in trying to establish this connection in theoretical terms, he is led, it seems to me, into the same impasse where the liberal–communitarian debate has been stuck. To explain why the civic community only exists in some regions of northern Italy and not in others, Putnam has to move into a historical investigation going back to the thirteenth century. He must then say that the civic community can only function where it already exists as a part of historical tradition. On the other hand, the examples he cites of the working of social capital come from traditions that belong to places—Indonesia (then under Suharto's military rule), Nigeria, and Mexico—which not even the most starry-eyed modernization theorist would name as havens of good democratic governance. In other words, while modern Western political institutions appear to need a grounding in community in order to be successful, the only contemporary examples through which community can be made sense of have to be borrowed from non-modern and non-Western cultural traditions. It is not surprising, therefore, that Putnam's work has come under fire from critics who have found it unduly pessimistic, because it suggests that good democratic government cannot be established by institutional modernization unless civic community already exists as part of the historical tradition. He has also been criticized for being unduly romantic in his portrayal of the associational life of the community. And finally, it has been pointed out that, contrary to Putnam's rosy picture, community life is usually conservative and resistant to change.[14] Traditionalism, romanticism, conservatism: all of these, one will remember, were familiar epithets used by liberal individualists against the communitarians. Evidently, we have not moved even a single step ahead of that debate.

Community and New Institutions of the State

To give a sense of what political theory must cope with in countries where the history of the modern state is short, let me present some findings of a study of community-formation among poor migrants in an Indian city.[15] These migrants form a group of about 1500 people living in a row

[14] All these criticisms have been made in an otherwise highly appreciative review by Margaret Levi, "Social and Unsocial Capital: A Review Essay of Robert Putnam's *Making Democracy Work*," *Politics and Society*, 24, 1 (March 1996), pp. 45–55.

[15] I have discussed this, and similar, cases at greater length in my book *The Politics*

of shanties perilously close to a railway track on the south-eastern fringes of Calcutta. The land on which they have built their shacks belong to the state-owned railways. They are, therefore, illegal squatters on public land. The settlement has grown here since the early 1950s. The migrants have come from various rural areas of southern Bengal, and some from Bangladesh. Since they migrated from different places at different times, the settlers had no prior network of attachments given to them as a collective. The community, such as it exists here, was built from scratch.

The overwhelming reason why they have acted as a collective is the very survival of their habitation. Ever since the emergence of the settlement some sixty years ago, there have been periodic attempts by the railway authorities to evict them. These attempts have been resisted, as the settlers will proudly tell a visitor, by the concerted efforts of the community as a whole. The most common metaphor by which the settlers speak about their community is that of a family. They do not talk of the shared interests of the members of an association, but of the more compelling bonds of a shared kinship. Nevertheless, there are concrete associational forms through which the collective functions. The most important of these is a welfare association which has its own office where it runs a small library and a medical clinic and which acts as the centre of community activity. It organizes sports and recreation activities and community festivals (including religious ones) and resolves disputes (even family disputes). It is also the body through which the community negotiates with the outside world—with government agencies such as the railways, the police, and the municipal authorities, with voluntary agencies offering welfare and developmental services, with political parties and leaders.

But apart from this formal body, there are other networks of community support that are vital in securing work or financial help. Many men here work as unskilled labourers in the construction business and depend on mutual contacts to find work. Most women in the settlement work as domestic help in middle-class houses in the neighbourhood for which again mutual references are important. Caste and village networks are sometimes activated for negotiating marriages, but everyone agrees that these obligations are much less stringent here than in the village. Although all members of the settlement see themselves as poor labourers, some

of the Governed: Reflections on Popular Politics in Most of the World (New York: Columbia University Press, 2004).

are less poor than others, and in fact some live as tenants in rooms let out by those who originally built the shacks. Most are unhappy with the conditions in which they live in the settlement and would love to move out. A few who have had the chance have indeed moved to other places in the city. But most stay on, struggling collectively "as a single family," desperately clinging on to their uncertain status as illegal squatters.

There are several conceptual problems raised by these findings. First, it is difficult to think of the collective form evolved by the settlers as a civic association. The association itself springs from a collective violation of property laws and civic regulations. The state cannot recognize the rationale for the association's existence as having the same validity as that of other economic and cultural associations of citizens pursuing more legitimate objectives. On the other hand, given the fact that this is only one of numerous other groups of population in Indian cities whose very livelihood or habitation is premised on violations of state law and civic regulations, the state cannot altogether ignore the collective claims of the association in making its own policies. Thus, state agencies such as the police or the railways and non-governmental development agencies deal with the collective body of squatters not as a body of citizens but as convenient instruments for the administration of welfare to marginal and underprivileged population groups.

Second, although the squatters accept that their occupation of public land is both illegal and contrary to the requirements of good civic life, they make a claim to a habitation and a livelihood as a matter of right. State agencies, on the other hand, are prepared to concede that this claim has a moral force that should be borne in mind when carrying out welfare policies but are strongly opposed to recognizing it as a justiciable right since, given the paucity of resources at the disposal of the state, it cannot be effectively delivered to the whole population of the country. Since places of residence and sources of livelihood are likely to remain in short supply in the foreseeable future, a general and principled recognition of the claim, as opposed to a contextual and instrumental one, say state officials, would only act as an invitation to further violations of public property and civic regulations.

Third, when the squatters demand the right to livelihood and habitation, they demand it as a collective right which they claim belongs to them as a community. This impinges upon a question that has vexed the modern state in postcolonial countries, especially those that have been modelled on Anglo-American constitutional procedures: can citizens have rights that belong to them by virtue of their membership of particular communities, defined by ethnic, religious, linguistic, or other criteria? Many states have recognized such rights for specific purposes, creating numerous legal anomalies and a theoretical defence of the practice that is hesitant and shamefaced. That equal homogeneous citizenship ought to be the norm seems to be conceded; current practices that do not conform to this norm are seen as deviations produced by colonial legacy or social backwardness or cultural exceptionalism.

Finally, the site on which our community of squatters have managed to conduct their struggle for survival is not that of a civil society of citizens dealing with a state in whose sovereignty they participate but rather that of a political society where claims and benefits can be negotiated between governmental agencies responsible for administering welfare, and groups of population that count according to calculations of political efficacy. The settlers, therefore, have to pick their way through a terrain where they have no standing as citizens; rather, their strategies must exploit, on the one hand, the political obligations that governments have of looking after poor and underprivileged sections of the population and, on the other, the moral rhetoric of a community striving to build a decent social life under extremely harsh conditions. These strategies, far from being inward-looking and isolationist, actually involve making a large array of connections outside the community—with other groups in similar situations, with more privileged and influential groups with whom the community has social or economic exchanges (such as employers or middle-class neighbours), with government functionaries, with political leaders and parties, and so on. These are the means through which the community has found a place in urban political society. It is by no means a secure place, for it is entirely dependent on the community's ability to operate within a field of strategic politics. I must add as an afterword to my story, this particular squatter settlement was finally removed in 2006 on the orders of the Calcutta High Court, with the government providing alternative housing several kilometres away, outside the peripheries of the city.

Many of the connections the squatters had established with other forces in political society seem to resemble the supposedly traditional forms of patron–client relations, but—and this is my claim regarding the ineluctable modernity of this political experience—they are enmeshed in an entirely new set of governmental practices that are the functions only of the modern state in the late twentieth century. The most significant feature of the survival strategies adopted in the last few decades by thousands of marginal groups, such as the one I have talked about, is the way in which the imaginative power of a traditional structure of community, including its fuzziness and capacity to invent relations of kinship, has been wedded to the modern emancipatory rhetoric of autonomy and equal rights. These strategies, I am suggesting, are not available within the liberal space of the associations of civil society transacting business with a constitutional state. In fact, in the particular case I have described, civic groups representing middle-class citizens were the ones who were better able to use the powers of the law to finally remove the settlement. For the majority of people in postcolonial societies, the normative status of the virtuous citizen will remain infinitely deferred until such time as they can be provided with the basic material and cultural prerequisites of membership of civil society. Until the arrival of that liberal millennium, however, they can only deal with a governmental system with the resources they can muster in political society. As we have seen before, community has a very tenuous place in the Western liberal theory of civil society and state; in the new political societies of the East, communities are some of the most active agents of political practice.

Undoubtedly, the possibilities of strategic politics by numerous groups representing perhaps the majority of the population in India are greatly facilitated by the existence in that country of an electoral democracy and a liberal constitutional system. However, I have little doubt that other groups of population in other Asian, African, and South American countries also adopt strategies of a similar sort to deal with governmental systems which, in this globalized age, tend to function largely through similar procedures and with similar technologies. The most significant feature of this strategic politics of the communities is the increasingly overriding importance of notions such as autonomy and representation, for which reason, I think, it is entirely valid to see in this politics a desire for democratization. The important differences of this politics with the classical history of democracy in the West are, first, that autonomy and representation are being claimed on behalf not only of individuals but of communities; and, second, that these democratic claims are being made in relation to a state whose governmental functions already encompass the bulk of the population well before the latter have been socialized into the institutions of civil society, this being a sequence of modernity different from what was experienced in the West. The politics of democratization must therefore be carried out not in the classical transactions between state and civil society but in the much less well-defined, legally ambiguous, contextually and strategically demarcated terrain of political society. A symmetrical theory of modernity would not, as Sudipta Kaviraj has pointed out, be of much help for us in explaining a different historical sequence of modernity in the East.[16]

This, I am suggesting, is one of the principal tasks of political theory today: to provide a conceptual map of the emerging practices of the new political societies of the East. The normative models of Western political theory have, more often than not, only served to show non-Western practices as backward or deviant: as I explained in Chapter One of this book, the norm-deviation structure is intrinsic to the modern liberal theory of government. What we need is a different conceptualization of the subject of political practice—neither as abstract and unencumbered individual selves nor as manipulable objects of governmental policy, but rather as concrete selves necessarily acting within multiple networks of collective obligations and solidarities to work out strategies of coping with, resisting, or using to their advantage the vast array of technologies of power deployed by the modern state. In the received history of Western political theory, as I have said before, capital and community have been antithetical. When the new history of Eastern modernity gets written in the twenty-first century, perhaps capital will at last find a resting place in community.[17] In the course of that journey, political theory as we have known it for so long will also get rewritten.

---

[16] Sudipta Kaviraj, "An Outline of a Revisionist Theory of Modernity," *Archives européennes de sociologie,* 46, 3 (2005), pp. 497–526.

[17] Need I add that I, a historical victim of Orientalist discourses, am using the term "Eastern" here with a twinkle in my eye and tongue firmly in cheek?

10

Democracy and Economic Transformation

Peasant Society Today

The first volume of *Subaltern Studies* was published in 1982. I was part of the editorial group that launched, under the leadership of Ranajit Guha, this critical engagement with Indian modernity from the standpoint of the subaltern classes, especially the peasantry. In the quarter of a century that has passed since then, there has been, I believe, a fundamental change in the situation prevailing in postcolonial India. The new conditions under which global flows of capital, commodities, information, and people are now regulated—a complex set of phenomena generally clubbed under the category of globalization—have created both new opportunities and new obstacles for the Indian ruling classes. The old idea of a Third World, sharing a common history of colonial oppression and backwardness, is no longer as persuasive as it was in the 1960s. The trajectory of economic growth taken by the countries of Asia has diverged radically from that of most African countries. The phenomenal growth in recent years of China and India, involving two of the most populous agrarian countries of the world, has set in motion a process of social change that, in its scale and speed, is unprecedented in human history.

In this context, I believe it has become important to revisit the question of the basic structures of power in Indian society, especially the position of the peasantry, under conditions of postcolonial democracy. This is not because I think that the advance of capitalist industrial growth is inevitably breaking down peasant communities and turning peasants into proletarian workers, as has been predicted innumerable times in the last century and a half. On the contrary, I will argue that the forms of capitalist industrial growth now under way in India will make room for the preservation of the peasantry, but under completely altered conditions. The analysis of these emergent forms of postcolonial capitalism in India under conditions of electoral democracy requires new conceptual work.

Let me begin by referring to the recent incidents of violent agitation in different regions of India, especially in West Bengal and Orissa, against the acquisition of agricultural land for industry. There have also been agitations in several states against the entry of corporate capital into the retail market for food and vegetables. The most talked about incidents occurred in Nandigram in West Bengal in 2007–8, on which much has been written. If these incidents had taken place twenty-five years ago, we would have seen in them the classic signs of peasant insurgency. Here were the long-familiar features of a peasantry, tied to the land and small-scale agriculture, united by the cultural and moral bonds of a local rural community, resisting the agents of an external state and of city-based commercial institutions by using both peaceful and violent means. Our analysis then could have drawn on a long tradition of anthropological studies of peasant societies, focusing on the characteristic forms of dependence of peasant economies on external institutions such as the state, and dominant classes such as landlords, moneylenders, and traders, but also of the forms of autonomy of peasant cultures based on the solidarity of a local moral community. We could have also linked our discussion to a long tradition of political debates over the historical role of the peasantry under conditions of capitalist growth, beginning with the Marxist analysis in Western Europe of the inevitable dissolution of the peasantry as a result of the process of primitive accumulation of capital, Lenin's debates in Russia with the Narodniks, Mao Zedong's analysis of the role of the peasantry in the Chinese Revolution, and the continuing debates over Gandhi's vision of a free India where a mobilized peasantry in the villages would successfully resist the spread of industrial capitalism and the violence of the modern state. Moreover, using the insights drawn from Gramsci's writings, we could have talked about the contradictory consciousness of the peasantry in which it was both dominated by the forms of the elite culture of the ruling classes and, at the same time, resistant to them. Twenty-five years ago, we would have seen these rural agitations in terms of the analysis provided by Ranajit Guha in his classic work *Elementary Aspects of Peasant Insurgency in Colonial India.*[1]

I believe that analysis would be inappropriate today. I say this for the following reasons. First, the spread of governmental technologies in India in the last three decades, as a result of the deepening reach of the developmental state under conditions of electoral democracy, has meant that the state is no longer an external entity to the peasant community. Governmental agencies distributing education, health services, food, roadways, water, electricity, agricultural technology, emergency relief, and dozens of other welfare services have penetrated deep into the interior of everyday peasant life. Not only are peasants dependent on state agencies for these services, they have also acquired considerable skill, albeit to varying degrees in the different regions, in manipulating and pressurizing these agencies to deliver these benefits. Institutions of the state, or at least governmental agencies (whether state or non-state), have become internal aspects of the peasant community. Second, reforms since the 1950s in the structure of agrarian property, even though gradual and piecemeal, have meant that, except in isolated areas, for the first time in centuries small peasants possessing land no longer directly confront an exploiting class within the village, as under feudal or semi-feudal conditions. This has had consequences that are completely new for the range of strategies of peasant politics. Third, since the tax on land or agricultural produce is no longer a significant source of revenue for the government, as in colonial or pre-colonial times, the relation of the state to the peasantry is no longer directly extractive, as it often was in the past. Fourth, with the rapid growth of cities and industrial regions, the possibility of peasants making a shift to urban and non-agricultural occupations is no longer a function of their pauperization and forcible separation from the land, but is often a voluntary choice, shaped by the perception of new opportunities and new desires. Fifth, with the spread of school education and expanded exposure to modern communications media such as the cinema, television, and advertising, there is a strong and widespread desire among younger members, both male and

[1] Ranajit Guha, *Elementary Aspects of Peasant Insurgency in Colonial India* (Delhi: Oxford University Press, 1983).

female, of peasant families not to live the life of a peasant in the village and instead to move to the town or the city, with all its hardships and uncertainties, because of its lure of anonymity and upward mobility. This is particularly significant for India where the life of poor peasants in rural society is marked not only by the disadvantage of class but also by the discriminations of caste, compared to which the sheer anonymity of life in the city is often seen as liberating. For agricultural labourers, of whom vast numbers are from the Dalit communities, the desired future is to move out of the traditional servitude of rural labour into urban non-agricultural occupations.

A New Conceptual Framework

I may have emphasized the novelty of the present situation too sharply; in actual fact, the changes have undoubtedly come more gradually over time. But I do believe that the novelty needs to be stressed at this time in order to ask: how do these new features of peasant life affect our received theories of the place of the peasantry in postcolonial India? Kalyan Sanyal has attempted a fundamental revision of these theories.[2] In the following discussion, I will use some of his formulations in order to present my own arguments on this subject.

The key concept in Sanyal's analysis is the *primitive accumulation of capital*—sometimes called primary or original accumulation of capital. Like Sanyal, I prefer to use this term in Marx's sense to mean the dissociation of the labourer from the means of labour. There is no doubt that this is the key historical process that brings peasant societies into crisis with the rise of capitalist production. Marx's analysis in the last chapters of Volume One of *Capital* shows that the emergence of modern capitalist industrial production is invariably associated with the parallel process of the loss of the means of production on the part of primary producers such as peasants and artisans.[3] The unity of labour with the means of labour, which is the basis of most pre-capitalist modes of production, is destroyed and the mass of labourers

---

[2] Kalyan Sanyal, *Rethinking Capitalist Development: Primitive Accumulation, Governmentality and Post-Colonial Capitalism* (New Delhi: Routledge, 2007).

[3] Karl Marx, *Capital*, vol. 1, tr. Samuel Moore and Edward Aveling (1887; Moscow: Progress Publishers, 1968), chs xxvi–xxxiii.

that emerges does not any more possess the means of production. Needless to say, the unity of labour with the means of labour is the conceptual counterpart in political economy of the organic unity of most pre-capitalist rural societies by virtue of which peasants and rural artisans are said to live in close bonds of solidarity in a local rural community. This is the familiar anthropological description of peasant societies as well as the source of inspiration for many romantic writers and artists portraying rural life. This is also the unity that is destroyed in the process of primitive accumulation of capital, throwing peasant societies into crisis.

The analysis of this crisis has produced, as I have already indicated, a variety of historical narratives ranging from the inevitable dissolution of peasant societies to slogans of worker–peasant unity in the building of a future socialist society. Despite their differences, the common feature in all these narratives is the idea of transition. Peasants and peasant societies under conditions of capitalist development are always in a state of transition, whether from feudalism to capitalism or from pre-capitalist backwardness to socialist modernity.

A central argument made by Sanyal in his book is that under present conditions of postcolonial development within a globalized economy, *the narrative of transition is no longer valid.* That is to say, although capitalist growth in a postcolonial society such as India is inevitably accompanied by the primitive accumulation of capital, the social changes that are brought about cannot be understood as a transition. How is that possible?

The explanation has to do with the transformations in the last two decades in the globally dispersed understanding about the minimum functions as well as the available technologies of government. There is a growing sense now that certain basic conditions of life must be provided to people everywhere and that if national or local governments do not provide them, someone else must—other states, or international agencies, or non-governmental organizations. Thus, while there is a dominant discourse about the importance of growth, which in recent times has come to mean almost exclusively capitalist growth, it is, at the same time, considered unacceptable that those who are dispossessed of their means of labour because of the primitive accumulation of capital should have no means of subsistence. This produces, says Sanyal, a curious process in which, on the one side, primary producers such as peasants, craftspeople, and petty manufacturers lose their land and other means of production, but, on the other, are also provided by governmental agencies with the conditions for meeting their basic needs of livelihood. There is, says Sanyal, primitive accumulation as well as a parallel process of the *reversal of the effects of primitive accumulation.*

It would be useful to illustrate this process with some examples. Historically, the process of industrialization in all agrarian countries has meant the eviction of peasants from the land, either because the land was taken over for urban or industrial development or because the peasant no longer had the means to cultivate the land. Market forces were usually strong enough to force peasants to give up the land, but often direct coercion was used by means of the legal and fiscal powers of the state. From colonial times, government authorities in India have used the right of eminent domain to acquire lands to be used for "public purposes," offering only token compensation, if any. The idea that peasants losing land must be resettled elsewhere and rehabilitated into a new livelihood was rarely acknowledged. Historically, it has been said that the opportunities of migration of the surplus population from Europe to the settler colonies in the Americas and elsewhere made it possible to politically manage the consequences of primitive accumulation in Europe in the eighteenth and nineteenth centuries. No such opportunities exist today for India. More importantly, the technological conditions of early industrialization which created the demand for a substantial mass of industrial labour have long passed. Capitalist growth today is far more capital-intensive and technology-dependent than it was even some decades ago. Large sections of peasants who are today the victims of the primitive accumulation of capital are completely unlikely to be absorbed into the new capitalist sectors of growth. Therefore, without a specific government policy of resettlement, peasants losing their land face the possibility of the complete loss of their means of livelihood. Under the globally prevailing normative ideas, this is considered unacceptable. Hence, the old-fashioned methods of putting down peasant resistance by armed repression have little chance of gaining legitimacy. The result is the widespread demand today for the rehabilitation of displaced people who lose their means of subsistence because of industrial and urban development. It is not, says Sanyal, as though primitive accumulation is halted or even slowed, for primitive accumulation is the inevitable companion to capitalist growth. Rather, governmental agencies have to find the resources to, as it were, reverse the consequences of primitive accumulation by providing alternative means of livelihood to those who have lost them.

To soften the blows dealt by primitive accumulation, several governmental technologies have become widespread in the second half of the twentieth century. They have become part of the political-economic technologies of democracy in India. Thus, it is not uncommon for developmental states to protect certain sectors of production that are currently the domain of peasants, artisans, and small manufacturers against competition from large corporate firms. But this may be interpreted as an attempt to forestall primitive accumulation itself by preventing corporate capital from entering into areas such as food crop or vegetable production or handicraft manufacture. However, there are many examples in many countries, including India, of governments and non-government agencies offering easy loans to enable those without the means of sustenance to find gainful employment. Such loans are often advanced without serious concern for profitability or the prospect of the loan being repaid, since here the motive for the money advanced is not the further accumulation of capital, but rather to provide the livelihood needs of the borrowers—that is to say, the motive is to reverse the effects of primitive accumulation. In recent years, these efforts have acquired the status of a globally circulating technology of poverty management: a notable instance is the micro-credit movement initiated by the Grameen Bank in Bangladesh and its founder, the Nobel Prize winner Mohammed Yunus. Most of us are familiar now with stories of peasant women in rural Bangladesh forming groups to take loans from the Grameen Bank. The loans enable small activities supplementing livelihoods, and the existence of a group puts pressure on the individual to repay the loan so that the group qualifies for another round of credit. Similar activities have been introduced quite extensively in India in recent years.

Finally, as in other countries, government agencies in India provide some direct benefits to people who, because of poverty or related reasons, are unable to meet their basic consumption needs. This could be in the form of special poverty-removal programmes, or schemes of guaranteed employment in public works, or even the direct delivery of subsidized or free food. Thus, there are programmes for supplying subsidized foodgrains to those designated as "below the poverty line," guaranteed employment for up to one hundred days in the year for those who need it, and free meals to children in primary schools. All these may be regarded, in terms of our analysis, as direct interventions to reverse the effects of primitive accumulation.

It is important to point out that, except for the last example of direct provision of consumption needs, most of the other mechanisms of reversing the effects of primitive accumulation involve the intervention of the market. This is the other significant difference in the present conditions of peasant life from the traditional models we have known. Except in certain marginal pockets, peasant and craft production in India today is fully integrated into a market economy. Unlike a few decades ago, there is almost no sector of household production that can be described as intended wholly for self-consumption or non-monetized exchange within a local community. Virtually all peasant and artisan production is for sale in the market and all consumption needs are purchased from the market. This, as we shall see, has an important bearing on recent changes in the conditions of peasant politics.

It is also necessary to point out that "livelihood needs" do not indicate a fixed quantum of goods determined by biological or other ahistorical criteria. It is a contextually determined, socially produced, sense of what is necessary to lead a decent life of some worth and self-respect. The composition of the set of elements that constitute "livelihood needs" will, therefore, vary with social location, cultural context, and time. In this sense, it is not the same homogeneous average labour-time socially necessary to reproduce labour that Marx used to define the value of labour-power in capitalist production. Livelihood needs can be expected to vary according to the social form of labour. Thus, the expected minimum standards of healthcare for the family or minimum levels of education for one's children will vary, let us say, between cities and villages, or between organized and informal sectors of employment, as will the specific composition of the commodities of consumption such as food, clothes, and domestic appliances. What is important here is a culturally and contextually determined sense of what is minimally necessary for a decent life, one that is neither unacceptably impoverished nor excessive and luxurious.

Transformed Structures of Political Power

To place these changes within a structural frame that describes how political power is held and exercised in postcolonial India, I also need to provide an outline of the transformation that, I believe, has taken place in that structure in recent years. Twenty-five years ago, the structure of state power in India was usually described in terms of a coalition of dominant class interests. Pranab Bardhan identified the capitalists, the rich farmers, and the bureaucracy as the three dominant classes, competing and aligning with one another within a political space supervised by a relatively autonomous state.[4] Achin Vanaik also endorsed the dominant coalition model, emphasizing in particular the relative political strength of the agrarian bourgeoisie which, he stressed, was far greater than its economic importance. He also insisted that even though India had never had a classical bourgeois revolution, its political system was nevertheless a bourgeois democracy that enjoyed a considerable degree of legitimacy not only with the dominant classes but also with the mass of the people.[5] Several scholars writing in the 1980s, such as Ashutosh Varshney and Rudolph and Rudolph, emphasized the growing political clout of the rich farmers or agrarian capitalists within the dominant coalition.[6]

The dominant class coalition model was given a robust theoretical shape in a classic essay by Sudipta Kaviraj in which, by using Gramsci's idea of the "passive revolution" as a blocked dialectic, he was able to ascribe to the process of class domination in postcolonial India its own dynamic.[7] Power had to be shared between the dominant classes

---

[4] Pranab Bardhan, *The Political Economy of Development in India* (Delhi: Oxford University Press, 1984).

[5] Achin Vanaik, *The Painful Transition: Bourgeois Democracy in India* (London: Verso, 1990).

[6] Ashutosh Varshney, *Democracy, Development and the Countryside: Urban–Rural Struggles in India* (Cambridge: Cambridge University Press, 1995); Lloyd I. and Susanne H. Rudolph, *In Pursuit of Lakshmi: The Political Economy of the Indian State* (Chicago: University of Chicago Press, 1987).

[7] Sudipta Kaviraj, "A Critique of the Passive Revolution," *Economic and Political Weekly*, 23, 45–7, pp. 2429–44. Reprinted with revisions as "The Passive Revolution and India: A Critique," in Sudipta Kaviraj, *The Trajectories of the Indian State: Politics and Ideas* (Ranikhet: Permanent Black, 2010), pp. 100–43.

because no one class had the ability to exercise hegemony on its own. But "sharing" was a process of ceaseless push and pull, with one class gaining a relative ascendancy at one point, only to lose it at another. Kaviraj provided us with a synoptic political history of the relative dominance and decline of the industrial capitalists, the rural elites, and the bureaucratic-managerial elite within the framework of the passive revolution of capital. In my early work, I too adopted the idea of the passive revolution of capital in my account of the emergence of the postcolonial state in India.[8]

The characteristic features of the passive revolution in India were the relative autonomy of the state as a whole from the bourgeoisie and the landed elites; the supervision of the state by an elected political leadership, a permanent bureaucracy, and an independent judiciary; the negotiation of class interests through a multi-party electoral system; a protectionist regime discouraging the entry of foreign capital and promoting import substitution; the leading role of the state sector in heavy industry, infrastructure, transport, telecommunications, mining, banking, and insurance; state control over the private manufacturing sector through a regime of licensing; and the relatively greater influence of industrial capitalists over the central government and that of landed elites on the state governments. Passive revolution was a form marked by its difference from classical bourgeois democracy. But to the extent that capitalist democracy as established in Western Europe or North America served as the normative standard of bourgeois revolution, discussions of passive revolution in India carried with them the sense of a transitional system—from precolonial and colonial regimes to some yet-to-be-defined authentic modernity.

The changes introduced since the 1990s have, I believe, transformed this framework of class dominance. The crucial difference now

[8] Partha Chatterjee and Arup Mallik, "Bhāratīya gaṇatantra o burjoyā pratikriyā," *Anya Artha* (May 1975), tr. in Partha Chatterjee, *A Possible India: Essays in Political Criticism* (Delhi: Oxford University Press, 1997), pp. 35–57; Partha Chatterjee, *Nationalist Thought and the Colonial World: A Derivative Discourse?* (London: Zed Books, 1986); Partha Chatterjee, "Development Planning and the Indian State," in T. J. Byres, ed., *The State, Development Planning and Liberalisation in India* (Delhi: Oxford University Press, 1998), pp. 82–103.

is the dismantling of the licence regime, greater entry of foreign capital and foreign consumer goods; and the opening up of sectors such as telecommunications, transport, infrastructure, mining, banking, insurance, etc. to private capital. This has led to a change in the very composition of the capitalist class. Instead of the earlier dominance of a few "monopoly" houses drawn from traditional merchant backgrounds and protected by the licence and import-substitution regime, there are now many more entrants into the capitalist class at all levels and much greater mobility within its formation.[9] Unlike the earlier fear of foreign competition, there appears to be much greater confidence among Indian capitalists to make use of the opportunities opened up by global flows of capital, goods, and services, including, in recent times, significant exports of capital. The most dramatic event has been the rise of the Indian information technologies industry. But domestic manufacturing and services have also received a major spurt, leading to annual growth rates of eight or nine per cent for the economy as a whole in the last few years until the slump of 2008–9.

There have been several political changes as a result. Let me list a few that are relevant for our present discussion. First, there is a distinct ascendancy in the relative power of the corporate capitalist class as compared to the landed elites. The political means by which this recent dominance has been achieved needs to be investigated more carefully, because it was not achieved through the mechanism of electoral mobilization (which used to be the source of the political power of the landed elites).[10] Second, the dismantling of the licence regime has opened up a new field of competition between state governments to woo capitalist investment, both domestic and foreign. This has resulted in the involvement of state-level political parties and leaders with the interests of national and international corporate capital in unprecedented ways. Third, although the state continues to be the most important mediating apparatus in negotiating between conflicting class interests, the autonomy of the state in relation to the dominant classes appears to

---

[9] A recent study is Harish Damodaran, *India's New Capitalists: Caste, Business, and Industry in a Modern Nation* (Ranikhet: Permanent Black, 2008).

[10] For an account of the "stealthy" introduction of economic reforms in the 1990s, see Rob Jenkins, *Democratic Politics and Economic Reform in India* (Cambridge: Cambridge University Press, 1999).

have been redefined. Crucially, the earlier role of the bureaucratic-managerial class, or more generally of the urban middle classes, in leading and operating, both socially and ideologically, the autonomous interventionist activities of the developmental state has significantly weakened. There is a strong ideological tendency among the urban middle classes today to view the state apparatus as ridden with corruption, inefficiency, and populist political venality and a much greater social acceptance of the professionalism and commitment to growth and efficiency of the corporate capitalist sector. The urban middle class, which once played such a crucial role in producing and running the autonomous developmental state of the passive revolution, appears now to have largely come under the moral-political sway of the bourgeoisie.

It would be a mistake, however, to think that the result is a convergence of the Indian political system with the classical models of capitalist democracy. The critical difference, as I have pointed out earlier, has been produced by a split in the field of the political between a domain of properly constituted *civil society* and a more ill-defined and contingently activated domain of *political society*.[11] Civil society in India today, peopled largely by the urban middle classes, is the sphere that seeks to be congruent with the normative models of bourgeois civil society and represents the domain of capitalist hegemony. If this were the only relevant political domain, then India today would probably be indistinguishable from other Western capitalist democracies. But there is the other domain of what I have called political society, which includes large sections of the rural population and the urban poor. These people do, of course, have the formal status of citizens and can exercise their franchise as an instrument of political bargaining. But they do not relate to the organs of the state in the same way that the middle classes do, nor do governmental agencies treat them as proper citizens belonging to civil society. Those in political society make their claims on government, and in turn are governed, not within the framework of stable constitutionally defined rights and laws, but rather through temporary, contextual and unstable arrangements arrived at through direct political negotiations. The latter

---

[11] Partha Chatterjee, *The Politics of the Governed: Reflections on Popular Politics in Most of the World* (New York: Columbia University Press, 2004).

domain, which represents the vast bulk of democratic politics in India, is not under the moral-political leadership of the capitalist class.

Hence, my argument is that the framework of passive revolution is still valid for India. But its structure and dynamic have undergone a change. The capitalist class has come to acquire a position of moral-political hegemony over civil society, consisting principally of the urban middle classes. It exercises its considerable influence over both the central and the state governments not through electoral mobilization of political parties and movements but largely through the bureaucratic-managerial class, the increasingly influential print and visual media, and the judiciary and other independent regulatory bodies. The dominance of the capitalist class within the state structure as a whole can be inferred from the virtual consensus among all major political parties about the priorities of rapid economic growth led by private investment, both domestic and foreign. It is striking that even the CPI(M) in West Bengal, and slightly more ambiguously in Kerala, have, in practice if not in theory, joined this consensus. This means that as far as the party system is concerned, it does not matter which particular combination of parties comes to power at the centre or even in most of the states; state support for rapid economic growth is guaranteed to continue. This is evidence of the current success of the passive revolution.

However, the practices of the state also include the large range of governmental activities in political society. Here, there are locally dominant interests, such as those of landed elites, small producers, and local traders who are able to exercise political influence through their powers of electoral mobilization. In the old understanding of the passive revolution, these interests would have been seen as potentially opposed to those of the industrial bourgeoisie; the conflicts would have been temporarily resolved through a compromise worked out within the party system and the autonomous apparatus of the state. Now, I believe, there is a new dynamic logic that ties the operations of political society with the hegemonic role of the bourgeoisie in civil society and its dominance over the state structure as a whole. This logic is supplied by the requirement, explained earlier, of reversing the effects of primitive accumulation of capital. To describe how this logic serves to integrate civil and political society into a new structure of the passive revolution, let me return to the subject of the peasantry.

Political Society and the Management of Non-corporate Capital

The integration with the market has meant that large sections of what used to be called the subsistence economy, which was once the classic description of small peasant agriculture, have now come fully under the sway of capital. This is a key development that must crucially affect our understanding of peasant society in India today. There is now a degree of connectedness between peasant cultivation, trade and credit networks in agricultural commodities, transport networks, petty manufacturing and services in rural markets and small towns, etc. that makes it necessary for us to categorize all of them as part of a single, but stratified, complex. A common description of this is the unorganized or informal sector, recently given official recognition by the National Commission for Enterprises in the Unorganised Sector (NCEUS) which has treated agricultural and non-agricultural activities in the unorganized sector in both rural and urban areas, including farming and household work, as differentiated parts of the same economic category.[12]

Usually, a unit in the informal sector is identified in terms of the small size of the enterprise, the small number of labourers employed, or the relatively unregulated nature of the business. In terms of the analytical framework I have presented here, I will propose a distinction between the formal and informal sectors of today's economy in terms of a difference between corporate and non-corporate forms of capital. Interestingly, the NCEUS too has settled for a similar definition: "The unorganized sector consists of all unincorporated private enterprises . . . with less than ten total workers."[13] The classification by size, necessary for purposes of counting, is of course arbitrary; the identification of the unorganized with the unincorporated sector, however, is conceptual.

My argument is that the characteristics I have described of peasant societies today are best understood as the marks of *non-corporate*

---

[12] National Commission for Enterprises in the Unorganised Sector (NCEUS), *Report on Conditions of Work and Promotion of Livelihoods in the Unorganised Sector* (New Delhi: Government of India, 2007).

[13] NCEUS, *Report*, p. 3.

capital. To the extent that peasant production is deeply embedded within market structures, investments and returns are conditioned by forces emanating from the operations of capital. In this sense, peasant production shares many connections with informal units in manufacturing, trade, and services operating in rural markets, small towns, and even in large cities. We can draw many refined distinctions between corporate and non-corporate forms of capital. But the key distinction I wish to emphasize is the following. The fundamental logic that underlies the operations of corporate capital is further accumulation of capital, usually signified by the maximization of profit. For non-corporate organizations of capital, while profit is not irrelevant, it is dominated by another logic—that of providing the livelihood needs of those working in the units. This difference is crucial for the understanding of the so-called informal economy and, by extension, as I will argue, of peasant society.

Let me illustrate with a couple of familiar examples from the non-agricultural informal sector and then return to the subject of peasants. Most of us are familiar with the phenomenon of street vendors in Indian cities. They occupy street space, usually violating municipal laws; they often erect permanent stalls, use municipal services such as water and electricity, and do not pay taxes. To carry on their trade under these conditions, they usually organize themselves into associations to deal with the municipal authorities, the police, credit agencies such as banks, and corporate firms that manufacture and distribute the commodities they sell on the streets. These associations are often large and the volume of business they encompass can be quite considerable. Obviously, operating within a public and anonymous market situation, the vendors are subject to the standard conditions of profitability of their businesses. But to ensure that everyone is able to meet their livelihood needs, the association will usually try to limit the number of vendors who can operate in a given area and prevent the entry of newcomers. On the other hand, there are many examples where, if the businesses are doing particularly well, the vendors do not, like corporate capitalists, continue to accumulate on an expanded scale, but rather agree to extend their membership and allow new entrants. To cite another example, in most cities and towns of India the transport system depends heavily on private operators who run buses and auto-rickshaws. Here too there is frequent violation of regulations such as licences, safety standards, and pollution norms—violations that allow these units to survive economically. Although most operators own only one or two vehicles each, they form associations to negotiate with transport authorities and the police over fares and routes, and control the frequency of services and entry of new operators to ensure that a minimum income, and not much more than a minimum income, is guaranteed to all.

In my book *The Politics of the Governed* I have described the form of governmental regulation of population groups such as street vendors, illegal squatters, and others whose habitation or livelihood verges on the margins of legality, as *political society*. In political society, I have argued, people are not regarded by the state as proper citizens possessing rights and belonging to the properly constituted civil society. Rather, they are seen to belong to particular population groups with specific empirically established and statistically described characteristics, which are targets of particular governmental policies. Since dealing with many of these groups implies the tacit acknowledgement of various illegal practices, governmental agencies often treat such cases as exceptions, justified by very specific and special circumstances, so that the structure of general rules and principles is not compromised. Thus, illegal squatters may be given water supply or electricity connections but on exceptional grounds, so as not to club them with regular customers who have secure legal title to their property; or street vendors may be allowed to trade under specific conditions that distinguish them from regular shops and businesses which comply with the laws and pay taxes. All this makes the claims of people in political society a matter of constant political negotiation, and the results are never secure or permanent. Their entitlements, even when recognized, never quite become rights. These features of the everyday practices of government are now receiving increasing scholarly attention.[14]

To connect the question of political society with my earlier discussion on the process of primitive accumulation of capital, I now wish

[14] For example, Akhil Gupta, *Postcolonial Developments: Agriculture in the Making of Modern India* (Durham, N.C.: Duke University Press, 1998); C.J. Fuller and Véronique Bénéï, eds, *Everyday State and Society in India* (London: Hurst, 2001); Emma Tarlo, *Unsettling Memories: Narratives of the Emergency in India* (Berkeley: University of California Press, 2003).

to advance the following proposition. *Civil society is where corporate capital is hegemonic, whereas political society is the space of management of non-corporate capital.* I have argued above that, since the 1990s, corporate capital, and along with it the class of corporate capitalists, have together achieved a hegemonic position over civil society in India. This means that the logic of accumulation, expressed at this time in the demand that national economic growth be maintained at a very high rate and that the requirements of corporate capital be given priority, holds sway over civil society—that is to say, over the urban middle classes. It also means that the educational, professional, and social aspirations of the middle classes have become tied with the fortunes of corporate capital. There is now a powerful tendency to insist on the legal rights of proper citizens, to impose civic order in public places and institutions, and to treat the messy world of the informal sector and political society with a degree of intolerance. A vague but powerful feeling seems to prevail among the urban middle classes that rapid growth will solve all problems of poverty and unequal opportunities.

The informal sector, which does not have a corporate structure and does not function principally according to the logic of accumulation, does not, however, lack organization. As I have indicated in my examples, those who function in the informal sector often have large, and in many cases quite powerful and effective, organizations. They need to organize precisely to function in the modern market and governmental spaces. Traditional organizations of peasant and artisan societies are not adequate for the task. I believe this organization is as much of a *political* activity as an economic one. Given the logic of non-corporate capital that I have described above, the function of these organizations is precisely to successfully operate within the rules of the market and governmental regulations in order to ensure the livelihood needs of their members. One of the striking findings of the NCEUS was the huge predominance among unorganized enterprises, not merely in the rural but even in urban areas, of self-employed owners operating with family labour and virtually no hired employees. Resorting to self-exploitation by stretching out the working hours, their overwhelming goal is merely to sustain their livelihoods.[15] Most of those who provide leadership in organizing people, both owners and

---

[15] NCEUS, *Report*, especially pp. 49–57.

workers, operating in the informal sector are actually or potentially political leaders. Many such leaders are prominent local politicians and many such organizations are directly or indirectly affiliated to political parties. Thus, it is not incorrect to say that the management of non-corporate capital under such conditions is a political function carried out by political leaders. The existence and survival of the vast assemblage of so-called informal units of production in India today, including peasant production, is directly dependent on the successful operation of certain *political* functions. That is what is facilitated by the process of democracy.

The organizations that can carry out these political functions have to be innovative—necessarily so, because neither the history of the cooperative movement nor that of socialist collective organization provides any model that can be copied by these non-corporate organizations of capital in India. What is noticeable here is a strong sense of attachment to small-scale private property and, at the same time, a willingness to organize and cooperate in order to protect the fragile basis of livelihood that is constantly under threat from the advancing forces of corporate capital. These organizations of political society often borrow their forms from those of associations in civil society, but other modalities such as kinship, patron–client relations, and even protection rackets and mafia-like networks, are not entirely uncommon. The informal economy, regulated by political society rather than by the legal organs of the state, also creates its own domain of revenue generation and expenditure in the collective interest of the organized group. Thus, a particular group of employers or workers in the informal sector may form an association that requires each member to pay regular contributions, managed by the leadership, to meet expenses that may include benefits such as medical costs as well as payments of bribes, fines, etc. The circulation of such revenues and expenditures constitutes an economic domain parallel to that of the legal domain of the organized economy, and is one more indicator of its "negative" status from the standpoint of the formal domain of the state and civil society.[16]

---

[16] A graphic account of such illegalities in the informal economy of Delhi can be found in Ravi Sundaram, *Pirate Modernity: Delhi's Media Urbanism* (London: Routledge, 2010).

However, it appears that these organizations of non-corporate capital are stronger, at least at this time, in the non-agricultural informal sectors in cities and towns and less so among the rural peasantry. This means that while the organization of non-corporate capital in urban areas has developed relatively stable and effective forms and is able, by mobilizing governmental support through the activities of political society, to sustain the livelihood needs of the urban poor in the informal sector, the rural poor, consisting of small peasants and rural labourers, are still dependent on direct governmental support for their basic needs and are less able to make effective organized use of the market in agricultural commodities. This challenge lies at the heart of the recent controversies over "farmer suicides" as well as the ongoing debates over acquisition of agricultural land for industry. It is clear that, in the face of rapid changes in agricultural production in the near future, Indian democracy will soon have to invent new forms of organization to ensure the survival of a vast rural population increasingly dependent on the operations of non-corporate forms of capital.

What I have said here about the characteristics of non-corporate capital is, of course, true only in the gross or average sense. It is admittedly an umbrella category, hiding many important variations within it. Informal or non-corporate units, even when they involve significant amounts of fixed capital and employ several hired workers, are, by my description, primarily intended to meet the livelihood needs of those involved in the business. Frequently, the owner is himself or herself also a worker. But this does not mean that there do not exist any informal units in which the owner strives to turn the business towards the route of accumulation, seeking to leave the grey zones of informality and enter the hallowed portals of corporate capitalism. This too might be a tendency that would indicate upward mobility as well as change in the overall social structure of capital.

Peasant Culture and Politics

The sociologist Dipankar Gupta has taken note of many of these features of changing peasant life to argue that we need a new theoretical framework for understanding contemporary rural society.[17] One of

[17] Dipankar Gupta, "Whither the Indian Village: Culture and Agriculture in Rural India," *Economic and Political Weekly*, February 19, 2005, pp. 751–8.

the features he has emphasized is the sharp rise in non-agricultural employment among those who live in villages. Between 1983 and 2004–5, employment in agriculture fell in India from 68.6 to 56.6 per cent.[18] In almost half the states of India, more than 40 per cent of the rural population is engaged in non-agricultural occupations today and the number is rising rapidly. A significant part of this population consists of rural labourers who do not own land but do not find enough opportunity for agricultural work. But, more significantly, even peasant families that own land will often include members employed in non-agricultural occupations. In part, this reflects precisely the pressure of market forces that makes small peasant cultivation unviable over time because it is unable to increase productivity. As the small peasant properties are handed down from one generation to the next, the holdings are further subdivided. I have seen in the course of my own fieldwork in West Bengal in 2004–6 that there is a distinct reluctance among younger members of rural landowning peasant families—both men and women—to continue with the life of a peasant. There is, they say, no future in small peasant agriculture: they would prefer to try their luck in town, even if it means a period of hardship. Needless to say, this feeling is particularly strong among those who have had some school education. It reflects not just a response to the effects of primitive accumulation, because many of these young men and women are from landowning families that manage to provide for their basic livelihood needs. Rather, it reflects the sense of a looming threat, the ever-present danger that small peasant agriculture will, sooner or later, succumb to the larger forces of capital. If this feeling becomes a general feature among the next generation of rural families, it will call for a radical transformation in our understanding of peasant culture. The very idea of a peasant society whose fundamental dynamic is to reproduce itself, accommodating only small and slow changes, will have to be given up altogether. Here we find a generation of peasants whose principal motivation seems to be to stop being peasants.

Based on findings of this type that are now accumulating rapidly, Gupta has spoken of the "vanishing village": "Agriculture is an economic residue that generously accommodates non-achievers resigned to

[18] National Sample Survey, 61st Round, Employment Tables.

a life of sad satisfaction. The villager is as bloodless as the rural economy is lifeless. From rich to poor, the trend is to leave the village . . ."[19] I think Gupta is too hasty to conclude thus. He has noticed only one side of the process which is the inevitable story of primitive accumulation. He has not, I think, considered the other side, which is the field of governmental policies aimed at reversing the effects of primitive accumulation. It is in that field that the relation between peasants and the state has been, and is still being, redefined.

I have mentioned before that state agencies, or governmental agencies generally, including NGOs that carry out governmental functions, are no longer an external entity in relation to peasant society. This has had several implications. First, because various welfare and developmental functions are now widely recognized to be necessary tasks for government in relation to the poor—who include large numbers of peasants—these functions in the fields of health, education, basic inputs for agricultural production, and the provision of basic necessities of life are now demanded from governmental agencies as a matter of legitimate claims by peasants. This means that government officials and political representatives in rural areas are constantly besieged by demands for various welfare and developmental benefits. It also means that peasants learn to operate the levers of the governmental system, to apply pressure at the right places, and negotiate for better terms. This is where the everyday operations of democratic politics, organization, and leadership come into play.[20] Second, the response of governmental agencies to such demands is usually flexible, based on calculations of costs and returns. In most cases, the strategy is to break up the benefit-seekers into smaller groups, defined by specific demographic or social characteristics. This enables a flexible policy that does not regard the entire rural population as a single homogeneous mass but rather breaks it up into smaller target populations. The intention is precisely to fragment the benefit-seekers and hence divide the potential opposition to the state.[21] Third, this

[19] Gupta, "Whither," p. 757.

[20] There are many studies documenting this process. See, for example, Jean Drèze and Amartya Sen, *India: Development and Participation* (Oxford: Clarendon Press, 1995).

[21] For a study of this process, see Stuart Corbridge, Glyn Williams, Manoj Srivastava, and René Veron, *Seeing the State: Governance and Governmentality in India* (Cambridge: Cambridge University Press, 2005).

field of negotiations opened up by flexible policies of seeking and delivering benefits creates a new competitive spirit among the benefit-seekers. Since peasants now confront, not landlords or traders as direct exploiters, but rather governmental agencies from whom they expect benefits, the state is blamed for perceived inequalities in the distribution of benefits. Thus, peasants will accuse officials and political representatives of favouring cities at the cost of the countryside; and particular sections of peasants will complain of having been deprived while other sections belonging to other regions or ethnic groups or castes or political loyalties have been allegedly favoured. The charge against state agencies is not one of exploitation but discrimination. This has given a completely new quality to peasant politics, one that was missing in the classical understandings of peasant society. This is where the everyday operations of democratic politics, organization and leadership come into play.

Fourth, unlike the old forms of peasant insurgency which characterized much of the history of peasant society for centuries, there is, I believe, a quite different quality to the role of violence in contemporary peasant politics. While subaltern peasant revolts of the old kind had their own notions of strategy and tactics, they were characterized, as Ranajit Guha showed, by strong community solidarity on the one side and negative opposition to the perceived exploiters on the other. Today, the use of violence in peasant agitations seems to have a far more calculative, almost utilitarian, logic, designed to draw attention to specific grievances with a view to seeking appropriate governmental benefits. A range of deliberate tactics are followed to elicit the right responses from officials, political leaders, and especially the media. In other words, violence of this sort has become part of performative strategies for building chains of equivalence that might bring about a populist consolidation against the ruling authorities. This is probably the most significant change in the nature of peasant politics over the last two or three decades.

As far as peasant agriculture is concerned, however, things are much less clear. Small peasant agriculture, even though thoroughly enmeshed in market connections, also feels threatened by the market. There is, in particular, an unfamiliarity with, and deep suspicion of, corporate organizations. Peasants appear far less able to deal with the uncertainties of the market than secure governmental benefits. In the last few years there have been hundreds of reported suicides of peasants who suddenly fell into huge debts because they were unable to realize the expected price from their agricultural products, such as tobacco and cotton. Peasants feel that the markets for these commercial crops are manipulated by large mysterious forces entirely beyond their control. Unlike many organizations in the informal non-agricultural sector in urban areas that can effectively deal with corporate firms for the supply of inputs or the sale of their products, peasants have been unable thus far to build similar organizations. This is the large area of the management of peasant agriculture, not as subsistence production for self-consumption, but as the field of non-corporate capital, that remains a challenge. It is the political response to this challenge that will determine whether the rural poor will remain vulnerable to the manipulative strategies of capital and the state, or whether they might use the terrain of governmental activities to assert their own claims to a life of worth and dignity.

It is important to emphasize that, contrary to what is suggested by the depoliticized idea of governmentality, the quality of politics in the domain of political society is by no means a mechanical transaction of benefits and services. Even as state agencies try, by constantly adjusting their flexible policies, to break up large combinations of claimants, the organization of demands in political society can adopt highly emotive resources of solidarity and militant action. Democratic politics in India is daily marked by passionate and often violent agitations to protest discrimination and secure claims. The fact that the objectives of such agitations are framed by the conditions of governmentality is no reason to think that they cannot arouse considerable passion and affective energy. Collective actions in political society cannot be depoliticized by framing them within the grid of governmentality because the activities of governmentality affect the very conditions of livelihood and social existence of the groups they target. At least that part of Indian democracy which falls within the domain of political society is definitely not anaemic and lifeless.

Interestingly, even though the claims made by various groups in political society are for governmental benefits, these cannot often be met by the standard application of rules and frequently require the declaration of an exception. Thus, when a group of people living or cultivating on illegally occupied land or selling goods on the street claim the right to continue with their activities, or demand compensation for moving somewhere else, they are in fact inviting the state to declare their case an exception to the universally applicable rule. They do not demand that the right to private property in land be abolished or that the regulations on trade licences and sales taxes be set aside. Rather, they demand that their cases be treated as exceptions. When the state acknowledges these demands, it too must do so not by the simple application of administrative rules but rather by a political decision to declare an exception. The governmental response to demands in political society is also, therefore, irreducibly political rather than merely administrative.

Much confusion can be avoided if this characteristic feature of political society is borne in mind. Political society cannot exist autonomously of civil society; rather, it is always negatively constituted as an abnormal field of exceptional practices that deviate from those that are approved of in proper civil society. It is the desire of political agents in that field to give it a positive construction—an identity and a voice—usually in the moral rhetoric of community. But such constructions are often fleeting and seldom acquire stable forms of political organization—another mark of their deviance from civil society.

I must point out one other significant characteristic of the modalities of democratic practice in political society. This has to do with the relevance of numbers. Ever since Tocqueville in the early nineteenth century, it is a common argument that electoral democracies foster the tyranny of the majority. However, mobilizations in political society are often premised on the strategic manipulation of relative electoral strengths rather than on the expectation of commanding a majority. Indeed, the frequently spectacular quality of actions in political society, including the resort to violence, is a sign of the ability of relatively small groups of people to make their voices heard and register their claims with governmental agencies. As a matter of fact, it could even be said that the activities of political society represent a continuing critique of the paradoxical reality in all capitalist democracies of equal citizenship and majority rule on the one hand, and the dominance of property and privilege on the other.

But the underside of political society is the utter marginalization of those groups that do not even have the strategic leverage of electoral mobilization. In every region of India, there exist marginal groups of people who are unable to gain access to the mechanisms of political society. They are often marked by their exclusion from peasant society, such as low-caste groups who do not participate in agriculture, or tribal peoples who depend more on forest products or pastoral occupations than on agriculture. Political society and electoral democracy have not given these groups the means to make effective claims on governmentality. In this sense, these marginalized groups represent a world outside, beyond the boundaries of political society.

The important difference represented by activities in political society, when compared to the movements of democratic mobilization familiar to us from twentieth-century Indian history, is the lack of a perspective of transition. While there is much passion aroused over ending the discriminations of caste or ethnicity or asserting the rightful claims of marginal groups, there is little conscious effort to view these agitations as directed towards a fundamental transformation of the structures of political power, as they were in the days of nationalist and socialist mobilizations. On the contrary, if anything, it is the bourgeoisie, hegemonic in civil society and dominant within the state structure as a whole, which appears to have a narrative of transition— from stagnation to rapid growth, from backwardness and poverty to modernity and prosperity, from third-world insignificance to major world-power status. Perhaps this is not surprising if one remembers the class formation of the passive revolution: with the landed elites pushed to a subordinate position and the bureaucratic-managerial class won over by the bourgeoisie, it is the capitalist class that has now acquired a position to set the terms to which other political formations can only respond.

The unity of the state system as a whole is now maintained by relating civil society to political society through the logic of reversal of the effects of primitive accumulation. Once this logic is recognized by the bourgeoisie as a *necessary political condition* for the continued rapid growth of corporate capital, the state, with its mechanisms of electoral democracy, becomes the field for the political negotiation of demands for the transfer of resources, through fiscal and other means, from the accumulation economy to governmental programmes aimed at providing the livelihood needs of the poor and the marginalized. The autonomy of the state, and that of the bureaucracy, now lies in their power to adjudicate the quantum and form of transfer of resources to the so-called "social sector of expenditure." Ideological differences, such as those between the Right and the Left, for instance, are largely about the amount and modalities of social sector expenditure, such as poverty removal programmes. These differences do not question the dynamic logic that binds civil society to political society under the dominance of capital. Once again, it is significant, but not surprising, that despite the freedom acquired by the Congress Party in the 2009 elections in running the national government without any contrary pull exerted by the Left parties, there continues to be the same attention paid to social sector expenditure as a complement to the emphasis on economic reforms to promote growth.

Let me summarize my main argument. With the continuing rapid growth of the Indian economy, the hegemonic hold of corporate capital over the domain of civil society is likely to continue. This will inevitably mean continued primitive accumulation. That is to say, there will be more and more primary producers, i.e. peasants, artisans, and petty manufacturers, who will lose their means of production. But most of these victims of primitive accumulation are unlikely to be absorbed in the new growth sectors of the economy. They will be marginalized and rendered useless as far as the sectors dominated by corporate capital are concerned. But the passive revolution under conditions of electoral democracy makes it unacceptable and illegitimate for the government to leave these marginalized populations without the means of labour to simply fend for themselves. That carries the risk of turning them into the "dangerous classes." Hence, a whole series of governmental policies are being, and will be, devised to reverse the effects of primitive accumulation. This is the field in which peasant societies are having to redefine their relations with both the state and with capital. Thus far, it appears that whereas many new practices have been developed by peasants, using the mechanisms of democratic politics, to claim and negotiate benefits from the state, their ability to deal with the world of capital is still unsure and inadequate. This is where the further development of peasant activities as non-corporate capital, seeking to ensure the livelihood needs of peasants while operating within the circuits of capital, will define the future of peasant society in India. As far as I can see, peasant society will certainly survive in India in the twenty-first century, but only by accommodating a substantial non-agricultural component within the village. Further, I think there will be major overlaps and continuities in emerging cultural practices between rural villages and small towns and urban areas, with the urban elements gaining predominance.

I have also suggested that the distinction between corporate and non-corporate capital appears to be coinciding with the divide between civil society and political society. This could have some ominous consequences. We have seen in several Asian countries what may be called a revolt of "proper citizens" against the unruliness and corruption of systems of popular political representation. In Thailand, there have been two army-led coups in 2006 and 2009 that ousted popularly elected governments. The actions seemed to draw support from urban middle classes who expressed their disapproval of what they considered wasteful and corrupt populist expenditure aimed at gaining the support of the rural population. In 2007, there was a similar army-backed coup in Bangladesh, initially welcomed by the urban middle classes. In India, a significant feature in recent years has been the withdrawal of the urban middle classes from political activities altogether: there is widespread resentment in the cities of the populism and corruption of all political parties which, it is said, are driven principally by the motive of gaining votes at the cost of ensuring the conditions of rapid economic growth. There is no doubt that this reflects the hegemony of the logic of corporate capital among the urban middle classes. The fact, however, is that the bulk of the population in India lives outside the orderly zones of proper civil society. It is in political society that they have to be fed and clothed and given work, if only to ensure the long-term and relatively peaceful well being of civil society. That is the difficult and innovative process of politics on which the future of the passive revolution under conditions of democracy depends.

11

Empire and Nation Today

The New Nations

We are often told 'Colonialism is dead.' Let us not be deceived or even soothed by that. I say to you, colonialism is not yet dead." Those were the words of President Achmed Sukarno of Indonesia at the opening of the Asian-African conference in Bandung in 1955. He went on to elaborate:

> I beg of you, do not think of colonialism only in the classic form which we of Indonesia, and our brothers in different parts of Asia and Africa, knew. Colonialism has also its modern dress, in the form of economic control, intellectual control, actual physical control by a small but alien community within a nation. It is a skilful and determined enemy, and it appears in many guises. It does not give up its loot easily. Wherever, whenever and however it appears, colonialism is an evil thing, and one which must be eradicated from the earth.[1]

Do those words still have a ring of truth? Could they be said about the world today? I believe they can, even though in many crucial respects the world has changed rather drastically in the last half a century. Let me quickly recount some of the things that were said at the Bandung Conference, attended by such leading lights of the Afro-Asian world as Chou En-lai, Jawaharlal Nehru, Ho Chi Minh, Kwame Nkrumah, and Gamal Abdel Nasser. We should remember that, in 1955, most of the countries of Africa were still under British or French or Portuguese colonial rule. It is in that context that we should judge which of the

[1] *Africa-Asia Speaks from Bandong* (Djakarta: Indonesian Ministry of Foreign Affairs, 1955), pp. 19–29.

many things said at Bandung are still of relevance and which have gone into the trash folder of history.

On the economic side, the Bandung Conference stressed the need for economic development of the countries of Asia and Africa. "Development" was, of course, a concept very much in vogue fifty years ago, and along with it the idea of planned industrialization through the active intervention of the nation-state. The conference resolution shows that most countries in the region saw themselves mainly as exporters of primary commodities and importers of industrial products. The conference discussed the possibility of collective action to stabilize the international prices of primary commodities. This condition has largely changed, at least for the countries of Asia. While large pockets of subsistence agriculture and poverty still remain in many countries, the main economic dynamic is now a rapidly growing, principally capitalist, modern industrial manufacturing sector that is quite diversified in its products and use of technology, and which supports the growth of modern financial, educational, and other tertiary sectors. What must be emphasized, however, is that this transformation has been brought about everywhere in Asia, not only in China and India but also in South Korea, Taiwan, Singapore, Malaysia, and Indonesia by the direct, systematic, and active intervention of the postcolonial nation-state and its political leadership.

But the economy is also the one respect in which the historical trajectory in Asia seems to have diverged enormously in the last half a century from that in Africa. Sub-Saharan Africa today has become, in the popular media, synonymous with poverty, a blot on the conscience of the world, the last place where absolute poverty is not yet on the way to being eradicated. It is also the place where the nation-state is said to have utterly failed in delivering the promises made at the time of its birth. For Africa, the cry now is for the rest of the world to provide what the nation-state was supposed to have delivered. "More than any other region," as Achille Mbembe emphasizes, "Africa thus stands out as the supreme example of the West's obsession with, and circular discourse about, the facts of 'absence', 'lack' and 'non-being', of identity and difference, of negativeness—in short, of nothingness."[2] On the other

---

[2] Achille Mbembe, *On the Postcolony* (Berkeley: University of California Press, 2001), p. 4.

hand, it is hardly insignificant that of the key players at Bandung fifty-five years ago, China, India, Indonesia, Malaysia, and Singapore are now regular invitees to summit meetings of the world's most powerful economies. That is a dramatic measure of how much the world has changed since 1955. No one talks of an Afro-Asian economic world any more.

On the political side, the main discussions at the conference were on the subject of human rights. It is particularly interesting to re-read these discussions today because they show how radically the context as well as the framework of debate on this subject has changed. In 1955 at Bandung, no one had any doubt about the principal problem of human rights in the world: it was the continued existence of colonialism and racial discrimination that stood in the way of human rights. The economically advanced and, for the most part, democratic countries of Europe (not counting Spain and Portugal which were under the dictatorships of Franco and Salazar) were the principal violators of human rights on a global scale. There was also little doubt about the chief instrument by which human rights were to be established: it was the principle of self-determination of peoples and nations. That was the principle the United Nations had enshrined. The leaders assembled at Bandung declared that the UN charter and declarations had created "a common standard of achievement for all peoples and nations."[3] Accordingly, the conference supported the rights of the Arab people of Palestine. It called for the end to racial segregation and discrimination in Africa. It supported the rights of the peoples of Algeria, Morocco, and Tunisia to self-determination. It called for the admission to the United Nations of Japan, Ceylon, Nepal, Jordan, Libya, Laos, Cambodia, and a united Vietnam.

Further, the Bandung conference reaffirmed the five principles of promotion of world peace, namely, mutual respect of all nations for their sovereignty and territorial integrity, non-aggression, non-interference in internal affairs, equality and mutual benefit, and peaceful coexistence. Amplifying on these principles, the conference affirmed the right of each nation to defend itself singly or collectively, but warned that arrangements for collective defence must not be used to

---

[3] A. Appadorai, *The Bandung Conference* (New Delhi: Indian Council of World Affairs, 1955), p. 8.

serve the particular interests of the big powers. The leaders at Bandung thought that they could, as President Sukarno said, "inject the voice of reason into world affairs." Sukarno himself mentioned the role of some of the prime ministers of Asian countries in ending the war over the continued French occupation of Indo-China. "It was no small victory and no negligible precedent," he said. "The five Prime Ministers did not make threats. They issued no ultimatum, they mobilized no troops. . . . They had no axe of power-politics to grind. They had but one interest—how to end the fighting [in Indo-China]."[4] The president did not know at the time, of course, that he had spoken too soon: the war in Indo-China would, before long, resume and take a tortuous and brutal course over the next two decades, killing millions of people along the way.

Looking back, it seems clear that this was the time, in the two decades following the end of World War II, that the nation-state was established as the normal form of the state everywhere in the world. The normative idea was unequivocally endorsed in the principle of self-determination of peoples and nations. The fact that the norm had not been fully realized was pointed out as a shortcoming, something that had to be overcome. It presented to the peoples of Asian and African countries an object of struggle, a goal that had complete moral legitimacy. It also provided a criterion for identifying the enemy: the enemy was colonialism, the practices of racial superiority, and the lingering fantasies of world domination by the old imperial powers.

A Post-national Age?

How are things different today? There are still a few places where "national liberation" remains an emotive object of political struggle. Perhaps the most intractable as well as the most justified of such national struggles has been that of the Palestinian people. However, the reason why Palestinians do not yet have a state of their own is not that the principle of national self-determination is difficult to apply to their case but that every suggested solution has been blocked by one or the other big power on account of its crucial strategic interests in the region. In this sense, the Palestinian case is somewhat unique. But the

[4] *Africa-Asia Speaks*, pp. 19–29.

Kashmir question too has remained unresolved for more than sixty years. There is the question of the Kurds, a people whose claims as a nationality has, once again for unique reasons of colonial history, never been sufficiently recognized in the international arena. There has been a lot of bloodshed and bitterness in many of the regions of the former Soviet Union and former Yugoslavia over contending "national" claims. Such identities and claims had been successfully contained for several decades within a complex, and authoritarian, federal structure of socialist government. With the collapse of the socialist regimes, the container appears to have shattered into pieces. But all these examples of unresolved claims of national self-determination can be understood as remnants of an older order in which the nation-state became the universal norm in the second half of the twentieth century.

The new order, it is being claimed, seeks to go beyond the framework of nation-states. It attempts to preserve the achievements of the nation-state while overcoming its frequently disastrous shortcomings. These arguments from varying ideological positions have not yet cohered into a body of theoretical reasoning and empirical evidence that can be pointed to as the definitive description of this new order. But some of these arguments have come from very distinguished thinkers and scholars, mostly from Europe. Let me point out what I think are the significant features in this corpus of arguments.

First of all, there is a general recognition that significant changes occurred in the structure of capitalist production and exchange in the last two decades of the twentieth century. The most common name for this phenomenon is globalization. Superficially, this refers to the huge increases in international trade and flows of capital, in the movement of people across national borders, and in the spread of information and images enabled by the new communications technology. It has been pointed out, of course, that as far as trade, the export of capital, and migration are concerned, the two decades before World War I saw an equal if not higher degree of globalization. But the period from the 1920s to the 1970s, which is the period of consolidation of both the nation-state and the modern national economy, clearly produced a worldwide grid of economic activities defined over nation-states. Compared to the middle decades of the twentieth century, therefore, the changes in the last two decades were dramatic.

Those who have looked at globalization more carefully, however, point out that what changed decisively in the last two decades of the twentieth century was the emergence of a new mode of flexible production and accumulation and the rapid expansion of the international financial market. New developments in communications technology allowed for innovations in the management of production that could now disperse different components of the production process away from the centralized factory to smaller production and service units often located in faraway parts of the world, sometimes even in the informal household sector. Alongside, there was a huge rise in the speculative investment of capital in the international markets for stocks, bonds, and currencies. These two developments have jointly provided the basic economic push away from the old model of national economic autarky to one where global networks are acknowledged as exercising considerable power over national economies.

It is against this background that certain leading thinkers of Europe have been arguing for some time for a relaxation, if not dismantling, of the old structure of national sovereignty that became normative in the middle of the twentieth century and was identified by the leaders at Bandung as the unfinished agenda of the worldwide anti-colonial struggle. Many of these proposals have been driven by the experience of a successful integration of several European states, with long histories of antagonism, into a single European Union. There are now virtually no national controls over trade, travel, and employment across national borders within Europe. There are numerous ways in which the sovereign powers of the nation-state have been curtailed in the fields of law, administration, taxation, and the judicial system. There is now a single currency in use in a large number of European countries. More significantly, it has been argued that the relaxation of sovereign controls at the top has also facilitated the devolution of powers below the level of the nation-state. In Britain, for instance, Scotland and Wales now have their own parliaments, an idea that would have been regarded as hugely threatening even thirty years ago.

Not only sovereignty, the new post-national theorists have argued that notions of citizenship are also undergoing radical change. The idea that the nation-state is the only true home of the citizen, the only guarantor of his or her rights, and the only legitimate object of his or her loyalty is changing fast and, say these theorists, should change even more quickly. If we can take the idea of citizenship away from the exclusive domain of the nation-state and distribute it among different kinds of political affiliations, then we would have more effective and democratic means to deal with problems such as the rights of migrants, the rights of minorities, cultural diversity within the nation, and the freedom of the individual. There will be little need for separatism, terror, and civil war. It is in this spirit that Jürgen Habermas has spoken of the "post-national constellation" and David Held and Daniele Archibugi of "cosmopolitan democracy."[5]

Empire Today

If this is the passage of the idea of the nation-state in the last half of the twentieth century, how has the idea of empire fared in the same period? Imperialism of the old kind mentioned by President Sukarno in his speech at Bandung did come to an end by the 1960s. The transition was not peaceful everywhere. When the French and the Dutch reoccupied their colonies in South East Asia after the defeat of Japan in World War II, they were met by armed popular resistance. The Dutch soon gave up Indonesia. In Indochina, the French withdrew in the mid-1950s, but of course the region was soon engulfed in another kind of conflict. The nationalist armed resistance became victorious in Algeria in the early 1960s.

In the British colonies, the transfer of power to nationalist governments was generally more peaceful and constitutionally tidy. It is said that this was because the liberal democratic tradition of politics in Britain ultimately made it impossible for it to sustain the anomaly of a despotic colonial empire and resist the moral claim to national self-government by the colonized people. By acquiescing in a process of decolonization, it was asserted, British liberal democracy redeemed

[5] Jürgen Habermas, *Postnational Constellation: Political Essays*, tr. Max Pensky (Cambridge: Polity Press, 2001); Daniele Archibugi and David Held, eds, *Cosmopolitan Democracy: An Agenda for a New World Order* (Cambridge: Polity Press, 1995). The idea of cosmopolitanism has seen a resurgence outside Europe too: see, for example, Kwame Anthony Appiah, *Cosmopolitanism: Ethics in a World of Strangers* (New York: W. W. Norton, 2006).

itself. The claim has been celebrated once more by Niall Ferguson in his *Empire*, intended as a manual of historical instruction for aspiring American imperialists.[6]

Of course, alongside the question of the moral incompatibility of democracy and empire, another argument had come to dominate discussions on colonialism in the middle of the twentieth century. This was the utilitarian argument which claimed that the economic benefits derived from colonies were far outweighed by the costs of holding them in subjection. By giving up the responsibility of governing its overseas colonies, a country like Britain could secure the same benefits at a much lower cost by negotiating suitable economic agreements with the newly independent countries. However, not every section of ruling opinion in Britain took such a bland cost–benefit view of something as sublime and noble as the British imperial tradition. Winston Churchill, for instance, remained dogmatically opposed to proposals for decolonization, and he was not alone among the British ruling elite.[7] Conservative governments in the 1950s were hardly keen to give up the African colonies and, when President Nasser nationalized the Suez Canal in 1956, Britain and France decided to intervene with military force. It was American pressure that finally compelled them to pull back. By then, it had become clear that the future of British industry and trade was wholly dependent on the protective cover extended by the US dollar. The decolonization of Africa in the 1960s effectively meant the end of Britain as an imperial power. The cost–benefit argument won out, leaving the moral reputation of liberal democracy largely in the clear.[8]

The United Nations, as it emerged in the decades following World War II, was testimony to the historical process of decolonization and the universal recognition of the right of self-determination of nations. It was living proof of the universal incompatibility of democracy and empire.

The declared American position in the twentieth century was

---

[6] Niall Ferguson, *Empire: The Rise and Demise of the British World Order and the Lessons for Global Power* (New York: Basic Books, 2002).

[7] As documented, for instance, by Richard Toye, *Churchill's Empire: The World That Made Him and the World He Made* (New York: Henry Holt, 2010).

[8] Wm. Roger Louis and Ronald Robinson, "The Imperialism of Decolonization," *Journal of Imperial and Commonwealth History*, 22, 3 (1990), pp. 462–511.

explicitly against the idea of colonial empires. The imperialist fantasies of Theodore Roosevelt at the beginning of the century soon turned into the stuff of cartoons and comic strips. Rather, it was an American president, Woodrow Wilson, who enshrined the principle of self-determination of nations within the framework of the League of Nations. After World War II, US involvement in supporting or toppling governments in other parts of the world was justified almost entirely by the logic and rhetoric of the Cold War, not those of colonialism. If there were allegations of US imperialism, they were seen to be qualitatively different from old-fashioned colonial exploitation: this was a neo-imperialism without colonies.

In fact, it could be said that, through the twentieth century, the process of economic and strategic control over foreign territories and productive resources was transformed from the old forms of conquest and occupation to the new ones of informal power exercised through diplomatic influence, economic incentives, and treaty obligations. A debate that was always part of the nineteenth-century discourse of imperialism—direct rule or informal control—was decisively resolved in favour of the latter option.

Has globalization at the end of the twentieth century changed the conditions of that choice? The celebratory literature on globalization in the 1990s argued that the removal of trade barriers imposed by national governments, the greater mobility of people, and the cultural impact of global information flows made for conditions in which there would be a general desire all over the world for democratic forms of government and greater democratic values in social life. Free markets were expected to promote "free societies." It was assumed, therefore, as an extension of the fundamental liberal idea, that in spite of differences in economic and military power there would be respect for the autonomy of governments and peoples around the world precisely because everyone was committed to the free and unrestricted flow of capital, goods, peoples, and ideas. Colonies and empires were clearly antithetical to this liberal ideal of the globalized world.

However, there was a second line of argument that was also an important part of the globalization literature of the 1990s. This argument insisted that, because of the new global conditions, it was not only possible but also necessary for the international community to use its power to protect human rights and promote democratic values in countries under despotic and authoritarian rule. There could be no absolute protection afforded by the principle of national sovereignty to tyrannical regimes. Of course, the international community had to act through a legitimate international body such as the United Nations. Since this would imply a democratic consensus among the nations of the world (or at least a large number of them), international humanitarian intervention of this kind to protect human rights or prevent violence and oppression would not be imperial or colonial.

The two lines of argument, both advanced within the discourse of liberal globalization, implied a contradiction. At one extreme, one could argue that democratic norms in international affairs meant that national sovereignty was inviolable except when there was a clear international consensus in favour of humanitarian intervention; anything less would be akin to imperialist meddling. At the other extreme, the argument might be that globalization had made national sovereignty an outdated concept. The requirements of peace-keeping now made it necessary for there to be something like an Empire without a sovereign metropolitan centre: a virtual Empire representing an immanent global sovereignty. There would be no more wars, only police action. This is the argument presented eloquently, if unpersuasively, by Michael Hardt and Antonio Negri. [9]

What is New About Empire?

Since Hardt and Negri's analysis provides some ingenious and influential arguments about the place of Empire in the globalized world of the twenty-first century, let me briefly review their proposal before moving on to my own assessment of the situation today.

Hardt and Negri speak of two logics of sovereignty within the modern political imagination. One is the transcendent sovereignty of the nation-state, demarcated over territory, located either in a sovereign monarchical power (*à la* Hobbes) or a sovereign people (*à la* Rousseau). Its logic is exclusive, defining itself as identical to the people that constitutes a particular nation-state as distinct from other nation-states. Its dynamic is frequently expansionist, leading to territorial acquisitions and rule over other peoples that are known in

[9] Michael Hardt and Antonio Negri, *Empire* (Cambridge, Mass.: Harvard University Press, 2000).

modern world history as imperialism. The second logic is that of the immanent sovereignty of the democratic republic, located, they argue, in the constituent power of the multitude (as distinct from the people) working through a network of self-governing institutions embodying multiple mechanisms of powers and counter-powers. The logic of immanent sovereignty is inclusive rather than exclusive. Even when territorialized, it sees its domain as marked by open frontiers. Its dynamic tendency is towards a constantly productive expansiveness rather than the expansionist conquest of other lands and peoples. Germinating in the republican ideals of the US constitution, the logic of immanent sovereignty now points towards the global democratic network of Empire.[10]

It is necessary to point out that even in their description of the historical evolution of the United States as an immanent Empire, Hardt and Negri acknowledge that there were closed and exclusive boundaries. First of all, it was possible to conceive of the expansive open frontier only by erasing the presence there of Native Americans who could not be imagined as being part of the supposedly inclusive category of the constituent multitude. That was the first inflexible border. Second, there were the African-Americans who were, as Hardt and Negri point out, counted as unequal parts of the state population for purposes of calculating the state's share of seats in the House of Representatives but, of course, not given the rights of citizens until the late twentieth century. The latter became possible not by the operation of an open frontier expanding outwards but rather by the gradual loosening of an internal border through a pedagogical, and indeed redemptive, project of civilizing, i.e. making citizens. Hence, even in the paradigmatic case of the United States as an immanent Empire, there was always a notion of an outside that could not be wishfully imagined as an ever-receptive open space that would simply yield to the expansive thrust of civilization. This outside consisted of practices (or cultures) that were resistant to the expansion of Empire and which thus had to be conquered and colonized. As with all historical empires, there are only two ways in which the civilizing imperial force can operate: a pedagogy of violence and a pedagogy of culture.

From this perspective, one has to see the US myth of the melting pot as not one of hybridization at all, as Hardt and Negri would have it,

[10] Ibid., pp. 160–82.

but rather as a pedagogical project of homogenization into a new, internally hierarchized, and perhaps frequently changing, normative American culture. In this respect, the US empire is no different from other empires of the modern era for whom contact with colonized peoples meant a constant danger of corruption: an exposure to alien ways that could travel back and destroy the internal moral coherence of national life. Hence, the pedagogical aspect of civilizing has only worked in one direction in the modern era—educating the colonized into the status of modern citizens; never the other way, as in many ancient empires, of conquerors allowing themselves to be civilized by their subjects. It is hard to find any evidence that the US empire is an exception to this modern rule.

Hardt and Negri also make the argument that since the new Empire is immanent and inclusive, and its sovereignty de-territorialized and without a centre, the forms of anti-imperialist politics that had proved so effective in the days of national liberation and decolonization have become obsolete. Anti-imperialist nationalism, grounded in the transcendent reification of the sovereign people as actualized in the nation-state, can now only stand in the way of the global multitude poised to liberate itself in the ever-inclusive, hybrid, and intrinsically democratic networks of Empire.[11] Most readers have found this to be perhaps the least persuasive argument in *Empire*. But the point that needs to be made here is that although the transcendent and terri-torialized idea of sovereignty located in an actual people-nation is a predominant performative mode in most third-world nationalisms, the immanent idea of a constituent power giving to itself the appro-priate machineries of self-government is never entirely absent. Indeed, just as the "people" can be invoked to legitimize exclusive, and often utterly repressive, national identities held in place by nation-state structures, so can it be invoked to critique, destabilize, and sometimes overthrow those structures. One might even say that the relative lack of stable institutionalization of modern state structures in postcolonial countries—a matter of persistent regret in the political develop-ment literature—is actually a sign of the vital presence of this imma-nent notion of a constituent power that has still not been subdued into the banal routine of everyday governmentality. Think of an entire

[11] Ibid., pp. 114–36.

generation of Bengalis who went, from the 1930s to the 1970s, imagining themselves first as part of an anti-colonial Indian nationalism, then as part of a religion-based Pakistani nationalism, and finally as a language-based Bangladeshi nationalism, reinventing itself every time as a new territorial nation-state and yet, surely, remaining, in some enduring sense, the same constituent power giving itself the institutions of self-rule. If immanence and transcendence are two modes of sovereign power in the modern world, it is hard to see in what way the US constitution has a monopoly over them.

I do not think, therefore, that the new globalized networks of production, exchange, and cultural flows have produced, as Hardt and Negri claim, the conditions of possibility for a new immanent, deterritorialized, and centre-less Empire. I do not find this argument persuasive even for the period of the 1990s—from the first Persian Gulf war to the war over Kosovo, when there was a relatively high level of consensus in the so-called international community for armed interventions to enforce international law and protect human rights. In the period after the invasion of Iraq, the argument has lost all credibility. Despite the rhetoric of a so-called global war against terror, the policies of the Bush administration and those of each of its allies seemed to be perfectly explicable in terms of fairly old-fashioned calculations of ensuring national security and furthering national interests. Much of the resistance to US unilateralism, taking numerous forms from the diplomatic to the insurgent and cutting across ideological divides, also adopted the old logic of protecting the sovereign sphere of national power. The question we must ask, then, is: how are we to understand the relation between nation and empire today? If nations and empires were declared to be incompatible fifty-five years ago at Bandung, has that assessment changed?

Empire is Immanent in the Modern Nation

It is true that the era of globalization has seen the undermining of national sovereignty in crucial areas of foreign trade, property, and contract laws and technologies of governance. There is overwhelming pressure towards uniformity of regulations and procedures in these areas, overseen, needless to say, by the major economic powers through new international economic institutions. Can one presume a convergence of interests and a consensus of views among those powers? Or could there be competition and conflict in a situation where international interventions of various kinds on the lesser powers are both common and legitimate?

The situation has turned even more uncertain and unpredictable since 2008 because of the sudden appearance of a global financial crisis. The principal dynamic that drove consumption and growth in the world economy over the last two decades was provided by the predatory movements of speculative finance capital. The crisis has brought those movements to a screeching halt. This has not only resulted in recession and the fear of massive unemployment in the advanced Western economies, but also in a severe slowdown of growth in large developing economies dependent on exports to Western countries. We are witnessing, at least for the time being, a sudden retreat from the neoliberal ideologies that were dominant in the last two decades to a recourse to Keynesian policies of hugely expanded state expenditure to stimulate demand, and the greater regulation of financial markets. Faced with growing state involvement in the economy and political pressures to secure employment, there appears to be a resurgence in the sentiments of national autarky in many countries of Europe and North America.

Although there is much talk today of the current global financial crisis spelling the irreversible decline of the Western economies and the rise to dominance of the rapidly growing manufacturing economies of Asia, it is still too soon to make such predictions. More crucially, one must not ignore the implications of the gap that will then be opened up between on the one hand the declining economic influence of the United States and the European countries, and on the other their continued overwhelming military dominance in the world. What sorts of political judgements can they be expected to make in such a situation of asymmetry between their real economic capabilities and their ambitions to global power?

If there is a material substratum of conflicts of interest in the world today, then it becomes possible to talk of the cynical deployment of moral arguments to justify imperialist actions that are actually guided by other motivations. This is a familiar aspect of nineteenth-century imperial history, as noted in Chapter One of this book. It was in the context of an increasingly assertive parliamentary and public opinion, demanding accountability in the activities of the government in foreign affairs, especially those that required the expenditure of public money and troops, that the foreign and colonial policies of European imperial powers became suffused with a public rhetoric of high morality and civilizing virtues. And it was as an integral part of the same process that a "realist" theory of *raison d'état* emerged in the field of foreign affairs, as a specialist discourse used by diplomats and policy-makers, that would seek to insulate a domain of hard-headed pursuit of national self-interest, backed by military and economic power, from the mushy, even if elevated, sentimentalism of the public rhetoric of moral virtue. This was the origin of ideological "spin" in foreign and colonial affairs—a specific set of techniques for the production of democratic consent in favour of realist and largely secretive decisions made in the pursuit of the so-called national interest by a small group of policy-makers.

But why should such duplicitous arguments be credible in a world where the form of the nation-state has become normative and universal? After all, nation-states have equal rights under international law and each has one vote in the General Assembly of the United Nations. Curiously, it is the very form of the universal equality of nation-states that has provided the common measure for comparing them according to various criteria. Thus, we are all familiar today with the statistical comparison of nations by indices such as the gross national product, economic growth, human development, quality of life, levels of corruption, and what have you. These are statistical measures of differences between nations. But statistical measures create norms and allow for the attribution of qualitative meanings, and even moral judgements. Thus, a norm may represent an average value of the empirical distribution of, let us say, literacy or infant mortality among the nations of the world. But a norm may also represent a certain desirable standard that is set as a target to be achieved. This allows for certain moral judgements to be made about the capacity, willingness, and actual performance of nations in relation to such ethical standards. It is not surprising, therefore, that many of these judgements become judgements about culture. Necessarily, therefore, the normalization of the nation-state as the universal form of the political organization of humanity contains within itself a mechanism for measuring cultural difference and for attributing moral significance to those differences. I must add that the process of normalization also allows one to track differences over time, so that nations which did badly before could be seen to be improving, just as others could be seen to be slipping behind. The theoretical structure of normalization constructed on the basis of these two senses of the norm was, one may recall, described in Chapter One.

I think it can be demonstrated that the history of the normalization of the modern nation-state is inseparable from the history of modern empires. It was in the course of the worldwide spread of the European empires that virtually all of the forms and techniques of modern governance were developed, transported, and adapted—not just in one direction, i.e. from Europe to elsewhere, but also in the reverse direction, i.e. from the colonies to the metropolis. But it was also as part of the same process of the normalization of the nation-state that the rule of colonial difference was invented. Even as the universal validity of the norms of modern governance was asserted, the rule of colonial difference allowed for the colony to be declared, on grounds of cultural difference, an exception to the universal norm. Thus, just as the deputies of the revolutionary National Assembly in France declared the universal validity of the rights of man, they had few difficulties in announcing at the same time that the rebellious slaves of Saint Domingue (present-day Haiti) could not have those rights. John Stuart Mill, in the middle of the nineteenth century, could write a whole book expounding the universal superiority of representative government, but not without inserting a chapter explaining why Indians and the Irish were not ready for it. One could easily fill an encyclopedia with examples of the application of the rule of colonial difference in the last two hundred years.

I wish to propose a general definition of empire that does not tie it with annexation and occupation of foreign territories and, therefore, is able to capture the new forms of indirect and informal control that have become common in recent decades. The imperial prerogative, I suggest, is the power to declare the colonial exception. Everyone agrees that nuclear proliferation is dangerous and should be stopped. But who decides that India may be allowed to have nuclear weapons, and also Israel, and maybe even Pakistan, but not North Korea or Iran? We all know that there are many brutally repressive regimes which are also sources of international terrorism, but who decides that it is not Saudi Arabia or Burma but the regime of Saddam Hussein in Iraq that must be overthrown by force? Those who claim to decide on the exception are indeed arrogating to themselves the imperial prerogative.

Declaring an exception, within the framework of normalization, immediately opens up a pedagogical project. The imperial power must then take on the responsibility of educating, disciplining ,and training the colony in order to bring it up to the norm. There have been in history only two forms of imperial pedagogy—a pedagogy of violence and a pedagogy of culture. The colony must either be disciplined by force or educated ("civilized") by culture. We have seen both of these forms in recent times, long after the era of decolonization and Bandung.

Let me add that with the evident decline of US unilateralism following the end of the Bush presidency and the global financial crisis, it is entirely conceivable that the imperial prerogative may now be shared among several powers. There could well emerge regional hegemons claiming to declare the colonial exception within their own spheres of influence, and seeking to discipline deviant states by the instruments of violence and pedagogy. There is no reason to believe that a postcolonial democracy such as India will not harbour ambitions of playing such an imperial role, just as democracies of the nineteenth century did. That would resemble in some ways a structure of international politics familiar in the imperial age of balance of power in the nineteenth century.

It is also worth pointing out that the norm-deviation and norm-exception structures for the application of policy are in principle available over all normalized comparative entities that might be objects of policy. In our discussion so far, we have confined the analysis to the case of nation-states. Seen historically, an interesting difference emerges between the colonial and postcolonial situations. Until the middle of the twentieth century, when the Western powers were the unquestioned arbiters of global power and international law, they also claimed the legitimate imperial authority to declare the colonial exception. From the latter half of the twentieth century, with the universalization of the nation-state, that authority came to be challenged. The imperial power, when it had to be used, needed the fig leaf of ratification by some entity that could claim to represent an international community. This is an important difference that defines the global practice of empire in the postcolonial age. But normalized comparisons can also be made between regions or population groups within actually consti-tuted nation-states: the structure of pedagogy, whether through viol-ence or culture, is not fundamentally different. However, since the policy field there is not constituted by putatively sovereign entities called nation-states, the term "imperial" is not appropriate in that situ-ation, even though arguments such as "internal colonialism" are not unknown in the context of postcolonial politics.

Talking of Bandung and what it might mean to us today, I wish to end with one more quote from President Sukarno at the 1955 conference. "We are living in a world of fear," he said. "The life of man today is corroded and made bitter by fear. Fear of the future, fear of the hydrogen bomb, fear of ideologies. Perhaps this fear is a greater danger than the danger itself, because it is fear which drives men to act foolishly, to act thoughtlessly, to act dangerously."[12] It is not clear from his speech who specifically the president thought might act foolishly out of fear. But speaking of our situation today, we hear daily of angry men from ordinary backgrounds with little power who choose to act dangerously out of fear and resentment. But we often forget how much more thoughtless and dangerous people in power can be when, driven by fear, they choose to arrogate to themselves the prerogative of declar-ing the exception. The nation-state may not be at its healthy best any more, but empire is certainly not dead.

[12] *Africa-Asia Speaks*, pp. 19–29.

Bibliography

Abu Taleb Khan, *Travels of Mirza Abu Taleb Khan in Asia, Africa, and Europe during the Years 1799 to 1803*, tr. Charles Stewart (1814; rpntd New Delhi: Sona Publications, 1972)

Africa–Asia Speaks from Bandong (Djakarta: Indonesian Ministry of Foreign Affairs, 1955)

Alam, Muzaffar, *The Languages of Political Islam in India, c. 1200–1800* (Delhi: Permanent Black, 2004)

Alavi, Seema, *Islam and Healing: Loss and Recovery of an Indo-Muslim Medical Tradition 1600–1900* (Ranikhet: Permanent Black, 2008)

Anderson, Benedict, *Imagined Communities: Reflections on the Origins and Spread of Nationalism* (London: Verso, 1983; revised ed. 1991)

———, *The Spectre of Comparisons: Nationalism, Southeast Asia and the World* (London: Verso, 1998)

Appadorai, A., *The Bandung Conference* (New Delhi: Indian Council of World Affairs, 1955)

Appiah, Kwame Anthony, *Cosmopolitanism: Ethics in a World of Strangers* (New York: W.W. Norton, 2006).

Archibugi, Daniele, and David Held, eds, *Cosmopolitan Democracy: An Agenda for a New World Order* (Cambridge: Polity Press, 1995)

Asad, Talal, *Genealogies of Religion: Discipline and Power in Christianity and Islam* (Baltimore: Johns Hopkins Press, 1993)

Attewell, Guy, *Refiguring Unani Tibb: Plural Healing in Late Colonial India* (New Delhi: Orient Longman, 2007)

Aurobindo, Sri, *Bande Mataram: Early Political Writings* (Pondicherry: Sri Aurobindo Ashram, 1973)

Avineri, Shlomo, and Avner de-Shalit, eds, *Communitarianism and Individualism* (Oxford: Oxford University Press, 1992)

Ayub, Abu Sayeed, *Ādhunikatā o rabīndranāth* (Calcutta: Dey's, 1968; revised ed. 1971)

Bakhle, Janaki, *Two Men and Music: Nationalism in the Making of an Indian Classical Tradition* (New York: Oxford University Press, and New Delhi: Permanent Black, 2005)

Bardhan, Pranab, *The Political Economy of Development in India* (Delhi: Oxford University Press, 1984)

Baviskar, Amita, and Nandini Sundar, "Democracy versus Economic Transformation," *Economic and Political Weekly*, 43, 46, pp. 87–9

Bayly, C.A., *Indian Society and the Making of the British Empire* (Cambridge: Cambridge University Press, 1988)

———, *Imperial Meridian: The British Empire and the World 1780–1830* (London: Longman, 1989)

Benjamin, Walter, "Critique of Violence," in Benjamin, *Selected Writings*, eds Marcus Bullock and Michael W. Jennings (Cambridge, Mass.: Harvard University Press, 1996), pp. 244–300

Bentham, Jeremy, *Principles of Morals and Legislation* (1789; Buffalo, N.Y.: Prometheus Books, 1988)

———, *The Works of Jeremy Bentham*, ed. John Bowring, vol. 1 (Edinburgh: William Tait, 1843)

Bhabha, Homi, "DissemiNation," in Homi Bhabha, ed., *Nation and Narration* (New York: Routledge, 1990), pp. 291–322

Bhaduri, Nrisingha Prasad, *Daṇḍanīti: prācīn bhāratīya rājśāstra* (Calcutta: Sahitya Samsad, 1998)

Bhargava, Rajeev, ed., *Secularism and Its Critics* (Delhi: Oxford University Press, 1998)

Bhattacharya, Dwaipayan, Partha Chatterjee, Pranab Kumar Das, Dhrubajyoti Ghosh, Manabi Majumdar, and Surajit Mukhopadhyay, *Strengthening Rural Decentralization* (Calcutta: Centre for Studies in Social Sciences, 2006)

Bhattacharya, Pradyumna, *Ṭīkā ṭippaṇī* (Calcutta: Papyrus, 1998)

Bhattacharya, Sabyasachi, ed., *The Mahatma and the Poet: Letters and Debates between Gandhi and Tagore 1915–1941* (New Delhi: National Book Trust, 1997)

Bose, Pradip Kumar, "Pujor kalkātār bikalpalok", *Bāromās* (1997)

Bourdieu, Pierre, *Distinction: A Social Critique of the Judgment of Taste*, tr. Richard Nice (Cambridge, Mass.: Harvard University Press, 1984)

Boxer, C.R., *João de Barros: Portuguese Humanist and Historian of Asia* (New Delhi: Concept, 1981)

Buck-Morss, Susan, *Hegel, Haiti, and Universal History* (Pittsburgh: University of Pittsburgh Press, 2009)

Chakrabarty, Dipesh, *Rethinking Working Class History* (Delhi: Oxford University Press, 1989)

———, *Provincializing Europe: Postcolonial Thought and Historical Difference* (Princeton: Princeton University Press, 2000)

Chatterjee, Partha, *Nationalist Thought and the Colonial World: A Derivative Discourse?* (London: Zed Books, 1986)

————, "A Response to Taylor's Modes of Civil Society," *Public Culture*, 3, 1 (Fall 1990), pp. 119–32

————, *The Nation and Its Fragments: Colonial and Postcolonial Histories* (Princeton: Princeton University Press, 1993)

————, ed., *Texts of Power: The Disciplines in Colonial Bengal* (Minneapolis: University of Minnesota Press, 1995)

————, "Development Planning and the Indian State," in T.J. Byres, ed., *The State, Development Planning and Liberalisation in India* (Delhi: Oxford University Press, 1998), pp. 82–103

————, *The Politics of the Governed: Reflections on Popular Politics in Most of the World* (New York: Columbia University Press, 2004)

————, *Prajā o tantra* (Calcutta: Anustup, 2005)

————, *Empire and Nation: Selected Essays 1985–2005* (Ranikhet: Permanent Black, and New York: Columbia University Press, 2010)

————, and Arup Mallik, "Bhāratīya ganatantra o burjoyā pratikriyā," *Anya Artha* (May 1975), translated in Chatterjee, *A Possible India: Essays in Political Criticism* (Delhi: Oxford University Press, 1997), pp. 35–57

Chattopadhyay, Sobhakar, *Bhārater itihās* (Calcutta: Narmada Publication, 1987)

Chaudhuri, K.N., *The Trading World of Asia and the English East India Company, 1660–1760* (Cambridge: Cambridge University Press, 1978)

————, *Trade and Civilisation in the Indian Ocean: An Economic History from the Rise of Islam to 1750* (Cambridge: Cambridge University Press, 1985)

Cohen, Jean L., and Andrew Arato, *Civil Society and Political Theory* (Cambridge, Mass.: MIT Press, 1994)

Coleman, James S., *Foundations of Social Theory* (Cambridge, Mass.: Harvard University Press, 1990)

Corbridge, Stuart, Glyn Williams, Manoj Srivastava, and René Veron, *Seeing the State: Governance and Governmentality in India* (Cambridge: Cambridge University Press, 2005)

Dale, Stephen Frederic, *The Mappilas of Malabar 1498–1922: Islamic Society on the South Asian Frontier* (Oxford: Clarendon Press, 1980)

Damodaran, Harish, *India's New Capitalists: Caste, Business, and Industry in a Modern Nation* (Ranikhet: Permanent Black, 2008)

Das Gupta, Chidananda, *The Painted Face: Studies in India's Popular Cinema* (New Delhi: Roli Books, 1991)

Datta, Bhabatosh, *Aitihya o rabīndranāth* (Santiniketan: Viswabharati, 1996)

Deb Sahitya Kutir, *Biśva paricay* (Calcutta: Deb Sahitya Kutir, 1953)

Drèze, Jean, and Amartya Sen, *India: Development and Participation* (Oxford: Clarendon Press, 1995)

Dumont, Louis, *Homo Hierarchicus: The Caste System and Its Implications*, tr. Mark Sainsbury, Louis Dumont, and Basia Gulati (1970; rpntd Delhi: Oxford University Press, 1998)

Fabian, Johannes, *Moments of Freedom: Anthropology and Popular Culture* (Charlottesville: University Press of Virginia, 1998)

Ferguson, Niall, *Empire: The Rise and Demise of the British World Order and the Lessons for Global Power* (New York: Basic Books, 2002)

Foucault, Michel, *Discipline and Punish: The Birth of the Prison*, tr. Alan Sheridan (Harmondsworth: Penguin, 1977)

———, *Power*, ed. James D. Faubion (New York: New Press, 2000)

Fuller, C.J., and Véronique Bénéï, eds, *Everyday State and Society in India* (London: Hurst, 2001)

Gandhi, M.K., *The Collected Works of Mahatma Gandhi*, vol.10 (New Delhi: Publications Division, 1958)

Gangopadhyay, Sachindranath, Pabitrakumar Ray, and Nripendranath Bandyopadhyay, *Rabīndradarśan* (Santiniketan: Centre of Advanced Study in Philosophy, 1969)

Geuss, Raymond, *Philosophy and Real Politics* (Princeton: Princeton University Press, 2008)

Ghosh, Anjan, "Durga Puja: A Consuming Passion," *Seminar*, 559 (March 2006)

Ghosh, Dilip Kumar, *Bhārat o bhāratbāsi* (Calcutta: New Book Stall, 1974)

Ghosh, Sankha, *Nirmāṇ ār sṛṣṭi* (Santiniketan: Viswabharati, 1982)

Ghulam Husain Tabtabai, *A Translation of the Sëir Mutaqherin; or View of Modern Times, being an History of India, from the Year 1118 to the Year 1194, (this Year answers to the Christian Year 1781–82) of the Hedjrah; etc. by Seid-Gholam-Hossein-Khan*, vols 1–4 (Calcutta: R. Cambray, 1902)

Gole, Nilufer, and Ludwig Ammann, eds, *Islam in Public: Turkey, Iran and Europe* (Istanbul: Istanbul Bilgi University, 2006)

Gramsci, Antonio, *Selections from the Prison Notebooks*, tr. by Quintin Hoare and Geoffrey Nowell-Smith (New York: International Publishers, 1971)

Guha, Ranajit, *A Rule of Property for Bengal: An Essay on the Idea of Permanent Settlement* (Paris: Mouton, 1963)

———, *Elementary Aspects of Peasant Insurgency in Colonial India* (Delhi: Oxford University Press, 1983)

———, "Discipline and Mobilize," in Partha Chatterjee and Gyanendra Pandey, eds, *Subaltern Studies VII* (Delhi: Oxford University Press, 1992), pp. 69–120

———, *Dominance without Hegemony: History and Power in Colonial India* (Cambridge, Mass.: Harvard University Press, 1997)

Guha-Thakurta, Tapati, *Monuments, Objects, Histories: Institutions of Art in Colonial and Postcolonial India* (New York: Columbia University Press, 2004)

———, *The Aesthetics of the Popular Print: Lithographs and Oleographs from 19th and 20th Century India* (Kolkata: Birla Academy of Art and Culture, 2006)

———, "From Spectacle to 'Art,'" *Art India Magazine*, vol. 9, no. 3, pp. 34–56

Gupta, Akhil, *Postcolonial Developments: Agriculture in the Making of Modern India* (Durham, N.C.: Duke University Press, 1998)

Gupta, Dipankar, "Whither the Indian Village: Culture and Agriculture in Rural India," *Economic and Political Weekly*, February 19, 2005, pp. 751–8

Gutman, Judith Mara, *Through Indian Eyes: Nineteenth and Early Twentieth Century Photography from India* (New York: Oxford University Press, 1982)

Habermas, Jürgen, *Postnational Constellation: Political Essays*, tr. Max Pensky (Cambridge: Polity Press, 2001)

Hacking, Ian, *The Taming of Chance* (Cambridge: Cambridge University Press, 1990)

Hall, Stuart, "Cultural Studies and its Theoretical Legacies," in Lawrence Grossberg, Cary Nelson, and Paula Treichler, eds, *Cultural Studies* (London: Routledge, 1992), pp. 277–94

Hansen, Thomas Blom, *Wages of Violence: Naming and Identity in Postcolonial Bombay* (Princeton: Princeton University Press, 2001)

Hardt, Michael, and Antonio Negri, *Empire* (Cambridge, Mass.: Harvard University Press, 2000)

Hegel, G.W.F., *Philosophy of Right*, tr. by T.M. Knox (London: Oxford University Press, 1967)

———, *Encyclopaedia of the Philosophical Sciences*, Part 1, tr. William Wallace (Oxford: Clarendon Press, 1975)

———, *Lectures on the Philosophy of World History*, tr. H.B. Nisbet (Cambridge: Cambridge University Press, 1975)

Ihtisamuddin, Mirza Shaikh, *Shigurf Namah i Velaët, or Excellent Intelligence concerning Europe; being the Travels of Mirza Itesa Modeen, in Great Britain and France*, tr. James Edward Alexander (London: Parbury, Allen and Co., 1827)

———, *Bilayetnama*, tr. A.B.M. Habibullah (Dhaka: Muktadhara, 1981)

————, *The Wonders of Vilayet: Being the Memoir, Originally in Persian of a Visit to France and Britain*, tr. Kaiser Haq (London: Peepal Tree Press, 2001)

Jain, Kajri, "More Than Meets the Eye: The Circulation of Images and the Embodiment of Value," in Sumathi Ramaswamy, ed., *Beyond Appearances? Visual Practices and Ideologies in Modern India* (New Delhi: Sage, 2003), pp. 33–70

Jameson, Fredric, *Singular Modernity: Essay on the Ontology of the Present* (London: Verso, 2002)

Jenkins, Rob, *Democratic Politics and Economic Reform in India* (Cambridge: Cambridge University Press, 1999)

Kapur, Geeta, *When Was Modernism: Essays on Contemporary Cultural Practice in India* (New Delhi: Tulika, 2000)

Kautilya, *The Arthasastra of Kautilya*, vol. 1, tr. R.P. Kangle (Delhi: Motilal Banarasidass, 1986)

Kaviraj, Sudipta, "A Critique of the Passive Revolution," *Economic and Political Weekly*, 23, 45–7, pp. 2429–44. Reprinted with revisions as "The Passive Revolution and India: A Critique," in Sudipta Kaviraj, *The Trajectories of the Indian State: Politics and Ideas* (Ranikhet: Permanent Black, 2010), pp. 100–43

————, "The Imaginary Institution of India," in Partha Chatterjee and Gyanendra Pandey, eds, *Subaltern Studies VII* (Delhi: Oxford University Press, 1992), pp. 1–39

————, *The Unhappy Consciousness: Bankimchandra Chattopadhyay and the Formation of Nationalist Discourse in India* (Delhi: Oxford University Press, 1995)

————, "An Outline of a Revisionist Theory of Modernity," *Archives européennes de sociologie*, 46, 3 (2005), pp. 497–526

Krieger, Leonard, *An Essay on the Theory of Enlightened Despotism* (Chicago: University of Chicago Press, 1975)

Laclau, Ernesto, *On Populist Reason* (London: Verso, 2005)

————, and Chantal Mouffe, *Hegemony and Socialist Strategy* (London: Verso, 1985)

Levi, Margaret, "Social and Unsocial Capital: A Review Essay of Robert Putnam's *Making Democracy Work*," *Politics and Society*, 24, 1 (March 1996), pp. 45–55

Louis, Wm. Roger, and Ronald Robinson, "The Imperialism of Decolonization," *Journal of Imperial and Commonwealth History*, 22, 3 (1990), pp. 462–511

Machiavelli, Niccolò, *The Prince*, tr. Luigi Ricci (New York: Mentor, 1952)

MacIntyre, Alasdair, *After Virtue: A Study in Moral Theory* (Notre Dame, Indiana: University of Notre Dame Press, 1984)

Maiti, Prabhatangshu, *Bhārater itihās* (Calcutta: Sridhar Prakashani, 2001)

Majumdar, Bijaychandra, *Bhāratbarṣer itihās* (Calcutta: Sen Brothers, 1924)

Mamdani, Mahmood, *Citizen and Subject: Contemporary Africa and the Legacy of Late Colonialism* (Princeton: Princeton University Press, 1996)

Mantena, Karuna, *Alibis of Empire: Henry Maine and the Ends of Liberal Imperialism* (Princeton: Princeton University Press, and Ranikhet: Permanent Black, 2010)

Marshall, P.J., ed., *The Writings and Speeches of Edmund Burke*, vol. 6 (Oxford: Clarendon Press, 1991)

Marx, Karl, "On the Jewish Question" (1843), in Karl Marx and Frederick Engels, *Collected Works*, vol. 3 (Moscow: Progress Publishers, 1975), pp. 146–74

——, *Grundrisse*, tr. Martin Nicolaus (Harmondsworth: Penguin, 1973)

——, *Capital*, vol. 1, tr. Samuel Moore and Edward Aveling (1887; rpntd Moscow: Progress Publishers, 1968)

——, *Capital*, vol. 1, tr. Ben Fowkes (London: Penguin, 1990)

Mbembe, Achille, *On the Postcolony* (Berkeley: University of California Press, 2001)

Mehta, Uday Singh, *Liberalism and Empire: A Study in Nineteenth-century British Liberal Thought* (Chicago: University of Chicago Press, 1999)

Menon, Nivedita, "Introduction," in Partha Chatterjee, *Empire and Nation: Selected Essays 1985–2005* (Ranikhet: Permanent Black, 2010; New York: Columbia University Press, 2010), pp. 1–20

Mill, John Stuart, *Considerations of Representative Government* (1861; rpntd Buffalo, N.Y.: Prometheus Books, 1991)

Miller, David, *Market, State and Community* (Oxford: Oxford University Press, 1989)

Mitra, Anandachandra, *Byabahār darśan* (Calcutta: Ray Press, 1876)

Mosley, Leonard, *The Last Days of the British Raj* (1961; rpntd Bombay: Jaico, 1971)

Moyn, Samuel, *The Last Utopia: Human Rights in History* (Cambridge, Mass.: Cambridge University Press, 2010)

Mukherjee, S.N., *Sir William Jones: A Study in Eighteenth-Century British Attitudes to India* (Cambridge: Cambridge University Press, 1968)

Mukherjee, Sanjeeb, "Civil Society in the East and the Prospects of Political Society," *Economic and Political Weekly*, 45, 5 (January 30, 2010), pp. 57–63

Mukherjee, Trailokya Nath, *A Visit to Europe* (Calcutta: Arunodaya Roy, 1902)

Mukhopadhyay, Jiban, *Svadeś paricay* (Calcutta: Nababharati, 2002)

Nag, Kalidas, *Svadeś o sabhyatā* (Calcutta: Modern Book Agency, 1950)

Nandy, Ashis, *The Intimate Enemy: Loss and Recovery of Self under Colonialism* (Delhi: Oxford University Press, 1983)

————, *Traditions, Tyranny and Utopias: Essays in the Politics of Awareness* (Delhi: Oxford University Press, 1987)

————, "The Political Culture of the Indian State," *Daedalus*, 118, 4 (Fall 1989), pp. 1–26

————, *The Illegitimacy of Nationalism: Rabindranath Tagore and the Politics of Self* (Delhi: Oxford University Press, 1994)

————, *The Savage Freud and Other Essays on Possible and Retrievable Selves* (Delhi: Oxford University Press, 1995)

————, "Introduction: Indian Popular Cinema as a Slum's Eye View of Politics," in Ashis Nandy, ed., *The Secret Politics of Our Desires: Innocence, Culpability and Indian Popular Cinema* (Delhi: Oxford University Press, 1998)

Nandy, Ashis, *et al., Creating a Nationality: The Ramjanmabhumi Movement and Fear of the Self* (Delhi: Oxford University Press, 1997)

National Commission for Enterprises in the Unorganised Sector (NCEUS), *Report on Conditions of Work and Promotion of Livelihoods in the Unorganised Sector* (New Delhi: Government of India, 2007)

Pal, Prasantakumar, *Rabijībanī*, vol. 4 (Calcutta: Ananda, 1988)

Pearson, M.N., *The Portuguese in India* (Cambridge: Cambridge University Press, 1987)

Pinney, Christopher, *Camera Indica: The Social Life of Indian Photographs* (Chicago: University of Chicago Press, 1997)

————, *Photos of the Gods: The Printed Image and Political Struggle in India* (Delhi: Oxford University Press, 2004)

Putnam, Robert D., Robert Leonardi, and Raffaella Y. Nanetti, *Making Democracy Work: Civic Traditions in Modern Italy* (Princeton: Princeton University Press, 1993)

Rajadhyaksha, Ashish, "The Phalke Era: Conflict of Traditional Form and Modern Technology," in Tejaswini Niranjana, P. Sudhir, and Vivek Dhareshwar, eds, *Interrogating Modernity: Culture and Colonialism in India* (Calcutta: Seagull, 1993), pp. 47–82

Rajagopal, Arvind, *Politics After Television: Religious Nationalism and the Reshaping of the Indian Public* (Cambridge: Cambridge University Press, 2001)

Ramaswamy, Sumathi, *The Lost Land of Lemuria: Fabulous Geographies, Catastrophic Histories* (Berkeley: University of California Press, 2004)

————, *Goddess and the Nation: Mapping Mother India* (Durham, N.C.: Duke University Press, 2010)

Rao, Velcheru Narayana, and Sanjay Subrahmanyam, "History and Politics in the Vernacular: Reflections on Medieval and Early Modern South India," in Raziuddin Aquil and Partha Chatterjee, eds, *History in the Vernacular* (Ranikhet: Permanent Black, 2008), pp. 25–65

Ray, Atulchandra, *Bhārater itihās* (Calcutta: Prantik, 2001)

Ray, Durgacharan, *Debganer martye āgaman* (1880; rpntd Calcutta: Dey's, 1984)

Ray, Nisith Ranjan, *Bhārat paricay* (Calcutta: Allied Book Agency, 2001)

Renan, Ernest, *Qu'est-ce qu'une nation?: conference faite en Sorbonne, le 11 mars 1882* (Paris: Calmann Lévy, 1882)

Rosanvallon, Pierre, *Counter-democracy: Politics in an Age of Distrust*, tr. Arthur Goldhammer (Cambridge: Cambridge University Press, 2008)

Roy, Ananya, *City Requiem, Calcutta: Gender and the Politics of Poverty* (Minneapolis: University of Minnesota Press, 2003)

Roy, Srirupa, *Beyond Belief: India and the Politics of Postcolonial Nationalism* (Durham, N.C.: Duke University Press, 2007)

Rudolph, Lloyd I., and Susanne H. Rudolph, *The Modernity of Tradition: Political Development in India* (Chicago: University of Chicago Press, 1967)

———, *In Pursuit of Lakshmi: The Political Economy of the Indian State* (Chicago: University of Chicago Press, 1987)

Sandel, Michael J., *Liberalism and the Limits of Justice* (Cambridge: Cambridge University Press, 1982)

———, ed., *Liberalism and Its Critics* (New York: New York University Press, 1984)

Sanyal, Kalyan, *Rethinking Capitalist Development: Primitive Accumulation, Governmentality and Post-Colonial Capitalism* (New Delhi: Routledge, 2007)

Sarkar, Dineschandra, and Kalipada Hore, *Bhārat-itihāser ruprekhā* (Calcutta: Vidyoday, 1973)

Sarkar, Sumit, *The Swadeshi Movement in Bengal 1903–1908* (1973; rpntd Ranikhet: Permanent Black, 2010)

Sen, Asok, "Rājnītir pāṭhakrame rabīndranāth," *Bangadarśan*, 11 (July–December 2006)

Sen, Nabinchandra, *Āmār jīban*, vol. 5 (1913), in *Nabīncandra racanābalī*, vol. 2, eds Santikumar Dasgupta and Haribandhu Mukhati (Calcutta: Dattachaudhuri, 1976)

Sen, Simonti, *Travels to Europe: Self and Other in Bengali Travel Narratives 1870–1910* (Hyderabad: Orient Longman, 2005)

Sen, Surendra Nath, "The Portuguese in Bengal," in Jadunath Sarkar, *The History of Bengal*, vol. 2 (Dhaka: University of Dacca, 1948)

Singh, K. Suresh, ed., *People of India*, 43 vols (Calcutta: Anthropological Survey of India, 1995–)

Sivaramakrishnan, Kavita, *Old Potions, New Bottles: Recasting Indigenous Medicine in Colonial Punjab 1850–1940* (New Delhi: Orient Longman, 2006)

Smith, Rogers M., *Civic Ideals: Conflicting Visions of Citizenship in U.S. History* (New Haven: Yale University Press, 1997)

Stein, Burton, "Eighteenth Century India: Another View," *Studies in History*, 5, 1 (January–June 1989), pp. 1–26

Subrahmanyam, Sanjay, *The Political Economy of Commerce: Southern India, 1500–1650* (Cambridge: Cambridge University Press, 1990)

———, *The Portuguese Empire in Asia, 1500–1700: A Political and Economic History* (London: Longman, 1993)

———, *The Career and Legend of Vasco da Gama* (Cambridge: Cambridge University Press, 1997)

Subramanian, Lakshmi, *From the Tanjore Court to the Madras Music Academy: A Social History of Music in South India* (Delhi: Oxford University Press, 2006)

Sundaram, Ravi, *Pirate Modernity: Delhi's Media Urbanism* (London: Routledge, 2010)

Tagore, Rabindranath, *Rabīndra racanābalī*, 15 vols (Calcutta: Government of West Bengal, 1961–8)

———, *Rabīndra-racanābalī*, vol. 10 (Calcutta: Government of West Bengal, 1989)

———, *The English Writings of Rabindranath Tagore*, ed. Sisir Kumar Das, 3 vols (New Delhi: Sahitya Akademi, 1996)

Tarlo, Emma, *Unsettling Memories: Narratives of India's 'Emergency'* (Delhi: Permanent Black, 2003)

Taylor, Charles, *Sources of the Self: Making of the Modern Identity* (Cambridge: Cambridge University Press, 1992)

Thompson, E.P., *Customs in Common* (London: Penguin, 1991)

Tocqueville, Alexis de, *Democracy in America*, vol. 1, tr. Henry Reeve, revised by Francis Bowen, ed. Phillips Bradley (New York: Vintage, 1990)

Toye, Richard, *Churchill's Empire: The World That Made Him and the World He Made* (New York: Henry Holt, 2010)

Trouillot, Michel-Rolph, *Silencing the Past: Power and the Production of History* (Boston: Beacon Press, 1995)

Tully, James, *Public Philosophy in a New Key, Vol. 1: Public Philosophy and Civic Freedom* (Cambridge: Cambridge University Press, 2009)

Vanaik, Achin, *The Painful Transition: Bourgeois Democracy in India* (London: Verso, 1990)

Varshney, Ashutosh, *Democracy, Development and the Countryside: Urban–Rural Struggles in India* (Cambridge: Cambridge University Press, 1995)

Vasudevan, Ravi S., "Introduction," in Vasudevan, ed., *Making Meaning in Indian Cinema* (Delhi: Oxford University Press, 2000), pp. 1–36

Walzer, Michael, *Spheres of Justice* (New York: Basic Books, 1983)

Washbrook, D.A., "Progress and Problems: South Asian Economic and Social History, *c.*1720–1860," *Modern Asian Studies*, 22 (1988), 1, pp. 57–96

Weidman, Amanda J., *Singing the Classical, Voicing the Modern: The Postcolonial Politics of Music in South India* (Durham, N.C.: Duke University Press, 2006)

Index

GPSR Authorized Representative: Easy Access System Europe, Mustamäe tee 50, 10621 Tallinn, Estonia, gpsr.requests@easproject.com